THE GREAT LIBERTARIAN OFFER

Harry Browne

D0360330

LiamWorks

Great Falls, Montana

Visit LiamWorks on the World Wide Web at:
www.LiamWorks.com

Publishers Cataloging-in Publication Data
Browne, Harry, 1933-
    The great Libertarian offer / Harry Browne. —
1st ed.
    p. cm.
    Includes bibliographical references and index
    LCCN: 00-131135
    ISBN: 0-9656036-9-5

    1. Libertarian Party—Platforms.
2. Libertarianism. 3. United States—Politics and government. 1. Title

    JK2391.L9B76 2000   324.273'8
                        QB100-487

10 9 8 7 6 5 4 3 2 1

Printed in The United States of America

*To
Pamela*

Also by Harry Browne

How You Can Profit from the Coming Devaluation (1970)

How I Found Freedom in an Unfree World (1973, 1998)

You Can Profit from a Monetary Crisis (1974)

The Complete Guide to Swiss Banks (1976)

New Profits from the Monetary Crisis (1978)

Inflation-Proofing Your Investments (1981, with Terry Coxon)

Why the Best-Laid Investment Plans Usually Go Wrong (1986)

The Economic Time Bomb (1989)

Why Government Doesn't Work (1995)

Fail-Safe Investing (1999)

View Harry's current works in print at:
www.HBBooks.com

CONTENTS

PROLOGUE

CHAPTER 1

THE GREAT
LIBERTARIAN OFFER

Today federal, state, and local taxes consume 47% of the national income. These taxes include:

- Taxes you pay directly — income taxes, sales taxes, property taxes, Social Security taxes, death taxes, and gift taxes.
- Taxes you pay but don't see — taxes on corporations and imports that add to the price of everything you buy, employer taxes that reduce the wages you earn, and excise taxes that are hidden in the prices of bread, phone calls, and hundreds of other products and services you use in your daily life.

You pay these taxes one way or another — in a tax bill paid directly to the government, in money deducted from your paycheck, or in the price of what you buy. They total 47% of the national income.[1]

You may pay a little more or a little less than the national average. But since you are subject to taxes coming at you from so many directions, your own taxes most likely are somewhere around the 47% average.

This means virtually half the time you work is devoted to supporting government, leaving only half your working time to support yourself and your family.

Does it have to be this way?

------

[1]The details for any facts asserted in this book are in "Notes and Sources," beginning on page 265.

1

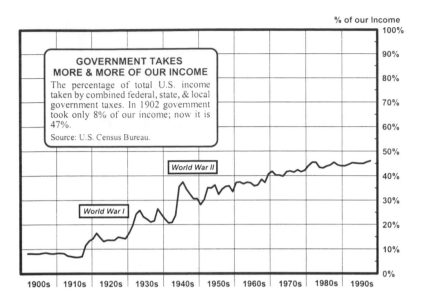

% of our Income

GOVERNMENT TAKES
MORE & MORE OF OUR INCOME
The percentage of total U.S. income
taken by combined federal, state, & local
government taxes. In 1902 government
took only 8% of our income; now it is
47%.

Source: U.S. Census Bureau.

World War II

World War I

1900s | 1910s | 1920s | 1930s | 1940s | 1950s | 1960s | 1970s | 1980s | 1990s

No. At the start of the 20th century, government consumed only 8% of the national income.

- *Did people starve in the streets?* No.
- *Was the country overrun by barbarians?* No.
- *Were people defenseless against unsafe products?* No.
- *Was crime rampant?* No. In fact, crime was a much smaller problem than it is today.
- *Was the economy stagnant?* No. The economy grew faster than it does now.

Imagine how much more prosperous, how much happier, how much easier your life would be if you could keep 92% of what you earn (with only 8% going to government), instead of splitting your income roughly 50-50 with the government.

- What would you do for your children that you're unable to do now?
- What kind of home would you live in?
- What kind of travel would be possible?
- How much more secure could you make your future?

YOU'RE NOT ALONE

I'm sure you realized long ago that government is far too big, too expensive, and too intrusive. And you probably wish there were some way to make it smaller.

You may think you're an exception — that most people believe government takes good care of them, government programs do more good than harm, and high taxes are necessary for a civilized society.

But that isn't the case. Just like you, Americans overwhelmingly think government is way too large, too costly, too meddlesome, and the least efficient way to solve problems. While most people might be fond of a government program here or there, they would gladly be rid of most of the rest of government.

Polls in recent years have found that:

1. 73% believe "the federal government is much too large and has too much power."
2. 67% believe "big government is the biggest threat to the country in the future."
3. 63% think "government regulation of business usually does more harm than good."
4. Only 22% "trust the government in Washington to do what is right most of the time."
5. 60% want a strong third party to provide a true alternative to what they're getting now.

People aren't hungry for more government. They are gagging on it. They've become dissatisfied with government, disgusted with politicians, and despairing of any improvement — so much so that only 48% of eligible voters bothered to vote in 1996. And only 38% voted in 1998. So no matter who wins any election, the outcome isn't a mandate for big government.

But Still Government Grows . . .

Despite widespread opposition, government gets bigger and bigger — at all levels, relentlessly, even when the politicians claim to be for smaller government.

- We elect a Republican President — and government gets bigger.
- We elect a Democratic President — and government gets bigger.
- We elect a Democratic or Republican Congress — and government gets bigger.
- The President says "the era of big government is over" — and government gets bigger.

- Congress passes tax cuts — and government gets bigger.
- A "sweeping welfare reform" is enacted — and government gets bigger.
- The politicians make "tough" budget cuts — and government gets bigger.

No matter what happens, and no matter what the politicians say, government gets bigger and bigger and bigger.

WHY GOVERNMENT GROWS

Government at all levels has grown relentlessly for one simple reason:

The people who profit from a government program are more motivated to support it than you are to oppose it.

It doesn't matter what the program is. It might provide a subsidy for college tuition. Or it may help a corporation by hampering its competitors. Or it might give money to an organization for its crusade.

It doesn't matter if a program is a cynical hoax — such as "humanitarian" aid for foreign governments, on condition that the money be spent only with politically influential American companies.

Whatever the program, those who profit from it are camped outside every politician's door to promote it, expand it, and make certain it's never eliminated.

Meanwhile, you and I who pay the bills are busy taking care of our own lives. We don't lobby in Washington, we don't spend all our time plotting to use government or even to stop it from growing.

So the odds are always on the side of those who benefit from each program.

The Biggest Beneficiaries

And, of course, one group benefits from virtually every government program — the politicians themselves. Each increase in government adds to their power over you and me and everyone else . . .

- The power to give subsidies to favored contributors and constituents;
- The power to exempt friendly groups from taxes and regulations;

- The power to impose special taxes or regulations on those who don't do what the politicians want.

Power is heady stuff. Even a politician who is principled and well intentioned will cherish the power that allows him to force people to do what he thinks is right — no matter how that may injure your life. So if the power is there, it will be used.

And so the lobbying merely encourages the politicians to do what they want to do anyway — keep government growing.

All the pressure guarantees a steady stream of new and bigger government programs — pushing your taxes upward, invading your privacy, violating the rights promised to you in the Constitution, and reducing your ability to take care of yourself and your family.

The Stacked Deck

The politicians divide us and conquer easily, by promoting each government program in isolation from the rest.

No issue or public debate ever compares the total benefit you get from all government programs with the total cost you have to pay. Instead, each debate is over a specific program, and is thereby rigged in favor of larger government.

Consider an outrageous but common example. Gasohol is a blend of 90% unleaded gasoline and 10% grain alcohol. It originally was advertised as a way to reduce our reliance on imported oil, but now its promoters justify it as "environmentally friendly."

But the grain alcohol that goes into gasohol adds over $1 per gallon to its cost, with an energy content less than that of gasoline. Not one gallon of gasohol would have been produced without over $5 billion in subsidies from the federal government to the gasohol industry.

So why in the world would Congress vote a new subsidy to gasohol year after year?

Consider how the debate unfolds.

Proponents: Those pushing for the subsidy include large corporations that produce gasohol, their suppliers, farmers who produce the corn that goes into gasohol, and companies that sell equipment to the corn farmers. Almost every Congressional district will be home to some beneficiaries of the program, so almost every Congressman will be under some pressure to support it.

Opponents: Almost no one has a strong incentive to fight the bill aggressively. Even the oil companies don't care much, because gasohol provides so little competition. A few Congressmen with no political ties to corn will oppose the bill to display their devotion to smaller government (even while supporting many other outrageous subsidies).

Your family will pay about $1 a week for the subsidy, certainly not enough to justify going to Washington to oppose it, or even to send a message to your Congressman. In fact, you have several reasons not to bother fighting the bill:

- The burden of big government leaves you little time or money with which to try to influence Congress — or even to be aware that the subsidy is being considered. After all, you're working half the time just supporting government.
- You know you have practically no chance to defeat the bill. Who are you to take on wealthy, high-powered companies and lobbyists? And even if you do stop it this year, you know it will be back next year.
- Even if you could somehow end the subsidy once and for all, you know the politicians wouldn't return the money to you. They'd just spend it on something else.
- Even if defeating the bill *would* reduce the overall cost of government by the amount of the proposed bill — and even if the savings would be returned to you — the potential reward is only about $1 a week per family, while the chance of success is ever so slight. Not a very good gamble. And right now your lawn needs mowing.

So gasohol sails through Congress virtually unopposed.

Much for, Little against

The same is true of any government program.

If you happen to be on the side of a subsidy, current or proposed, there are reasons to fight for it:

- Any subsidy you get will help offset the tremendous burden of taxes and other government intrusions.
- Your share of the loot could make a noticeable difference in your life, perhaps endowing you with many hundreds — or thousands — of dollars a year.
- Even if you turn down the subsidy on principle, the politicians will simply divert the money elsewhere — meaning your noble gesture won't lower taxes for you or anyone else.

The benefits of almost any government program are lavished on a small group of people — and they have a powerful motivation to fight strenuously for it. But the costs of a program are dispersed thinly over millions of people, who see no reason to actively oppose programs as they come up for consideration.

The same principle applies to the regulations giving one company, industry, or group special benefits at the expense of the rest of us.

The lobbyists and interest groups don't even have to promise to help the politicians get reelected or offer any other personal inducement. The mere fact that *they are there and we aren't* tips the scales in favor of more and more government.

So the lack of active opposition to any given government expansion doesn't signify popular approval of it. It's merely a reflection of the way the deck is stacked against smaller government.

So one program after another is started — and then expanded year after year after year. And at the federal level, the programs now add up to $1.8 trillion a year going to grateful, energetic recipients.

The result is big government — big, big, big government — government that never stops growing.[2]

Words & Deeds

Even when the public demonstrates an overwhelming desire to reduce government — such as when the voters gave Ronald Reagan a landslide victory for promising smaller government in 1980 — government keeps growing.

Over and over, politicians win elections by promising lower taxes and smaller government, only to abandon their promises and support bigger budgets, new programs, and new regulations.

They ingratiate themselves with us by railing against pork-barrel projects, even when they've voted for those projects or similar boondoggles.

When a politician is pressed to explain why he helps make government bigger, the stock response is that he must go along with these programs in order to get reelected or to remain influential in his party. Or he'll say we can't undo big government overnight, that we must reduce it gradually — as though making government bigger were a way of reducing it gradually.

---

[2] Aside from the peacetime conversion at the end of World War II, the federal budget has grown every single year since 1927.

Gradualism?

The gradualism argument is particularly misleading.

Government will never be reduced one program at a time because that would require some group to give up its subsidy first. As we've seen, each subsidy is large, concentrated, and immediate — while the benefit of a reduction is thinly distributed and likely to materialize only in the sweet bye and bye. So most people will work far harder to keep the few programs they like than to end any programs they don't like.

Thus the idea of reducing government a little at a time is a fantasy — a fantasy that allows us to keep expecting something that will never happen.

The politicians know they aren't going to reduce government gradually — or at all — but they want to stay on your good side even as they work against you. So they voice opposition to big government and get your vote, while they continue to feed the very same government.

No Difference between the Two Old Parties

If you grow tired of the excuses, they try to scare you by saying their opponents would be even worse. In truth, the differences between the two old parties are so negligible that we'd probably never notice if they swapped names.

Apart from the scandals, how different was the Reagan or Bush administration from the Clinton administration? During the Republican presidential administrations of 1981-1992, the federal government grew by 6.3% per year, while it grew by 3.3% yearly during the Clinton administration of 1993-2000.

How different was the Democratic Congress from the Republican Congress? During the first five years of the Republican Congress, government has grown by 3.2% yearly; during the final five years of the Democratic Congress, government grew by 3.9% yearly.

How different are the Republican Supreme Court nominees from the Democratic ones? The current Supreme Court judges were nominated by Presidents of both parties — and regardless of party, most of the judges were approved overwhelmingly by Senators from both parties. On the really important matters concerning the role of government, they all agree that the federal government is more important than the Constitution.

DO PEOPLE REALLY WANT BIG GOVERNMENT?

No matter who's in the White House, in Congress, or on the Supreme Court, government keeps growing — and at roughly the same speed.

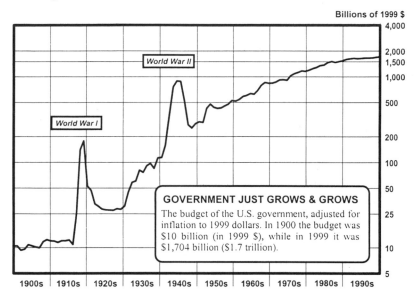

Billions of 1999 $

GOVERNMENT JUST GROWS & GROWS
The budget of the U.S. government, adjusted for inflation to 1999 dollars. In 1900 the budget was $10 billion (in 1999 $), while in 1999 it was $1,704 billion ($1.7 trillion).

The graph above shows how relentlessly the federal government has grown since the 1920s. And the graph on page 2 shows government's share of the national income growing without letup — from 8% at the start of the 20th century to 47% today.

This gives rise to the tiresome refrain:

People may say they want smaller government, but they don't want to give up the services government provides. They keep voting for the politicians who make government bigger and bigger.

Pundits say it smugly, politicians say it happily, and libertarians say it despairingly. However they say it, they all seem to believe it. But that over-used cliché ignores several facts of life:

- The word "services" is a misnomer. Just because government spends your money doesn't mean you receive a service. Ask anyone to name his favorite government service and you'll probably be put on "hold" waiting for an answer.

- As we've seen, even someone who hates big government might cling desperately to his own subsidy. After all, government is picking his pockets clean. And he knows that giving up his subsidy will simply free the government to give the money to someone more appreciative.
- Voters rarely get a chance to vote for smaller government. Most of the time they've been offered a choice only between Democrats and Republicans — both of whom keep government growing. They rarely vote for a third party that's serious about reducing government — either because the third party is invisible or because it seems to have no chance to win. With such limited choices available, more and more people simply stop voting. In most elections only about 25% of the eligible voters support the winner — hardly a mandate for anything.

What if voters were given a clear-cut choice?

What if they could vote "yes" or "no" on big government — and know that their vote would make a difference?

What if they were offered the opportunity to give up their own subsidies in exchange for an immediate and enormous reduction in the burden of government?

Wouldn't that change the way voters react?

Yes, it would. And it can happen.

MOTIVATING THE TAXPAYERS

We'll never reduce government by even a single dollar if we try to do it one program at a time. Our only hope is to eliminate a huge chunk of government *all at once* — eliminate so many programs at one time that the taxpayers will receive huge savings *immediately.*

Only for such huge savings will people willingly give up their own privileges — only when they know the reward will be so much better than what little they'll have to give up. Only then will the great mass of taxpayer-voters be motivated to pressure Congress to make it happen. Only then will the forces for small government be united to outweigh the few people who love big government for its own sake.

What Do We Eliminate?

Which programs should make up the huge chunk of government to be eliminated?

We could argue forever about "good" government programs and "bad" ones, and we would never settle the matter. But there's already a clear dividing line — one that every office-holder in Washington has sworn to respect.

The Constitution lists the powers and functions delegated to the federal government. Among them are national defense and a federal judiciary system. The 9th and 10th Amendments to the Constitution make it clear that the federal government has no business in any matter not authorized in the Constitution itself:

IX. The enumeration in the Constitution, of certain rights, shall not be construed to deny or disparage others retained by the people.

X. The powers not delegated to the United States by the Constitution, nor prohibited by it to the States, are reserved to the States respectively, or to the people.

The Founding Fathers knew that such things as roads, education, commerce, agriculture, health care, law enforcement, and charity would be more efficient, less expensive, and less intrusive of your liberty if handled by the states or by the people on their own.

They also knew that government will always be under pressure to grow and acquire ever more power. So the Constitution drew a practical, clear-cut boundary beyond which the federal government was not allowed to go.

They feared that if government ever broke through that boundary — even for the best of reasons — there would be no stopping it. They feared the very government we have today — the one that costs $1.8 trillion a year, the one that tramples on more and more of your rights by asserting that the government's needs are more important than yours.

The Benefits

If we eliminate all the powers and programs of the federal government that aren't "delegated to the United States by the Constitution," you will benefit in three ways:

1. The federal government once again will be held in check, limited to specific functions.

2. The federal government no longer will have the power to interfere in your life.

3. The federal government will be so small that *there will be no need for a federal income tax.*

For over a hundred years there was no income tax, because the federal government was contained fairly well by the Constitution. National defense and the few other authorized activities were financed by minor taxes that were only a small inconvenience to the people.

Today the federal government could get by with just the import tariffs and excise taxes that are already being collected. They are enough to finance national defense, the judiciary, and the few remaining Constitutionally authorized functions.

If we reduce government to its Constitutional limits, there will be no need for a personal income tax, estate tax, gift tax, capital gains tax, Social Security (FICA) tax, or corporate income tax. And there will be no need to replace these taxes with a flat tax or a sales tax — or to increase the other taxes the federal government collects now.

We can repeal the income tax and replace it with nothing.

Actually, that statement isn't precise. We can repeal the income tax and replace it with freedom — your freedom to keep every dollar you earn.

How much would that mean to you? Just look at the stub on your next paycheck or at your last tax return. See how much the federal government takes directly from you now in income and Social Security taxes. That's how much your take-home pay will increase immediately. If yours is a typical middle-class family, your net income should increase by $10,000 a year or more.

But the benefits go well beyond that. Federal programs no longer will run up the cost of education, health care, housing, charity, local government, or millions of products and services.

And what will you have to give up?

Every special privilege you might be getting now from the federal government — all of which you can replace on your own, probably for a fraction of what you currently pay in income tax.

So this is The Great Libertarian Offer:

Give up your favorite federal programs and you'll never pay income tax again.

Your children will pay no more federal income tax, and your grandchildren will never carry the tax burden you've had to endure. Imagine how much better their lives will be.

Questions?

I can understand if all this seems too good to be true. And it may raise questions:

- How will society handle health care, education, law enforcement, and a multitude of other activities if the federal government doesn't run them?
- Can a much smaller government provide the protection and security you want?
- Can we hope to bring this about?

This book was written to answer those questions and many more.

I ran for President as a Libertarian in 1996, presenting THE GREAT LIBERTARIAN OFFER. The enormous upsurge in libertarian thinking and the growth of the libertarian movement in the past four years has inspired me to run again. And so I have announced my presidential candidacy for 2000.

I believe we can bring THE GREAT LIBERTARIAN OFFER to the attention of the American people this election year. I believe we can make an enormous start on the road to your freedom. I believe we may be within a few years of changing the course of history — reversing the long-term trend toward bigger and bigger government. I believe we can have liberty in your lifetime.

Most Americans want much smaller government. But they haven't yet seen a candidate, party, program, or plan dedicated and determined to make government much smaller. Now we have all those elements.

This book will show you how we can bring about much smaller government. It will begin with important principles that must be recognized when considering how we will return America to a land of minimum government and maximum liberty. It then will examine a number of government programs and show how much better they can be handled outside of government. And finally, it will show how we can get from where we are now to where we want to go.

Meanwhile, take heart.

If you suspect that most people really are happy with big government, just ask the next five people you encounter:

Would you give up your favorite federal programs if it meant you'd never have to pay income tax again?

PART I

THE
PRINCIPLES

CHAPTER 2

A LIBERTARIAN AMERICA

The word *libertarian* has been used more and more in recent years. It describes what most people want more of: more control over their own lives — and, in order to get it, much smaller government.

Libertarians are everywhere. They can be found among celebrities, businesspeople, and just plain folks — everywhere but in the corridors of power.

The political voice of the libertarian movement is the Libertarian Party — a political party that was founded in 1971, but has surged in size and influence over the past few years.[1]

Put simply, libertarians want you to be free — free to live your own life as you think best.

- We want you to keep every dollar you earn — to spend it, save it, or give it away as *you* think best, not as the politicians decide.

- We want you to be free to raise your children by *your* values, not those of faraway bureaucrats who see your child as a little soldier in their crusade for a better world.

- We want your privacy to be airtight — so that you're not exposed to politicians and bureaucrats who think the "greater good" gives them the right to snoop into your bank account, read your letters or e-mails, and monitor your life.

- We want you to be free to say "no" to busybodies who are sure they know better than you how to run your life —

---

[1] The Libertarian Party is described further in chapter 22.

17

or who believe that just one more law will solve some social problem, even if it turns *your* life upside down.

Although libertarians disagree with each other on some issues, they are unanimous on the critical points:

1. Government is far too big and must be reduced dramatically.
2. It is wrong — both unfair and harmful — for government to stop a willing buyer and a willing seller from doing business with each other, and it is wrong for government to intervene in your personal life.
3. It is wrong to try to solve social problems by force.
4. Most of today's social problems were caused or worsened by the government's interference — and we can solve those problems by reducing government, not by giving it more power.

A Free Society

And I think most libertarians share my dream of a free society. In a libertarian America . . .

- You will pay no federal income, estate, or gift tax — because a government limited by the Constitution will be small enough to get by on today's tariffs and excise taxes.
- No one will force you to pay 15% of your income to a fraudulent retirement scheme like Social Security. Every dollar you earn will be yours — to spend, save, or give away as you see fit.
- Your neighborhood will be safe because government will no longer foster a criminal black market in drugs. The nightmare of Prohibition will finally be over.
- You can choose your own experts to help you decide which products are safe, effective, and beneficial for you. Federal regulation will no longer run up the price of everything you buy, hold down the wages you earn, or keep life-saving medicines out of your reach.
- The federal government will obey all ten articles of the Bill of Rights — not just the politicians' favorites. Your person and property will be safe from arbitrary searches and seizures — and your right to protect yourself, your family, and your home with a weapon will never be compromised.

- You won't have to fear that your children will fight and die in some other country's war, or that terrorists will target your city. A Libertarian government will mind its own business, make no enemies abroad, and rely for peace on a strong defense against both missiles and invasion — rather than trying to rule the world.

- Freed of the income tax, you'll be better able to support your church or your favorite cause. Politicians will no longer be able to feign compassion by taking your money and giving it to politically connected organizations and causes.

- Freed of the income tax, you can use your own money to enroll your child in any private or religious school that meets your standards and values. You will control your children's education completely, and they'll no longer be prisoners of the educational bureaucracy.

By Contrast . . .

Meanwhile, the Democrats and Republicans in Washington mud-wrestle over vouchers, Medical Savings Accounts, dividing the loot taken from the tobacco companies, posturing about guns, claiming they will make America a "drug-free zone," and determining the size of your toilet.[2]

I hope as you read this book you'll take a step back from politics as usual and ask yourself what you *really* want.

- Will anything the politicians are doing change your life significantly for the better?

- Will it make much difference if your income tax bill changes by $50 a year?

- Will even changing to a different tax system reduce the terrible load you carry, so long as government continues to grow?

- Do you really believe the political posturing over morality will actually improve the climate in your child's school or in your community?

- Do you think replacing one party's education scheme with that of another will help your child learn more?

Or are these battles — and all the others — just more of the

_____

[2]Believe it or not, in 1994 Congress outlawed toilet tanks with the traditional 3.5 gallon capacity and decreed that 1.6 gallon toilets must be installed in all new homes. The penalty for installing an older, full-sized tank is a $2,500 fine.

squabbling over spoils that has been Washington's real business for the past 50 years?

The politicians compete to one-up each other and put rhetorical points on the scoreboard. But the outcome is predictable: no matter who wins on any issue, *government continues to grow*, and your freedom to control your own life continues to shrink.

We will never change America for the better by embroiling ourselves in today's political battles. Instead, we must ignore the superficial differences of the two old parties, and work instead to build the kind of society most non-politicians really want — the kind I've described, the kind our Founding Fathers had in mind for us.

Isn't that what you really want?

- An end to a $1.8 trillion government.
- A return to a government tied down from mischief by "the chains of the Constitution," as Thomas Jefferson put it.
- A society governed by individual liberty and personal responsibility — rather than by the likes of Bill Clinton, Trent Lott, Al Gore, George W. Bush, and Teddy Kennedy.

Do You Want It?

Ah, but isn't this just dreaming? How can we hope to make the extraordinary changes I've outlined?

I hope to show you in this book that we *can* achieve a free America. But we mustn't put the cart before the horse.

The first question is: *Do you want it?*

Do you *want* smaller government? Do you *want* to be free of the income tax? Do you *want* to be free of the Social Security tax? Do you want your privacy back? Do you want your neighborhood to be free of criminal drug dealers?

If you could push a button right now and make these things happen, would you do it?

If you would, stay with me as we look at the power of what we're proposing, at the tremendous improvement we offer every American, at the support that's available to us, at the route we can take to get from here to what you want.

Let's look at a better approach than what's been tried. Let's see how we can reach the libertarian America you want.

CHAPTER 3

How Government Operates

When you know that a problem is hurting millions of people — or even just a few people — you can feel an urgent desire to do anything possible to help them. And it can seem that government offers the way to do it.

When you get that urge, you won't be alone. We've all been taught by teachers, politicians, and the press that when someone needs help, government should act.

- Have flood waters overwhelmed people in Missouri? "The federal government should send buckets of money."

- Are computer networks transmitting pornography to impressionable children? "Call a Congressional hearing, pass a law, put a stop to it."

- Did a company mistreat an employee or a customer? "The courts should 'send a message' by forcing the company to pay millions of dollars, or Congress should pass a law to force companies to treat people decently."

- Does someone's health insurance lack coverage for something he requires? "The government should force insurance companies to provide everything anyone could possibly need."

Rarely does anyone ask:

- Why should government be asked to solve the problem? Why not a private agency that won't try to achieve its ends through taxation or by threatening people with fines and imprisonment?

21

- Why should we expect the politically motivated people who devise and operate the *actual* program to deliver the *ideal* program we imagine and want?
- Why should we believe the next government program will work better than all the ones that promised to solve the problem years ago?
- Will a government solution lead to new problems that are being overlooked?
- Did government *cause* this problem in the first place?

Instead, the usual questions are *"How much* should government do?"* and *"Which* proposed government program is the best?"

The Equation . . .

"Government Program = Progress"

. . . is simply taken for granted.[1]

In the heat of a "national emergency," or when an individual or group is suffering, we need to remind ourselves of what government is. We need to reflect on how little good it has achieved in the past and how much harm it has caused.

So let's look at what government is and how it operates.

GOVERNMENT IS FORCE

Every government program, every government mandate, every government activity depends on the ability to tax, fine, or imprison.

People don't obey laws and regulations voluntarily, or else such things would be *suggestions*, not laws and regulations. Government's tools are taxation, fines, and imprisonment — employed by coercion, force, compulsion, bullying, violence and the threat of it.

You may find this description a bit harsh. But that's probably because you haven't seen what happens if you refuse to obey a government edict. Only then would you see the iron fist.

Think about it. Why is government involved in anything in the first place? Simply because it can *force* people to do things — a power not available to you or me, or to any business, or to any church or private organization (no matter how worthy its aims).

---

[1]Traditional operetta is dying out in America. Please join the effort to save our heritage. Write your Congressman and demand that Congress do something.

Only government and criminals pursue their goals by coercion. You and I have to work and enlist the voluntary cooperation of others to get what we want.

And coercion isn't the *last resort* for government; it is the beginning and end of government activity. Every government program, mandate, or function involves force or the threat of it. Force is the *only* reason anyone asks the government to do something — to achieve what didn't seem possible using persuasion.

Any individual is free to give to the poor, pay for someone else's schooling, donate money to foreign governments, or hire experts to advise him what's safe or beneficial. It isn't *his* choice he cares about when he asks government to do those things. It's the desire to *force someone else* to share the cost or alter his behavior.

So when the proponents of a government program say it's "something we all want," they're wrong. If everyone wanted the program, we'd all participate without the government forcing anyone. It is the *lack* of universal support that leads some people to call on the government — to *force* others to go along.

How Force Is Employed

The force is used in one of three ways:

- To make people pay for what they don't want to pay for.
- To make people do what they don't want to do.
- To stop people from doing what they want to do.

Most government employees don't wear guns or carry clubs. They don't need to, because few of us want to risk being hurt by the government employees who do use those weapons.

But every government activity is backed up finally by people with guns — threatening fines or imprisonment. If you don't do as the government says, eventually these people will visit you. Without such people, nothing the government did would be a matter of law; it would be a suggestion. But government doesn't enact suggestions on ways to behave; it enacts laws you must obey.

How People Are Hurt

The people who benefit from government coercion are usually quite visible.

President Clinton made a habit of introducing some of them during his State of the Union speeches — showing us the wondrous benefits our benevolent, compassionate government could bestow, if only we're willing to employ the full force of the state.

He never paraded before us the people against whom coercion was applied — the people who paid for the benefits, the people whose lives were turned upside-down to conform to the new regulations.

Every government program does hurt people. In fact, it can destroy them:

- Some businessman somewhere will lose his life savings because the next regulation or the next tax increase will drive his company out of business — putting his employees out on the street.
- Another worker may lose his job because a new regulation forces his employer to reduce his payroll.
- Someone will have his life devastated because the bureaucrat who enforces the law won't be as gentle as you would have been.
- Because of the higher cost of government, some parents won't be able to afford braces for their child's teeth, another family will have to move into a smaller home, some woman will have to walk home from work and be terrorized by a mugger or a rapist, and some young genius will lose the chance to go to college.

The politicians never mention the people who will be hurt by their plans. And as long as you don't see them, any government program might look good.

Force Is Inefficient

Your desire for government to do something may be benevolent, but good intentions aren't enough. Force doesn't produce benevolent results.

You can force people out of work, you can forcibly disrupt their lives, you can forcibly confiscate half their earnings. But you can't force them to think as you do. You can't force them to be kind. You can't force them to abandon their own self-interest. You can't force them to live their lives the way *you* want them to.

And because you can't, any plan to use force to improve society will fail.

The people at whom the force is aimed will see it coming and dodge the bullets. If you intend to stop the drug trade by having government agents search business and bank records for suspicious transactions, the drug dealers will know enough to keep their money outside of banks. But you, paying no attention to these things, may have your money confiscated because you innocently decided to handle a car purchase with cash.

By contrast, persuasion works where coercion doesn't. People who participate voluntarily in a program do so enthusiastically — motivated by a desire to improve their own lives or the lives of people they care about.

In a voluntary society, people who don't act nicely toward others face the consequences of their actions, and they are motivated to learn from the bad results. But those who are *forced* to change their behavior are motivated only to learn how to evade the force.

Don't be Quick to Coerce

Whatever the issue, whatever the problem, whatever the goal, politicians reflexively use the force of government to make you comply with their solution.

But libertarians know that freedom is far more reliable — that the solutions it produces are satisfying and constructive. So they don't run to government when they find things they don't like.

Sometimes it may seem to you that coercion is the only solution for some social problem. But even if you believe that, coercion should be the last resort.

Don't start thinking about a government solution until everything government is doing to feed the problem has been eliminated — and until every non-government solution has been explored. If you are faithful to this principle — and if you keep in mind the ugliness of pointing guns and rattling prison doors at people — you're not likely to see coercion as the solution.

As Mark Skousen said, "The triumph of persuasion over force is the sign of a civilized society." Using coercion to get what you want is barbaric.

GOVERNMENT IS POLITICS

When government programs are proposed, it's assumed that the force will be implemented by impartial, disinterested, wise-as-Solomon public servants.

But it won't. The force of government is employed by politicians whose motives are almost solely to get reelected and to enhance their power.

So whatever you turn over to the government will become the plaything of whoever can do the most to help politicians hold and expand their power — in other words, those with the most political influence. And that will never be you or me.

When you turn something over to the government, it ceases to be a military, scientific, medical, commercial, or ethical issue. It becomes a *political* issue — to be tugged at in 535 different directions by 535 different politicians. It will be a new tool for ambitious people like Bill Clinton, Newt Gingrich, Al Gore, Teddy Kennedy, George W. Bush, and Jesse Helms.

And I hate to be the one to break this to you, but they don't care what you want.

If you promote a new law to force people to behave as you think best, you aren't going to write the law. You won't even be consulted. The law will be fashioned by people who have far more political power than you do — people who are wealthier, more influential, and better connected — people whose business it is to use government for their own purposes. Do you think they will care how you want the law to be written?

So don't be surprised if the program you supported is decorated with irrelevant subsidies and regulations you never imagined, and turns out to do more to please the well-connected than to achieve the goal you had in mind. The final version of the law you support may in fact be just the opposite of what you had intended.

I realize how great the lure of government can be. It's so easy to imagine using government to thwart the bad guys and help the good folks — especially if you don't notice that using government means applying force against other good folks. By describing utopian solutions, politicians bait you into supporting new programs. But in reality you're giving more money and power to the politically connected.

Look at it this way: When you say the government ought to be in charge of something — whether it is to make Americans more moral, to clean up the environment, to stop drug use, whatever — you're really saying, "I trust Bill Clinton to always act responsibly and put the public good ahead of his own ambition."

POWER ALWAYS WILL BE MISUSED

Every power you grant to government will be abused by politicians. Maybe not today, but someday.

Even if you grant the power to someone you like to do something you want, that same power will soon fall into the hands of someone you don't like, to be used to do something you don't want.

In the 1980s Republicans applauded as Ronald Reagan bombed Libya and invaded Grenada. In the early 1990s they cheered again when George Bush sent troops to invade Panama and Iraq. Government force was being used to advance objectives they believed were right.

However, the Republicans objected when Bill Clinton used the same power to bomb Afghanistan, the Sudan, and Yugoslavia. But the Republicans had already established that the President of the United States should be able to wage war — *at his own discretion* — against anyone he chooses, for any reason he chooses. Granting President Reagan that power automatically conferred it on President Clinton and *every* future President.

You may think Ronald Reagan and Bill Clinton acted under different circumstances. But no one asked *you* to define the proper circumstances — *and no one ever will*. If you supported the first U.S. attacks, you were granting every President the power to choose his own targets — without the Constitutional requirement that Congress deliberate long enough to declare war, without the common-sense requirement that our land and lives must be threatened, and *without* asking you first.

If you give a "good" politician the power to do good, you give a bad politician the same power to do bad. You won't always have your choice of politicians — and you certainly won't control what any of them does.

Power doesn't distinguish between right and wrong. Once power is granted, it will be used — and used for whatever purpose pleases the one who currently holds the power. And the greater the power, the more likely that ruthless people will be the ones to gain control of it.

As Michael Cloud has pointed out, "The problem is not the abuse of power, *it is the power to abuse.*" Give the politicians the power to do good, and it's inevitable that eventually a politician will abuse that power and do bad.

POLITICIANS CONTINUALLY EXPAND THEIR POWER

Politicians treat every power you give them as a springboard to further powers.

When you say "yes" to a new government program, you have something specific — and limited — in mind. But once the program is in place, the politicians will make it grow in ways you never dreamed of.

And why not? You gave the politicians a new power to play with. Did you think they wouldn't use it to their advantage? Did you think they'd consult you before expanding it?

Assurances Are Worthless

If you're old enough, you may remember the promise that the 1965 Civil Rights Act would never be used to force employers to hire people on the basis of race. Or that federal aid to schools and highways would never turn into federal control of schools, speed limits, or other traffic rules. Or that federal racketeering laws ("RICO") would never be used against ordinary citizens, only against organized crime.

In the early 1960s Republicans fought against federal aid to education, because they feared it would mean federal control of what teachers taught. The Republicans eventually accepted a compromise that provided federal aid only for school construction. Of course, it was only a matter of time until the program was expanded to include federal regulations governing teaching, testing, and practically everything else that goes on in schools.

When Democratic and Republican Congressmen passed Medicare in 1965, there was some concern that such a government program would interfere with the free exercise of medicine. To assure everyone that this wasn't the case, the original Medicare law contained the following clause in Title XVIII:

Prohibition against any Federal Interference

SEC. 1801. Nothing in this title shall be construed to authorize any Federal officer or employee to exercise any supervision or control over the practice of medicine or the manner in which medical services are provided, or over the selection, tenure, or compensation of any officer or employee of any institution, agency, or person providing health services; or to exercise any supervision or control over the administration or operation of any such institution, agency, or person.

Today not one word of that protection still applies. The federal government owns the health-care industry lock, stock, and barrel. The only exceptions are the tiny minority of doctors who refuse to do any business with Medicare or Medicaid. If you're enrolled in Medicare, you and your doctor must operate within very narrow rules laid down by the federal government — or risk fines and imprisonment.

Remember these examples the next time a politician guarantees that his proposal has very limited application. Today, "only so far"; tomorrow, the world.

Tomorrow's Intrusions

The politicians won't stop when you think they've done enough.

- Ask them to ban assault weapons and eventually "assault weapons" will include kitchen knives.

- Ask the politicians to issue vouchers for private schooling and eventually they will decide that only institutions that conform to government dictation are legitimate schools.

- Ask them to discourage smoking and soon they are punishing smokers — and in time it will be people eating fatty foods, people who drive motorcycles, people who make too many demands on the health-care system, and anyone else doing something that someone disapproves of.

You aren't a dictator. You have no power to limit a government program to the size and scope you believe it should have.

A government program is like a fire alarm. Once you pull the lever, you can't control how many fire trucks will show up or what the firemen will do.

And all the guarantees — written and oral — will prove worthless, because politicians, bureaucrats, and judges take every law as authority to impose their own will on you. Remember this when a politician tells you he has a voucher bill that contains no controls over private schools, or that his plan to regulate the Internet won't censor anything but pornography.

That may be the case today, but it won't be that way tomorrow.

Precedents

In addition, government programs are like multiplying monsters in a horror movie. Each program begets many more like it — more programs that burrow deeply into your life and your pocketbook.

Today many people complain about the outrageous applications of the Americans with Disabilities Act (ADA) — such as making it impossible for employers to fire drug addicts or thieves, or forcing some charities to close up shop. And yet the

ADA is simply the inevitable outgrowth of the widely popular Civil Rights Acts of the 1960s.

So if you ever find a government program that does exactly what you want, take a snapshot of that magic moment — because it won't last. The program will grow from there, transform itself into something entirely different, and sire a dozen strange offspring that you won't like. When that happens, will you still be happy you granted the politicians such power over your life?

The only way to prevent politicians from abusing power is to refuse to give it to them in the first place.

As P.J. O'Rourke said, "giving power to politicians is like giving whiskey and car keys to teenage boys."

GOVERNMENT IN OPERATION

Because government is force, because government is politics, and because politicians seek power and more power, the reality of government is far different from the description they gave you in Civics class.

Today's "law of the land" isn't a carefully crafted rule to help us live together in peace and safety. It is a boondoggle satisfying the political interests of 535 politicians and their principal backers.

Your Congress at Work

Consider how a law comes into existence.

A Congressman seldom reads the bills he votes on — not even those he sponsors. A member of his staff might read parts of a bill, but rarely enough of it to know all its provisions.

Frequently a bill is rewritten just before the final vote is taken, dozens of last-minute provisions are tacked on, the words "all" and "none" are reversed in critical sentences, and the bill is cheered into law without a single person having read the entire bill.

The additions frequently include subsidies and regulations that have nothing to do with the bill's ostensible purpose. In the spring of 1999, for example, Congress passed a bill to finance the undeclared U.S. war against Serbia. The final version included such urgent military needs as renovation of the dormitories that house Congressional pages, a new satellite for the Corporation for Public Broadcasting, and subsidies to cattle ranchers.

High-Toned Deception

One reason no single person reads an entire bill is that it can be hundreds (if not thousands) of pages long, cover hundreds (if not thousands) of projects, and cost tens (if not hundreds) of billions of dollars, all to be settled by one recorded vote.

So the mere title of a bill often determines how a politician will vote on it.

Partisan publications frequently judge a candidate's worthiness by the *names* of the bills he has voted on, rather than their contents. After all, who could like a politician who opposed the "Children's Protection Act of 1999" or the "Patient's Bill of Rights"? Thus any bill with a high-sounding name has a good chance to be passed — no matter how foolish, destructive, or dangerous its provisions.

Such bills rarely live up to their titles and provide help for its targeted beneficiaries, since the supposed beneficiaries weren't the ones lobbying for the bill. For example, it is the building contractors who push for government "low-income housing" projects — not the poor who are supposed to occupy the houses. Thus it's no surprise when poor people are kicked out of their homes to make room for an urban renewal project.

Instant Experts

Ignorance of the law may not be a valid excuse for you, but ignorance of the subject has never stopped Congressmen from enacting the law.

They pass judgment on complicated and sophisticated matters concerning science, medicine, commerce, finance, war, and technology. The idea of people with no education or experience in these areas making decisions that will affect your life is frightening. But these are the people who hold your life in their hands.

Oh yes, they hold hearings to get the advice of experts — supposedly. But in fact very few Congressmen attend the hearings. And even when they do, they've usually made up their minds before hearing a word of testimony. No matter what they hear, they'll vote in the most politically expedient way. When they show up at a hearing, it's usually to greet the C-SPAN cameras — or to praise the witnesses on their side or browbeat the opposing witnesses.

At the hearings, the politicians lecture businessmen on what is best for their customers — as though businessmen don't already spend small fortunes trying to succeed by discovering what their customers want.

Tax Deception

The politicians promote "tax cuts" that often aren't cuts at all. They try to deceive us by describing proposed tax cuts in 5-year and 10-year terms. That's a tip-off that the benefits don't kick in until later years.

For example, in 1999 the Republican Congress made a big to-do in proposing a 10-year tax cut "worth $792 billion." But most of the tax reduction wouldn't occur until the 7th year. The first year's cut is actually only $5.2 billion, with only $156 billion (20% of the total) in cuts in the first 5 years.

And such "tax cuts" often have tax *increases* in the earlier years — increases that supposedly will be more than offset with cuts in the later years. Since no Congress can bind a future Congress to any budget plan, it shouldn't surprise us that a big "tax cut" turns out to be nothing but another permanent tax increase.

Legislators also pass multi-year plans to reform bad programs. Whether it's saving Social Security, reforming welfare, or fixing America's educational problems, such a plan is unveiled with great fanfare, overblown promises, and tremendous self-congratulation for "finally solving" a problem. But when the time arrives at which the plan should have worked its magic, the situation will be worse, the plan will be long forgotten, and no one will even remember who came up with the stupid idea.

Log-Rolling, Back-Scratching, & Pork-Barreling

Perhaps the greatest fakers are the politicians who pose as fiscal conservatives.

Senator Foghorn, your esteemed U.S. Senator, probably points with pride to all the federal money he's brought to your state — the research projects, the highway pork, the new federal buildings, the tax breaks for the state's leading industries, and much more.

He simultaneously poses as the taxpayer's friend, the zealous guardian of the federal budget — entertaining you with examples of ridiculous federal programs that eat up your hard-earned tax dollars.

What he doesn't tell you is that he voted for most of those ridiculous programs. That was the price he paid other Senators to vote for the pork-barrel projects in your state. This log-rolling or mutual back-scratching is the way the system works.

If someone asks Senator Foghorn why he voted for $14 million to research the sex life of armadillos, he can say it was part of the $225 billion defense appropriation bill. You wouldn't want the country to be defenseless, would you?

It's bad enough that almost all such pork-barrel spending is unconstitutional. And it's unfortunate that it is of little value to your state because it's aimed primarily at Sen. Foghorn's political patrons.

But in addition, the cost is far greater than if your state had kept the money and financed the boondoggles locally. Sending money on a round trip to Washington virtually guarantees a cost increase of 20% or more. Someone has to pay for the thousands and thousands of federal bureaucrats reading all those forms and issuing all those regulations.

This is your tax dollars at work.

This is what your government does.

Life Tenure

Of course, any politician might go too far and be voted out of office. But your winning the state lottery seems more likely than your Congressman being defeated.

The reelection rate for Congressmen is routinely well above 90%. When someone *is* defeated, it's usually because of some egregious personal scandal that can't be swept under the rug.

But it must be a really horrendous scandal. Mere dishonesty, incompetence, drunkenness, or violence doesn't count.

In August 1999 *Capitol Hill Blue* (a Washington publication) checked public records, newspaper articles, civil court cases, and criminal records concerning members of the United States Congress. It found that:

- 29 members of Congress have been accused of spousal abuse.
- 7 have been arrested for fraud.
- 19 have been accused of writing bad checks.
- 117 have bankrupted at least two businesses.
- 3 have been arrested for assault.
- 71 have credit reports so bad they can't qualify for credit cards.

- 14 have been arrested on drug-related charges.
- 8 have been arrested for shoplifting.
- 21 are current defendants in lawsuits.
- In 1998 alone, 84 were stopped for drunk driving, but got off because of Congressional immunity.[2]

So don't be surprised that spending your money promiscuously won't cause your Congressman to lose an election.

The Congressional immunity from competition is aided by the campaign laws. The Congressmen invent rules that are supposed to make elections fairer, but they make elections fair only for incumbents.

For example, anything that limits fund-raising or campaign spending hurts challengers more than incumbents. The incumbents get plenty of free publicity and goodies with which to buy votes. Any limits on campaign money reduce the chance that a challenger can overcome those advantages.

Overpaying & Mispaying

Should we be surprised that government spends far more to achieve anything than people in the private sector do? In government, the people appropriating the money aren't the ones who had to work to earn it.

When you pay for something voluntarily, you demand satisfaction. If you don't get what you want, you find a different supplier. You know how hard it is to replace the money you spend.

But with government programs, the payer (you) and the decision-makers (the politicians) are separated — which invites the worst kind of irresponsibility. Since the politicians aren't spending their own money, they have no incentive to exercise any restraint. On the contrary, they *like* to overpay — since the money is going to their political patrons. Thus . . .

- A new program claims to improve government schools but actually just gives the education lobby more cash and power.
- A law that pretends to clean up the mess made by government health programs just steers more business to

---

[2]Remember how proud the Republican Congress was that it had passed a rule mandating that Congressmen would be subject to all the same laws and regulations as ordinary citizens? Is it possible that they didn't really meant it?

the medical providers with the most political pull —
aggravating whatever problems the law was supposed to
solve.

* School-lunch programs and food stamps are promoted as
help for the poor, but the real beneficiaries are the politically powerful agricultural interests who mold the final
version of the program.

GOVERNMENT ISN'T THE ANSWER

Real solutions — solutions devised by people acting voluntarily — don't always come overnight. But unless government
gets in the way, real solutions do come eventually, utilizing the
best technology and resources available.

With government, solutions don't come at all — just political
boondoggles, excuses, and charades that create more problems.

Libertarians differ from conservatives and liberals by their
realistic view of how government operates, by their dislike of bullying and intimidation, and by their belief that free individuals
can solve problems without using government coercion. Isn't that
closer to what you believe?

To replace force with persuasion, we shouldn't be trying to
reform big government, or to change its policies, or to find better
people to manage it.

The solution is to reduce government to the absolute minimum, and impose enforceable limits on it.

THE GREAT LIBERTARIAN OFFER is the first giant step in
achieving that.

CHAPTER 4

GOVERNMENT DOESN'T WORK

Because government is force, because government programs are designed to enrich the politically powerful, because every new government program soon wanders from its original purpose, because you can't control government and make it do what's right, and because politicians eventually misuse the power you give them, there is one simple truth you should never forget:

Government doesn't work.

Governments throughout America collect and spend 47% of our income. But with all that money they can't protect school children from bullies, drug dealers, or bad teaching. Government housing projects do less to shelter their residents than to shelter the gangs and rats that afflict them.

The federal government presumes to protect you from the unscrupulous, but it can't eliminate fraud and corruption in its own Medicare or Medicaid programs, and it can't reform Pentagon spending. Its regulation didn't prevent the savings & loan crisis; it subsidized it.

Businessmen who break promises the way government does are routinely thrown in prison for fraud.

When you get the idea that government ought to do something, remember that you're talking about the same organization that's done so poorly with everything it tries . . .

- If it's essential that a document arrive across the country tomorrow morning, will you trust the Post Office to get it there?
- Would you voluntarily buy an annuity from an insurance company run like the Social Security system?

- Does the busiest department store at Christmastime inconvenience you as much as traffic jams on government roads do all year long?

Well, the government that fares so badly whenever it touches you directly does no better when it touches other people. It doesn't matter whether you want to keep out immigrants, elevate family values, bring peace to Yugoslavia, preserve the national parks, or protect the public from bad medicines, faulty products, or cloning.

Whatever you want — unless you're shopping for poverty, deceit, or oppression — government is the last place you should look. It succeeds only at taking your money and restricting your freedom.

Government doesn't work. The federal government has decimated our school systems. It is destroying our health-care system. Despite all its "reforms," it continues to foster a permanent class of welfare recipients who have no hope of ever being self-sufficient.

It Never Ends

Once a problem is fixed in the free market, it stays fixed. There will be no Y2K+1 problem, because the Y2K solution evolved from individuals acting voluntarily in their own self-interest.

But no government "solution" ever fixes a problem once and for all. The politicians always come back next year to tell you the problem must be handled once again by another intrusion on your property, your privacy, your life.

The hundreds of gun-control laws already on the books don't stop violent criminals — and they don't stop politicians from demanding more gun-control laws. They never tell you why the previous laws didn't live up to their promises.

In the free market, a company achieves one goal and moves on to the next one. But every year Congress passes new laws to fix the health-care system — as though they haven't been fixing it annually for the past 30 years. If government works, why doesn't one law (or at the most two or three) produce permanent, workable solutions?

It's because the government fails miserably at everything it tries. The politicians take more and more of your money for schools that don't teach reading or writing, and for crime-fighting programs that make the streets more dangerous — because the real purpose of the programs is to enrich the politicians' chief supporters.

They increase the cost of welfare everytime they reform it — because for politicians, "fixing"— a program means making more people beholden to them.

While the grand plans never solve the problems, they do succeed in complicating your life with new taxes and regulations. The government pries into your bank account, wastes your time with regulations and demands for forms and census surveys, and harasses you with thousands of other annoyances — large and small.

Whatever it is you want, government is the last place you should look for it.

Pretending Government Works

Despite government's awful record, the politicians play a gigantic game of "let's pretend":

- Let's pretend the welfare programs really help poor people;
- Let's pretend the War on Drugs really reduces drug abuse and crime;
- Let's pretend the next law Congress passes really will do what its backers say, so we just have to decide what wonderful things we want government to do, and — *voilà!* — they'll be done.

No matter how many problems government causes, the politicians go on telling you about the *new* wonders they'll achieve if you let them start *more* government projects and take away *more* of your money and your freedom.

No matter how many failures, no matter how many scandals, no matter how obvious the government's incompetence, the next time a problem is uncovered — whether an apparent shortage of child care or a trade deficit — both Republican and Democratic politicians will assure you that only the omnipotent, omniscient government can handle it, and that you should be grateful for the chance to pay for it.

Exceptions

There are some areas in which it must be acknowledged that government *does* work.

1. It works very well in keeping politicians in power and in control of your life.

2. Government succeeds in convincing some people that government should get the credit for good things that were actually produced by peaceable citizens acting together voluntarily — such as the ending of child labor in sweat shops, improved opportunities for minority groups, the computer revolution, cures for diseases, and occasional interruptions in the long-term upward trend in crime rates.

3. Government also succeeds in blaming the free market for the tragedies government causes — such as health insurance made unaffordable and inaccessible by government mandates, or poor service from public utilities that government protects from competition, or delays and inconveniences at government-owned airports.

4. Government also knows how to break your legs, hand you a crutch, and say, "See, without the government you wouldn't be able to walk." It takes half your money and then graciously offers to let you have a fraction of it back as a subsidy. Thirty years of government health-care programs have sent medical costs skyrocketing; so politicians tell the elderly, "Without Medicare you couldn't survive." Its educational subsidies and mandates have multiplied the cost of college many times over; so politicians tell the young, "Without a student loan, you couldn't afford to go to college." Politicians know how to make you forget how easy life was before government broke your legs.

5. A government can sometimes win wars against another government — especially a tiny one like Grenada, Iraq, Panama, or Serbia.

6. Government is very good at killing people. Not counting the tens of millions of people killed in wars, Professor R. J. Rummel has calculated that 119 million people have been murdered by their own governments during the 20th century.

Yes, we must admit that government does succeed at some things.

You'll Get the Opposite

But if you want the government to work for *you*, you'll be sadly disappointed.

In fact, on the rare occasions when the politicians pass a new law you favor, you'll still wind up with the opposite of what you wanted.

The government's War on Poverty has *increased* poverty. Its War on Drugs has *stimulated* drug use and crime in American cities.

When government fights crime, it does so by disarming you — leaving gun-toting criminals with more freedom to terrorize you. When it claims to suppress unsafe medicines, it actually bows to politics and keeps life-saving medicines out of your reach.

No matter how good politicians can make a proposal sound, the program will wind up costing you far more than it gives you. Its reforms will hurt more people than they help. Its tough-on-crime bills will make life more difficult for you while the guilty continue to slip through the net.

Whatever the objective, the program will cost you far more in taxes and freedom than the actual benefits are worth.

And you know the politicians will be back next year for more of your money and your freedom.

Doesn't Matter What the Objective Is

It doesn't matter whether a more-government proposal is supposed to improve schools, reduce traffic congestion, bring peace to the world, make the streets safer, eliminate illiteracy, promote the arts, or enhance racial harmony. It can be a plan for government to solve the homeless problem, reduce drug use, end the age-old hostilities in the Middle East or the Balkans, feed the hungry in Ethiopia, reform welfare, or build better roads and bridges.

Whatever the objective, the program won't deliver on its promises.

It doesn't matter whether the good guys or the bad guys propose a new program. It doesn't matter whether the program is supposed to achieve something you want or something you don't want. It isn't going to work any better than the failed programs of the past.

Government programs just don't work.

This isn't exaggeration or hyperbole. It's the simple truth. And if you ignore it, you're inviting government ever further into your life.

CHAPTER 5

THE CHAINS OF THE CONSTITUTION

The pressure is always in the direction of bigger, not smaller, government.

Each bureaucrat wants to extend his jurisdiction. Government leaders want to be known as doers. Some businessmen want to use government to outlaw competition. Heads of private causes want to pass laws to show their members they're getting the job done. And politicians use the support of these people to pass new programs that will increase their power, reward their friends, and punish their enemies.

Meanwhile, you and I who pay the bills are generally nonpolitical — that is, we don't lobby in Washington, we don't spend all our time plotting to use government or even to stop it from growing.

We're busy tending to our own lives and earning the money to meet the enormous tax burden. Thus we're out-gunned by the bureaucrats, leaders, and lobbyists who live and breathe politics — the people who are always Johnny-on-the-spot to support the politicians when they want to initiate new programs, protect existing programs, and expand them.

So even the most egregious, wasteful, and harmful government programs become immortal. And most proposals to expand government are cheered into law by this determined minority.

The pressure is always for government to grow.

The Serpent in the Garden

Our wants are infinite, while our resources are limited. There always will be things we want but can't have.

43

Government is like the serpent in the Garden of Eden, tempting us by promising to give us more than our resources would allow — if we will just turn our lives over to the government. It's understandable that people so easily give into the temptation.

And once government starts handing out goodies taken from someone else, the demands on government start growing — and they never stop.

Because it's so easy for government to grow — and because government programs, once in place, rarely are terminated — government eventually will suffocate us unless there are absolute, enforceable limits on what government can do.

FREEDOM COMES FROM LIMITS ON GOVERNMENT

America's unique success stems from the Constitution the Founding Fathers created to limit the federal government.

The Constitution permitted the federal government to provide a few services — national defense, a court system, legal tender, a postal system — but nothing more. The government was given no blanket authority to manage society or run your life.

The Founding Fathers knew that such things as education, commerce, agriculture, law enforcement, and charity would be more efficient, less expensive, and less intrusive of our liberty if handled by the states or by the people on their own. So the 9th and 10th amendments to the Constitution made it clear that the federal government was strictly prohibited from doing anything not specifically authorized in the Constitution.

Thus was government bound down by the chains of the Constitution, as Thomas Jefferson put it. The chains on government allowed Americans to feel free. And they *were* free. Not free from want, nor from care, nor from discrimination, nor from insults.

But they had a freedom that citizens in no other country of the world had: *freedom from government.* Free from officious bureaucrats who wanted to direct every aspect of their lives — free from tax-collectors who wanted to take greater and greater parts of their earnings — free of directives from distant rulers.

Yes, freedom from government.

Our American heritage is one of individual liberty, personal responsibility, and freedom from a government strictly limited by a written Constitution.

The Limits Are Gone

Unfortunately, that heritage has been discarded.

Americans no longer have the liberty to direct their own lives. They no longer are responsible for their own choices because bureaucrats choose for them.

The Constitution has been relegated to something the politicians refer to in a 4th-of-July speech or a political argument. It has no real force and effect in preserving your freedom.

In truth, the Constitution is dead, and politicians no longer are restrained by anything. When was the last time your Congressman voted against a bill because he judged it to be unconstitutional?

In fact, almost every time he votes, your Congressman is voting *against* the Constitution.

And the Supreme Court is quite willing to ratify that vote.

The Court decides whether government has a "compelling interest" in overruling the Constitution — and most of the time the Court rules that it does. The judges do this even though nothing in the Constitution says it can be ignored in favor of the government's interests.

WHAT THE CONSTITUTION SAYS

Politicians and political pundits act as though the Constitution were an arcane document that only legal scholars can decipher.

They argue over such things as whether the 1st amendment was meant to cover pornography or "commercial speech." Or whether the 2nd amendment extended gun rights only to state militias. Or whether there's a "penumbra" of privacy somewhere in the Constitution.

These arguments ignore the plain language of the Constitution. Although we keep hearing about the need to interpret the Constitution, the fact is that the Constitution was written in plain English — not Chinese, or Esperanto, or Pig Latin. It doesn't require the Supreme Court or anyone else to interpret it for us.

The 9th amendment to the Constitution says very clearly:

The enumeration in the Constitution, of certain rights, shall not be construed to deny or disparage others retained by the people.

In other words, you retain every right that hasn't been expressly restricted by the Constitution. And the Constitution doesn't include a single restriction on your rights to speech, religion, self-protection, privacy, or most anything else.

Thus the Constitution granted the government no power to restrict advertising, to ban any kind of literature (no matter how much you or I might find it offensive), to take away your right to privacy, or to impair your ability to defend yourself against aggressors.

The Bill of Rights is a simple, straightforward, literal, and absolute document:

- The 1st Amendment says you have a right to speak out even if the government thinks it has a "compelling interest" in shutting you up.
- The 2nd Amendment says you have the right to keep and bear arms even if some madman somewhere uses a gun for a bad purpose.
- The 4th Amendment says you have a right to be safe from search and seizure even if some DEA agent thinks you fit the profile of a drug dealer.
- The 9th Amendment says you retain every right that hasn't been expressly taken from you by the Constitution.
- The 10th Amendment says the government has no authority to engage in any activity that isn't specifically permitted by the Constitution.

The government was never given the power to interfere with your freedoms under any circumstances. Presidents, Congressmen, and judges have taken that power without constitutional authority.

NOW GOVERNMENT IS FREE

And so now the politicians decide for themselves when they will respect the Constitution and when they will ignore it.

To get to where we are now, the politicians needed to violate the Constitutional limits only once. Once they did that, even if it was for a good program, it was just a matter of time until they could pass *any* program they wanted — *good or bad.*

Once the government enacts even one program beyond the constitutional limits, sooner or later you'll have a $1.8 trillion government and a $5 trillion debt. And that's where we are today, with no Constitutional protection against big government.

As Michael Cloud has pointed out, "either the government is in chains or the people are. And when the federal government slipped out of the chains, it slapped them onto us."

So now government is free — free to do whatever it wants — and we are not.

As a result, America is little different from most other nations — nations in which government dominates the lives of its citizens. All the old-world abuses the Founding Fathers wanted to avoid — government extorting a percentage of your income, officious bureaucrats asking to see your papers, government referring to you by number, and more — have come to be taken for granted in America.

America's problems today don't stem from a lack of patriotism, devotion, charity, or goodness. They stem from a lack of individual freedom — from a government without limits.

THE CONSTITUTION MUST BE RESPECTED

Until we recapture the American heritage of limited government, you can expect government to continue to grow, and your liberty to continue to shrink.

You won't get smaller government by proposing new government programs or arguing for the retention of *any* current program not authorized by the Constitution — no matter how beneficial you imagine the program to be.

You really have only two choices. Either:

- We stop the federal government from doing *anything* not authorized in the Constitution, or . . .
- You resign yourself to a government that will continue to grow ever larger, taking more and more of your income, invading more and more of your life.

Either government is free or you are. There is no middle ground.

As Thomas Jefferson put it:

To take a single step beyond the boundaries specially drawn around the powers of Congress is to take possession of a boundless field of power, no longer susceptible to definition.

Libertarians know the goal isn't to pass only the right programs, or to assure that only the right people get elected to positions of power. We realize that's impossible. The goal is to minimize the politicians' power — to limit it by the Constitution. The only power that can never be abused is the power the politicians don't possess.

Once government is again limited to the Constitution, we can each decide for ourselves whether government is too big, too small, or just the right size. And each of us can, if he chooses, work to shrink government further or work to amend the Constitution to give government more power.

But first we must use THE GREAT LIBERTARIAN OFFER to reestablish the constitutional limits.

CHAPTER 6

FREEDOM VS. GOVERNMENT

The world includes people who are greedy and dishonest — people who love money or power much more than they love anything else — people who will lie and cheat, or even worse, to get what they want. Some of these people run private companies.

But a business can survive only by persuading you to buy, and so every business has an incentive to give you what you want. If it fails to do so, it opens the door for a competitor to offer you something better.

It doesn't matter whether a business fails you because of incompetence, fraud, laziness, or just bad luck. You don't have to know the reason. If you don't get what you want, you look elsewhere. So no private business operating on its own is a threat to you — even if it's run by the worst sort of people.

Government, on the other hand, doesn't tolerate competition. You can't choose to pay your taxes to someone else, or to invest your Social Security money with a different organization, or to look for a different agency to regulate your business. Whatever government offers, it forces you to buy — even if the people running it are incompetent, fraudulent, lazy, or chronically unlucky.

If all human beings were honest, benevolent, and efficient, it might be safe to let politicians run your life — since you wouldn't have to worry about incompetence or fraud. But human beings aren't angels. Greed, incompetence, and dishonesty do exist. And it's a terrible mistake to give greedy, incompetent, or dishonest people control over your life — especially since they'll never let you fire them.

If they aren't consistently good, efficient, and charitable, you suffer. You are *forced* to pay their taxes, *forced* to deal with their monopolies, and *forced* to refrain from doing what would be best for you and your family. You have no choice.

By contrast, in the free market it's not essential that everyone be honest and competent, because you don't *have* to deal with any particular person or company. A competitor usually will be there to offer whatever you think the others lack. And one good supplier is usually all you need for anything.

Since not everyone is well-intentioned and competent, which would you prefer — having the freedom to distance yourself from fools and cheats, or giving fools and cheats the power to force you to do their bidding?

Dealing with Reality

Utopia would be the world exactly as you want it. Obviously, that isn't possible. So you must look for the system that's likely to give you the most of what you want.

If you're free of government coercion, you can choose the products, services, solutions, and opportunities you think are best — independent of the choices others make. You can change suppliers whenever you want. And you can patronize several different companies simultaneously, to get exactly the combination of services you want.

But if government is at the center of your life, you will get very little of what you want — because what you get will depend upon who has the most political influence.

What is truly utopian is the hope that the next government program will work better than the last, or that politicians will ignore their own interests when they make decisions about your life, or that we can have an all-powerful government that doesn't attract greedy and dishonest people who cherish that power.

BIG BUSINESS & THE WEALTHY

Some people say you're helpless against wealthy companies. But unless those companies enlist the coercive power of government, they can't force you to do business with them.

Big companies spend big money trying to persuade you to buy from them. But even with enormous advertising budgets, success is never assured.

After spending $250 million, the Coca-Cola Company gave

up when their customers refused to switch from Coke Classic to the New Coke in the 1980s. Before that, Ford Motor Company spent a billion dollars trying unsuccessfully to convince people that the Edsel was the car of their dreams. And Microsoft spent a mint of its own money on the Microsoft Network while the public continued to ignore it.

But the government always gets your business, no matter what. The failure and expense of the Post Office, foreign aid, the Drug War, and the War on Poverty go on and on. Despite the public's disgust, the public is forced to keep paying. Anyone can say "no" to America's biggest companies, but no one can refuse the government.

So you don't have to be afraid of the people with the most money. It makes more sense to fear the people with the most guns — the government.

Who Helps the Poor?

Many people believe the free market is biased against the poorer elements of society — and that government must help the poor. Precisely the opposite is true. It is the rich that do the most for the poor.

As you know, many rich people endow foundations and other charities to provide for those less fortunate. But they also help the poor in less altruistic and less obvious ways.

Look at the products the poor enjoy today — automobiles, cellular phones, computers, even air conditioning in many cases. Every one of these came on the market because of massive investments made either by wealthy people or by large combinations of middle-class investors. Such investments were made because of an expectation that the products could be sold to people who could afford them.

But the early versions of these products were too expensive for the average person. For example, only ten years ago a typical personal computer was priced in the $5,000 to $15,000 range. When automobiles, cellular phones, air conditioning, and fax machines first appeared, they too were priced out of the reach of most people.

It was the purchases of wealthier people that made it possible for these products to survive. Then, as the market broadened, competition drove the prices down until they were within reach of virtually everyone in society.

Because the market is still relatively free to introduce most new products without government interference, the poor eventually have access to products and services that middle-class people can't get in many other countries. In fact, in many ways America's "poor" are poor only by comparison to better off Americans — but not poor relative to the rest of the world.

UNLEASHING FREEDOM

Because freedom works, you and virtually everyone else can enjoy air travel, antibiotics, inexpensive fax machines, cellular phones, and satellite dishes — products and services that yesterday's millionaires could find only in science fiction.

For $1,000 you can buy a computer far more powerful than the one used to design the first hydrogen bomb. You can make a long-distance phone call for 5% to 10% of what it cost 20 years ago.

What has government done for you during the past few decades?

- Is postal service faster or less expensive?
- Is your children's school system twice as efficient at half the cost?
- Is your community safer?
- Have the drug warriors reduced the damage done by drugs?
- Is government less expensive than it was in 1980 or 1990?

Is *any* government program better today than it was a decade or two ago? Does any city, town, or state in America pay less for government than it did a decade ago?

Please keep in mind the free market's achievements and the government's failures when you hear the next plea for a government program. It will be far more expensive and much less efficient than promised — and not nearly as satisfying as what could be achieved privately if government would get out of the way and stop taking our money.

Removing the Obstacle

The biggest obstacle to getting what you want today is the government — with its taxes, regulations, prohibitions, and mandates.

Reducing government and getting it out of our way will unleash the incentives that produce what you want:

- The companies that increase your standard of living with new products, and services and better-paying jobs;
- The private charities that actually help the needy, rather than turn them into permanent dependents;
- The innovative people who make their fortunes by identifying what you want and helping you get it.

It is said "The government should do for the people only what they cannot do for themselves." But there's nothing the government can do for you that you can't do for yourself. And you can do it far less expensively, far more easily, far more securely, and far more to your liking by calling on the help of people seeking to make a profit. In addition, you can choose whatever you want for yourself, without first having to obtain the approval of the electorate, the establishment, or anyone else.

But suppose there's something you just can't imagine getting in the free market — something you feel must be done by government. Is that one program worth opening the door to an organization that charges $1.8 trillion per year and strangles us in nightmarish laws and regulations?

Wouldn't you be willing to forgo that program in exchange for much smaller government and no income tax?

DO YOU REALLY WANT GOVERNMENT TO DO IT?

The next time a government program or a new law seems attractive, please ask yourself these questions:

1. Do you really want to make this a matter of fines and prison terms?
2. Do you really want to transform this matter into a political issue — to be decided by whoever has the most political influence?
3. Do you really expect this program to retain its original size and scope, without spreading into other areas of your life?
4. Do you really think the program will operate in the way you imagine — knowing that you won't control it?
5. Do you really want to hand the government power that can be misused in the future by a politician you may despise?

6. Do you really believe this program or law will achieve its goal — knowing that no existing government program has matched the promises made for it?

7. Are you willing to breach the Constitution to have your way — opening the door ever wider to whatever tomorrow's politicians want?

Wouldn't You Rather Have the Free Market Do it?

After reflecting on government's drawbacks, consider the virtues of the free market:

1. **You don't have to find the solution yourself.** Maybe you don't know how to solve a particular problem, but there are people who do — people with the talent, skills, and experience to find the solution. The opportunity for profit — in money or in satisfaction — will propel them to find the best way and offer it to you. It doesn't matter whether it's a need for products, services, charity, research, security, or anything else. If there's something people want but aren't getting, the opportunity to get rich will attract someone who will figure out how to provide it.

2. **Competition will assure the best.** If one company falls down on the job, eager competitors will move in. No government service has ever satisfied users more than one freely developed by individuals in pursuit of a profit. If we want the best, it will come from private companies competing for profit, not from politicians feigning benevolence.

3. **It will cost much less without government.** Competition prods companies to lower their costs and share the savings with their customers. Even five years ago, no one expected computer prices to go as low as they have. Politicians, on the other hand, have no motivation to reduce costs and every incentive to increase their budgets.

4. **If you leave this to the free market, no one will force anything on you.** You won't have to pay for anything, you won't have to participate in anything — not until *you* are satisfied that you're getting what you want. You will be free to choose the alternative you judge best — and

free to delay your choice until you're sure of what you're getting.

5. **If you can keep your own money, you can get what you need.** Once we have made THE GREAT LIBERTARIAN OFFER a reality, you will have additional thousands of dollars a year available to get whatever you want — how you want it, when you want it.

MOVING FORWARD, INSTEAD OF BACKWARD

Freedom has given you everything you treasure. Government has given you problems you don't want. Still, the government's public relations machine convinces many people that only government can provide what we need.

A popular joke in the Soviet Union told of two women standing in line waiting to buy bread at a government store. One of them said, "Isn't this disgraceful — having to wait three hours to buy a loaf of bread?!"

"Yes, but still we really are fortunate," the other responded. "At least our government produces bread. The government doesn't do that in capitalist countries."

So, too, here in America there are people who believe that whatever the government does now could never be done by private companies. No matter how badly government handles a service, they think it would be even worse without the government — that there would be no electricity, water, education, highways, help for the poor, medical care for the aged, or even farms if the government didn't produce, subsidize, or regulate these things.

If government had taken over the production of cars in 1920, today we'd all be driving expensive, uncomfortable, unreliable, hard-to-get Model-T cars — and saying, "We really are fortunate; if it weren't for the government, we'd have no cars at all."

PART II
THE ISSUES

CHAPTER 7

DO YOU WANT FREEDOM
OR SYMBOLISM?

In this part of the book we will look at a number of today's issues.

As we examine them, we must separate symbolism from substance. We must continually remind ourselves of what we really want — freedom — and not be lured into supporting whatever seems to be the least bad choice.

I say this because politicians know how to propose "solutions" that are purely symbolic — achieving nothing except to convince you they are on your side.

- When a politician supports a "school choice" bill to provide vouchers for a handful of children in a poor neighborhood (at an extremely high cost), he is playing with symbols. How will the program help *your* children? Why, instead of applying a few Band-Aids, isn't he working to end all federal meddling with local schools? Why isn't he working to repeal the income tax — so you can afford to send your child to any school, secular or religious, that meets your qualifications?

- When a politician supports a "Patient's Bill of Rights," he is making a symbolic gesture — pretending to care about the difficulty you face in getting adequate health care. Why isn't he trying to get the federal government entirely out of health care — instead of trying to paper over the problems the politicians have caused?

- When a politician "fights crime" by supporting more gun control laws or tougher prison sentences, he must know these measures have done nothing to make you safer. He's making a symbolic gesture — feigning a deep concern for "the children" and for your safety, but doing nothing effective for either.

- When Congress imposed economic sanctions on South Africa in 1986, the politicians knew they were destroying the jobs of thousands of black South Africans — the very people they were supposed to be helping. But who cares how many people went hungry? It's the symbol that counts.

Politicians propose to post the 10 Commandments in government schools, to finance big government with a sales tax instead of an income tax, to cut off trade with unpopular countries, to beat up on big business. But none of these proposals will change your life in any significant way. They are empty gestures — mere posturing to try to convince you that the politicians really care about you.

Let's Get Real

They don't. And the proof of that is revealed in the way they avoid proposing anything that could make a dramatic improvement in your life.

A politician in Congress or your state legislature can introduce any bill he wants. He isn't limited to symbolic gestures. He can push for the real thing — a bill that would actually get the government completely out of the areas where it's causing problems. Even if such a bill wouldn't pass today, introducing it can change the terms of debate and put us on the right road — one that leads to a real solution.

But if you examine the records of all those politicians who cozy up to you and tell you how hard they work for "smaller government," you will find many empty gestures and very few genuine attempts to eliminate specific government activities.

When a politician uses symbolic gestures, he's proving that *he isn't there to help you*; he's there to help himself. His symbolic gestures are an attempt to keep you on his side — not to change things for the better.

ASKING FOR WHAT WE WANT

The solutions I will propose in the chapters ahead might

seem too extreme to some people — who may say we should move more gradually.

But what has gradualism achieved? Of what value is it to propose a "solution" that doesn't actually solve anything?

If you want to change America for the better, don't begin by asking "What can we get?"

Ask "What do I want?"

- Do you want to get rid of the income tax entirely by reducing government dramatically? Or would you be satisfied just to change the method by which you pay for big government?

- Do you want to be free to save and invest *all* the money you earn? Or will you be satisfied with the freedom to divert a mere 2% of the current 15% Social Security tax to an alternative approved by the politicians?

- Do you want to end the criminal black markets in drugs, the addicts who are prohibited by law from seeking medical help, the gang warfare, the invasions of your liberty in the name of the War on Drugs? Or would you be satisfied with a few cosmetic changes that leave the drug market in the hands of criminals?

- Do you want to be free to buy the medicines, products, and services you think are best for you, and to control your own property completely? Or will you be satisfied with a promise by the regulators to apply "cost-benefit analysis" to new restrictions?

As you look at the proposals I'll make in the coming chapters, don't ask, "Is this politically possible today?" Ask yourself the essential first question: *Is this what you want?*

If it is, we can think about the best route to get it. But if you start by settling for less than what you really want, you give up all chance of ever getting it.

KEEPING YOUR FOCUS

Because we're human beings, we're bound to have differences in opinion. We all want different things, and we may have different ideas about how to change the government.

But where we do agree is that we want government to be much smaller than it is today.

We can get that smaller government only if we can rally enough people to a common goal. The goal must be limiting the federal government to what the Constitution authorizes, because only that will provide a reward — repealing the income tax — that's big enough to motivate large numbers of people.

Once that's achieved, you and your family will be much freer, far more prosperous, and living in a far more peaceful community. And then you can, if you choose, work to make government even more to your liking. If you think it's still too large, you can work to reduce it. If you think it's too small, you can work to amend the Constitution to add what you think is necessary.

But you throw away any chance to get smaller government if you start making exceptions for unconstitutional government programs that seem to provide some benefit.

Saying "Government is too big, it doesn't work well, it's stealing our freedom" and then proposing a government solution to any problem is a sure way to discredit yourself and start down the road to endless arguments about specific programs.

When you're tempted to make an exception for government intrusions in some area, I hope you'll remember:

- *Government is force.* Every government program is backed by the coercive power to compel people to alter their lives. For government to provide what you want, it must take it by force from someone else.

- *Government is politics.* Whenever you turn anything over to the government, you transform it into a political issue — to be decided by whoever has the most political influence. And that will never be you or me.

- *You don't control the government.* No government program will operate as you imagine it should. The politicians and bureaucrats will transform your wonderful idea to suit themselves — into something quite different from what you envision.

- *Power is sure to be misused eventually.* When you give a good politician the power to do good, you give many future politicians the power to do bad.

- *Government doesn't work.* Because government is force, because it is political, because your intentions won't matter, because power will always be misused, government simply won't deliver what you want. I don't know of any government program that has achieved what it promised.

• *Government must be subject to absolute limits.* Because politicians have every incentive to expand government, and with it their power, there must be absolute limits on government. The Constitution provides the obvious limits we must reimpose upon the federal government. Until the Constitution is enforced, we have no hope of containing the federal government.

And so, as you examine the issues in the chapters ahead, please realize that we defeat our attempt to make government smaller if we make exceptions — if we allow government to exceed the Constitution in *any* area.

Once we allow a single exception, the floodgates are open and we have a $1.8 trillion government and a $5 trillion federal debt.

That isn't what I want. And I doubt that you do either.

I believe what you want is the freedom to live your life as you want and to raise your children as you think best.

THE GREAT LIBERTARIAN OFFER will give you that freedom.

CHAPTER 8

FREEDOM FROM THE INCOME TAX

The income tax is the most oppressive method of paying for government programs.

To enforce an income tax — whether it is flat, bumpy, or progressive — the government must have the power to peer into every corner of your life — without a warrant and without evidence of a crime. Treasury agents enforcing the income tax routinely pore through customer records at your bank, and ask your banker to investigate "unusual" transactions.

Because the income tax and the IRS (Internal Revenue Service) are so widely despised, the politicians love to posture as friends of the downtrodden taxpayer. They've turned the public's disenchantment to their own advantage by proposing measures to ease the pain. The most prominent remedies are:

- Replace the graduated income tax with a flat tax (an income tax with a single rate for all taxpayers).
- Replace the graduated income tax with a national sales tax.
- Tame the IRS with reforms.
- Eliminate the IRS entirely, replacing it with a kinder, gentler tax-collector.

It's understandable that taxpayers hope to find relief in these proposals. But none of them will ever remove terror and force from the tax-collection business because of one simple fact:

The federal government spends $1.8 trillion every year.

Where is that $1.8 trillion going to come from?

Will the Russians provide it? Has a guardian angel stepped forward to pay it? I don't think so.

So who will pay the $1.8 trillion?

Obviously, you and I and other Americans will have to pay it. Whatever the tax system, we have to provide every dollar the politicians spend.

And since no prominent politician has offered a specific proposal to dramatically reduce the size of government, we must face up to two basic truths:

1. Any change in the tax code, the tax rates, or the method of taxation will change only the *method* of payment, not the *amount* of payment.
2. No matter what the tax system, big government requires a pitiless, oppressive, take-no-prisoners tax-collection agency. If the IRS were reined in, revenues would plummet and the politicians would have to get by with less. So despite the grandstanding, no one is going to "pull the IRS up by the roots" or "drive a stake through its heart." They may change its name to the Benevolent Service Agency, but its methods won't change.

Since smaller government isn't a part of the politicians' plans, a sales tax or flat tax will require a high single rate to cover the cost of big government. It will be far more expensive than its proponents suggest, and thus unlikely ever to become a reality.

But by championing either of those alternatives, a politician can pose as your friend — the tireless advocate who is working night and day to free you from the income tax.

The National Sales Tax

Some politicians say a 15% national sales tax will produce as much money as the existing income tax. But if Congress ever got serious about the plan, the simple 15% sales tax would become a complicated tax code with a rate far above 15%.

The compassionate caucus will complain that the sales tax falls more heavily on the poor; so there will have to be exemptions for food, rent, and other things that poor people rely on. Or low-income individuals will simply receive a free pass — perhaps ID cards exempting them from any sales tax.

And plausible arguments will be made to exempt various

"necessities" — which, coincidentally, will be products produced by politically powerful industries. Do you think building contractors won't lobby to get home purchases exempted? And what about new cars? And health care? And — well, you get the point.

The exemptions will leave fewer transactions to be taxed. So the tax rate will have to be higher than 15% — much higher — to cover all the costs of big government. How high will the rate have to be? I don't know, but 20% or more seems likely.

And that's just for starters. Everytime the politicians spend more than the tax produces, they will have to raise the tax in the name of "fiscal responsibility."

The tax rate also will rise because a 20% rate is a strong incentive for tax avoidance and evasion. We should expect a black market to develop in jewelry, cell phones, VCRs — any products that are relatively small and of large value. And so the number of transactions actually taxed will be smaller than expected, requiring a higher tax rate.

The actual rate could easily become 25% or higher — which, with state and local sales taxes, comes to 30% or more.

Do you think the American people will rally to the idea of paying the government 30% everytime they buy something?

I doubt it. And so the plan has little chance to succeed.

Some sales-tax advocates claim the plan's virtue is that Americans will revolt against big government once the sales tax makes plain how much they're paying to government, leading to a demand for smaller government. But that same revulsion against a 20-30% tax rate will remove the sales tax from serious consideration.

So why should we spin our wheels trying to a enact a sales-tax plan that is only an intermediate step toward smaller government and has little chance to succeed?

The Flat Tax

A flat tax is no more promising.

A single tax rate won't eliminate the IRS. You might file your return on a postcard, as flat-tax proponents claim, but your friendly IRS agent would still demand to see your records and put the burden on you to prove that you have no hidden income.

In order to get their ideas accepted, flat-tax politicians brag that their plans will remove millions of people from the income tax rolls entirely. But if you realize that *someone* has to pay for big government, you know that freeing specific people from paying income tax creates two problems:

1. You and other taxpayers will have to make up the difference somehow.
2. Anyone freed from the cost of government has an incentive to support new government programs, because *he* won't have to pay for them — *you* will. So this doesn't move us toward smaller government; it does just the opposite.

As with the proposed sales tax, after making room for a multitude of exemptions, the flat rate would be much higher than the 15% to 20% you hear about today.

Read the Fine Print

Even if there were no exemptions in a sales tax or a flat tax, either plan still would be unattractive to too many people. So long as we are wedded to big government, any new tax must generate as much revenue as the present system. So if anyone pays less under the new tax rules, someone else must be paying more. Will the latter person welcome the change?

Because the rates would have to be so high, neither the sales tax nor the flat tax has a chance to succeed. But politicians don't live off successes, they live off promises. When a proposal dies in a Congressional committee, an experienced politician will simply blame the failure on his opponents — and continue to promote his fantasy tax reform for years and years.

Freedom from oppressive taxes means getting rid of big government, not finding a new way to finance it. By reducing government dramatically, we can have the best kind of flat income tax imaginable — one with a flat rate of 0%.

And only that kind of rate is so clear, attractive, and immediate that the American people will be motivated to reduce government dramatically.

OTHER POLITICAL DECEPTIONS

Politicians love to propose tax cuts because proposing is free and involves no effort. But even when the tax cuts are enacted, your load doesn't get lighter. So long as government is expensive, you and I must pay through the nose. And politicians have no real interest in making government smaller.

A favorite specialty of politicians is buttering up the middle class. They continually cry out for "middle-class tax relief." But no matter how often the tax code is reformed, most income tax still is paid by people in the $19,000 to $100,000 range — by the great middle class the politicians claim to love so much. The middle class continues to pay most of the bill because it's the largest group from which to extract the revenue.

Whenever a politician tells you of tax cuts he sponsored, voted for, or signed, ask him how much he has reduced the overall size of government. If he can prove he actually reduced the overall burden of government, stuff him and put him in a museum — as an extraordinarily rare specimen.

Reforming the IRS

Every few years Congress publicizes horror stories of families destroyed by the tax-collectors. Then the politicians pass an IRS reform bill — as they did in 1988, 1996, and 1998.

But nothing ever changes — as we can see from the continued Congressional hearings with new horror stories.

After enacting the latest reform in 1998, the politicians congratulated themselves on shifting the burden of proof in tax controversies from you to the IRS.

But if the IRS audits your tax return, you still have to prove anything the IRS disputes; it has to prove nothing. If your case goes to a Tax Court, the IRS need only show some basis for making its assessment of the tax or penalty; the burden of proof is still on you to show the IRS wrong.

Only in criminal prosecutions does the burden of proof shift to the government, and such prosecutions are very rare.

There's a good reason the IRS is never truly reformed. The politicians have only two choices: either (1) let the IRS run roughshod over us, or (2) be unable to finance big government.

Which do you think they'll choose?

TWO SIDES OF REAL RELIEF

We don't need a simplified income tax. We don't need a replacement tax. Our lives will be better only when we reduce the burden of taxes by reducing dramatically the cost of government.

We've seen that you can't get rid of government spending so long as you try to do it one program at a time. The pressure to keep any one program will be concentrated and intense, while the incentive for eliminating the program will be dispersed and diluted among millions of people.

Americans will rally to large reductions in government only when they're offered a large reward.

And that reward is the total repeal of the income tax . . .

- Not a dinky tax cut that can be rescinded next year;
- Not a change to a lower, flat rate of tax — which can be raised soon afterward (as the 1986 flatter rate of 28% grew to 40% in only seven years);
- Not a switch to a sales tax you'll have to pay everytime you buy something.

We will never cut federal spending by even one dollar unless we offer the American people the complete repeal of the income tax as an incentive to reduce government. And we can't repeal the income tax without reducing federal spending dramatically. The two tasks are inseparable. To attempt one without the other is a formula for failure.

That's why THE GREAT LIBERTARIAN OFFER asks every American: Would you give up your favorite federal programs if it meant you'd never have to pay income tax again?

TOO MANY ON THE DOLE?

It may seem that we can't succeed because too many Americans seem to be net beneficiaries of government.

Nearly 50 million people have some income but pay no federal income tax. They would seem to have every reason to protect a system that bestows benefits without charging them anything. And there are other people who do pay income tax but seem to receive far more than they pay.

But please keep three points in mind.

Everyone Is a Prospect

First, while it may seem that many people won't benefit personally from THE GREAT LIBERTARIAN OFFER, we shouldn't write off anyone — even people who live off government payments.

There are many reasons someone might wind up on welfare, for example. Some like the idea of a permanent, if shabby, vacation — while others have undergone extraordinary personal tragedies. But one thing is true about most every welfare recipient: he doesn't want his children to be on welfare. It's not like a family business he wants to pass on to the next generation.

If we can show welfare recipients how much more rewarding the job market will be when we repeal the income tax, and how much better off they and their children will be when we get government completely out of welfare, they may rally to our side.

Plenty of government employees are allies as well. If you want to verify that government doesn't work, just ask a government employee to tell his own horror stories. Many of them feel tied to careers that aren't nearly as rewarding, emotionally or financially, as they'd expected when they began their jobs. Repealing the income tax will make it much easier for most of them to get a head start on a new career in the free market.

Retired people may not pay much income tax, but they have strong reasons to support us. What's the most important element in their lives? In most cases, their children and grandchildren. They advise them, they dote on them, they follow their progress closely, they pray for them.

And what are we offering? To lift the burden of income tax from their children's shoulders, to give them an immediate and permanent increase in take-home pay of 30% to 50% — and to enable their grandchildren to go through their entire careers free of the income tax.

Finally, no matter how many people currently pay no income tax, well over 100 million people aren't so lucky — and that's more than the number who vote in presidential and Congressional elections.

Poor Trade

Second, those who seem to get more in benefits than they pay in tax usually are worse off as a result.

Suppose you pay, say, $10,000 per year in income tax, while government spends $14,000 on you personally. Despite the numbers, you don't actually come out $4,000 ahead. You're giving up $10,000 you could have spent on anything you want — but the $14,000 is spent on "benefits" the politicians choose. The programs may *cost* $14,000, but their *value* to you may be a good deal less than the $10,000 you had to pay for them.

In the same way, we hear that some states are "net gainers"; they receive more in subsidies from the federal government than their citizens pay in federal taxes. But the subsidies are for what the politicians want — and are worth less to the citizens of the state than the taxes they pay.

In addition, the subsidies may be concentrated among a handful of large, politically connected companies in the state, while the average taxpayer remains a net loser. All those new federal buildings may enrich contractors and a few new federal employees, but the buildings' only benefits to most citizens are the shadows they cast.

Government Doesn't Work

Third, Americans as a whole receive far less from government than they give up.

If that weren't true, we'd have to say that government *can* create something from nothing, that there *is* such a thing as a free lunch, and — yes — that government does work.

Most Americans get far less from government than they pay into it. If they believe they're net winners, it's because many of the taxes they pay are hidden and because they're never asked to compare their overall tax load with their meager benefits.

THE GREAT LIBERTARIAN OFFER provides a more realistic comparison.

RELATED TAXES

THE GREAT LIBERTARIAN OFFER includes the repeal of all direct federal taxes — the personal income tax, taxes on interest and dividends, capital gains tax, estate tax, gift tax, corporate income tax, and Social Security taxes.[1]

Repealing the corporate income tax means employers will be able to offer more money to make sure you and other good employees don't go to work elsewhere, more money to invest in new tools that will make you more productive and more valuable, more money with which to develop new markets that will increase the demand for your work. If you're a valuable part of your company, repealing the corporate income tax should increase your earnings and other job benefits.

The estate tax must go as well. It licenses IRS agents to become grave-robbers — picking over the remains of the dead. You should be free to leave what you've accumulated to people and organizations that are important to you — even to your Congressman if you want.

---

[1]Social Security will be covered in the next chapter.

In the same way, you should be free to make gifts in any amount without incurring a tax.

No matter what you think of inherited wealth, the desire of talented people to leave large estates to their children or to charity has driven many of society's benefactors to work harder — providing benefits to you and me.

REMAINING TAXES

For over a hundred years there was no income tax, because the federal government stuck pretty closely to the Constitution. So the government survived easily on just tariffs (taxes on imports) and excise taxes (taxes imposed on the producers of particular goods and services).

Today those taxes produce more than enough to finance a strong national defense, the court system, and the few other functions the Constitution authorizes for the federal government.

Are these good taxes? I don't think so. In my mind, the only good tax is a dead tax. I don't want to force anyone to do anything.

Tariffs and excise taxes are neither voluntary nor fair. But they involve fewer intrusions on the average citizen than other, more direct taxes. And compared with the wholesale brutality of the income tax, they seem no more painful than an elbow in the ribs.

All imports should carry the same tax rate — which, if spread over all imported products, should be no more than 2%. Tariffs never should favor one industry over another — never be a tool by which politicians can hinder competition for politically connected industries.

Excise taxes include taxes on alcohol, tobacco, telephone service, gasoline, and dozens of other products and services. As soon as possible, these taxes should be reduced as well, and never should be used to put one industry at a disadvantage to another.

Chapter 21 describes a federal budget with enough revenue for national defense and other constitutional activities. Once we have limited the federal government to its constitutional functions, we can look for ways to reduce the cost of government even more — reducing the remaining taxes further and further.

Taxes & Lotteries

Despite my aversion to taxes, even a small federal government will need to be paid for. Government is force, and there is no obvious way to pay for it without taxes.

Most states now use lotteries to raise part of their budgets. Seeing this, some people believe a libertarian federal government could be financed in the same way — eliminating the need for any taxes.

But state lotteries have large profits to contribute to a state's budget only because they offer such poor odds to their customers. They couldn't get customers with those poor odds if they didn't forcibly exclude all competitors.

By contrast, Nevada has no state lottery because it couldn't compete with legal casinos that offer much better odds on Keno, roulette, and other games of chance.

In a free society, open competition would improve lottery odds and reduce the operators' profits, leaving no room to divert money to government programs.[2]

STATE TAXES & SPENDING

You might worry that state and local governments will offset federal reductions in taxes and spending with higher state taxes and spending.

That's possible, but not probable.

More likely, state income taxes will disappear shortly after the federal income tax is repealed.

Today a half-dozen states don't have an income tax. But there isn't a large migration of people to those states because people still have to pay federal income tax — which is a far greater burden.

But once the federal income tax is gone, moving to a no-income-tax state means complete freedom from the income tax — a much greater lure. California would have to repeal its income tax to keep some of the best companies and productive people from moving to Nevada — which has no income tax. And Georgia would have to repeal its income tax to keep high-earners from choosing Florida. Other states would have to compete with no-income-tax states like New Hampshire, North Dakota, Texas,

---

[2]In 1995 the average state lottery paid out only 58% of its gross receipts in prizes. The average Las Vegas casino, facing competition, pays out over 96% of its gross receipts to winners.

and Tennessee — or else face declining populations and dwindling property values.

Some states might try to raise other taxes to replace the income tax. But I believe competition among states will lead to much smaller government and lower taxes in almost all states.

WHERE THE MONEY COMES FROM

It is only during the last 60 years or so that people have come to assume that the government must spend money on school lunches or children will starve, that government must support single mothers or they'll die in the streets, that government must pay for research or progress will stop.

Having lived with this assumption for so long, people ask, "If the income tax is repealed, where will the money come from to take care of education, the poor, or [fill in the blank]?"

But where does the money come from now? From the people — from you and me. All the money the government spends was taken from those who earned it — people who are quite competent to spend it on anything they believe is important.

With much smaller government and no income tax, people will be free to decide for themselves where they want the money to go and how it will be spent. The money no longer will be routed through Washington — where people who didn't earn it can spend without limit, where goals are turned upside down to satisfy those with political influence, where "education" money is used to destroy schools, and where "welfare" money is used to cripple the poor.

Where the Money Could Go

Repealing the income tax will leave an extra trillion dollars a year in the hands of individual Americans — money now being poured down government rat holes.

That trillion dollars will buy a job for everyone who can work and charity for everyone who can't.

Can you envision the jobs that will be created? Can you imagine the increase in charity? Whatever the problem, the people most interested in solving it will have the means to do so.

Is there a shortage of day care? Repeal the income tax and you can take care of your children much better than government can.

Is the school system deaf to your demands for better academic training and safer facilities? Repeal the income tax and you'll have the wherewithal to put your child in whatever private or religious school you choose.

Are there people down and out and in need of help? Repeal the income tax so that those who really care will have the money to nurture them properly.

Whatever the issue, the answer is to free you and everyone else to keep all the money you earn — *all* the money, not just some of it.

Double Benefit

Government *taking* from us the money we could use to take care of ourselves is only half the problem. Government *spending* the money has doubled the damage. The federal government has destroyed American education, it is decimating our health-care system, and it has recruited millions of Americans into permanent welfare dependence.

THE GREAT LIBERTARIAN OFFER says: give up your favorite federal programs in exchange for never having to pay income tax again. Considering what the government does with those federal programs, perhaps THE GREAT LIBERTARIAN OFFER should be:

Would you be willing to end the destruction of education, the inflation of health-care costs, the decline in law enforcement, the erosion of your liberty, and the political contempt for the Constitution *and* never have to pay income tax again?

Truly, THE GREAT LIBERTARIAN OFFER lets you win both ways — with a huge and immediate increase in take-home pay plus an end to the steady destruction of American society by the federal government.

THE INCOME TAX MUST GO

Take a look at last year's form 1040 or at the stub on your paycheck. See how much you pay in income and Social Security taxes. If yours is a typical middle-class family, you probably pay at least $10,000 per year.

When we repeal those taxes, what will you do with all the extra money you'll have every year?

- Will you put your children in a private school where they'll get the kind of education you want for them?
- Will you make plans to start your own business?

- Will you support your church or your favorite charity in a way you've never been able to do before?
- Will you buy a new home, or take your family on that vacation you've always dreamed of but could never afford?

You should have every dollar you earn — including the $10,000 a year or more you're now losing to the income tax — to spend, to save, to give away as *you* think best.

Is any federal program more attractive than the freedom and prosperity you'll have when we repeal the income tax?

CHAPTER 9

FREE TO PLAN A
SECURE RETIREMENT

Social Security is not your ordinary insurance program. It dispenses with such old-fashioned concepts as saving and wealth-building. There is no salesman to talk to. No long, complicated contract with fine print — and no actuarial tables to get in the way. No decisions for you to make.

It operates on a very simple principle:

> *The politicians take your money from you and spend it as they please.*

For all your working years, 15% of what you earn (up to $60,600 of earnings per year) goes to the politicians as Social Security tax. They might spend your money on other people's retirements — or use it to buy votes, build monuments to themselves, or prop up the Russian government for another half hour. But the one thing they'll never do is put your money in an account with your name on it, where it can be invested and grow and build up for your retirement.[1]

No matter how much you've paid into Social Security, the politicians have put *nothing* aside for your retirement. Every dollar they've taken from you has already been spent.

Anything Social Security eventually pays you will be taken by force from the paychecks of younger people — probably including your own children and grandchildren.

---

[1]As of 2000, the Social Security tax is 7.65% taken from your paycheck and 7.65% paid directly by your employer. The employer's share is money that would otherwise have been paid to you. So the actual tax on you (as well as on any self-employed person) is 15.30% on the first $60,600 of your yearly earnings — for a maximum tax of $9,271 per year.

Of course, such a system is inherently unsound — robbing Peter to pay Paul, then robbing Patty to pay Peter, and then searching for someone to rob in order to pay Patty. Because the system is fueled by taxing and spending, rather than by saving and investing, keeping it going gets harder and harder.

So the politicians have to "save" Social Security every few years. They do this by changing the rules. The tax rate goes up. The amount of your wages subject to tax goes up. The retirement age goes up. And the benefit schedules change. If they keep "saving" Social Security this way, one day someone may have to pay 85% of his income in order to receive a pension of $100 a month when he retires at age 92[2].

In any event, keeping the program going is getting harder and harder as people stay alive longer and longer. And every advance in medical science makes the Social Security problem worse. Only for Social Security administrators would a cure for cancer be a catastrophe.

The latest forecast of the Government Accounting Office says that by 2014 Social Security will be unable to pay its bills if it doesn't get another fix soon.

The Future

Social Security isn't unique. It's a model of government in action — taking from some, giving to others, and promising more to everyone.

To keep the game going, the politicians make more and more promises without knowing who's going to pay for them. And so the liabilities mount up — until some future Congress has to deal with the situation by raising taxes, by reneging on some of the promises, and by restricting your freedom even further.

Economists have estimated that a young person entering the workforce today will have to pay 70% of his lifetime income in taxes just to cover all the promises *already* made for Social Security and other government schemes. But how many people will show up for work if 70% of their earnings is taken from them?

So eventually the government will be able to survive only by reducing drastically many of the "services" it has promised. One day your Social Security check will be cut. Or some banks will

---

[2]When the system started in 1935, the tax was 2% on the first $3,000 of your earnings — for a maximum tax of $60 per year.

fail but the government insurance system won't have the money to cover all the losses. Or you'll get sick in your old age but Medicare will be so broke it can only hand you a booklet of first-aid tips from Dear Abby.

Most people know intuitively that the government won't keep its promises — especially those for Social Security. In fact, one poll found that only 32% of all Americans who haven't yet retired believe they will ever collect Social Security benefits. In the under-30 age group, more believe in flying saucers than in the survival of Social Security. And, of course, their skepticism is well founded.

You can't trust politicians with your health, or to make sure banks are safe, or to manage welfare, or to put your safety or financial future ahead of their own interests. So it should be obvious that you can't trust politicians with your retirement money.

Turning anything over to politicians makes it a political issue — to be decided in favor of whoever has the most political influence. And that will never be you or me.

MAXIMIZING RETIREMENT

Social Security doesn't invest your money, it spends it. So it will always be a poor alternative to the simplest system of saving and investing. This makes the Social Security tax especially painful because you could do so much more with the 15% the politicians are taking from you.

If you pay money into a private retirement account, you have a guaranteed contract you can count on. The contract never changes without your permission, and no one can take anything away from you. And in addition to providing a retirement income for yourself, you accumulate capital you can pass on to your children.

Suppose you're 25 years old today, starting out on a career. And suppose, instead of paying 15% to Social Security, you could keep that and save it on your own — perhaps doing nothing more sophisticated than keeping it in a bank savings account, earning yearly interest of only 5%. And, lastly, suppose your first year's salary is $25,000, growing from there by 5% each year.

When you retire, your savings would produce a monthly income of $4,510 (compared with Social Security's maximum benefit of $1,433). In addition, you would leave an estate of over

$1 million for your heirs, whereas Social Security gives you no estate at all.

Or, if you'd be happy with Social Security's maximum benefit of $1,433, you could acquire that by saving only 5% of your income, rather than by pouring 15% of it into Social Security. And you'd still leave an estate of over $350,000 — compared with $0 for Social Security.[3]

POLITICAL REFORMS OF SOCIAL SECURITY

Politicians aren't interested in plans to make your retirement secure through private savings, however. They want to keep you locked into the present system. "Saving Social Security" is a mantra for both Democrats and Republicans. To them, it means saving their control over your life.

No politician is suggesting you have the right as a free American to drop out of Social Security whenever you want. Or that you be allowed to control completely your own earnings or your own retirement. Or that Social Security should be operated like any prudent private insurance company — one that guarantees to meet its obligations by saving and investing the money it collects.

No chance. All the suggestions for saving Social Security are about gaining power and ducking blame — putting off the problem, raising taxes, or giving the government more control and calling it reform.

Democratic proposals include having the Social Security Administration invest some of its tiny reserves in the stock market — instead of keeping them all in U.S. government bonds, as is done now. This supposedly would increase the return and eliminate the need to raise the Social Security tax. Just think, Al Gore will be your investment advisor.

Even if the politicians *could* invest sensibly in stocks, actually producing more money, this would serve only to give them more money to squander. And they'd still be back every few years, pushing another tax increase to bail out a bankrupt system.

The Republicans, on the other hand, talk about "privatizing" Social Security. Does that mean the 15% they've been taking

---

[3]The table on page 268 shows how well you can retire at age 65, based on when you start saving and how much of your income you set aside for investing.

from you will be yours to keep and invest however you want? Not on your life. They have in mind letting you keep, maybe, 2% of the 15% they've been taking from you — just as serfs were allowed to keep a small portion of the food they produced for their masters.

Of course, you'll have to invest that 2% in ways the government approves of — which means dealing only with companies that have ingratiated themselves with the politicians. And the government still will take the other 13% of the Social Security tax and send it down that big rat hole in Washington.

Some Republican proposals promise to increase the 2% gradually until one day you'll get to keep the entire 15%. When will that be? The foremost Republican plan estimates you'll have complete control in 60 years. Just think: your great-great-grandchildren might be completely free from the Social Security scheme.

Except, of course, that plans to reduce government control gradually are quickly discarded.

- In 1981 Congress enacted a plan to reduce taxes over three years. In the second year they *raised* taxes, and did so again in the third year.
- In 1997 Congress made a big show of putting "spending caps" into the federal budget — *permanent* limits on how much the government could spend on most items within the budget. The following year the politicians discarded the caps.
- In 1999 the President and Congress noisily pledged to set aside any surplus receipts from the Social Security tax to pay for future Social Security benefits. Three months later, spending the surplus on the war in Yugoslavia seemed like a better idea.

A multi-year transition program is usually a lie and always a failure. It's the diet you'll start next month and the weeds you'll pull when the weather's better.[4]

Even if the politicians stuck to such a plan for the full 60 years, why should we have to wait decades to be completely free of Social Security?

---

[4]Long-term privatization programs in countries like Chile have had more success partly because a dictatorship isn't subject to political pressure to abandon its plans.

Tax Increase Coming

When it's time to pay off on political promises, the money is almost never there. And if politicians can't weasel out of a promise, they have only one way to pay for it: raise taxes. In fact, they've raised Social Security taxes 16 times already. That's an average of once every four years since the program started in 1935.

Each payroll tax increase is touted as the final solution for Social Security, but it really is just one more in a continuing series. So if we let the politicians continue to control Social Security, the next tax increase is inevitable.

Excuses

Republican and Democratic politicians offer all kinds of reasons for hanging on to control over your retirement.

They say that some people don't know how to invest profitably. But, once again, government breaks your legs and then claims that only it can provide the crutch. Saving for your retirement is difficult only because the politicians have made it that way.

If they didn't tax interest earnings, and if their monetary policies didn't create inflation, you could assure a comfortable retirement simply by putting 5% to 10% of your paycheck into a bank savings account — or having your employer do it for you. Even if you know nothing about investing, you could easily take care of yourself — if the politicians would simply leave you alone.

They claim also that government must run your retirement because some people are too irresponsible to plan ahead.

Of course, some people wouldn't provide for their own retirement. But it is wrong to force *everyone* into a fraudulent system just because a few people won't take responsibility. It's like saying that since not everyone can drive well, *no one* should be allowed to drive — and we all have to ride in the government bus, even as it careens along the edge of a cliff.

Because government taxes away half our income, planning for retirement *is* difficult today. The obvious solution is to reduce taxes dramatically, end Social Security, and let you save the amount you think is right.

That was the system we had before Social Security was enacted. People saved for their own retirement. Those few people who wound up with nothing were taken care of by private charity; their retirement wasn't as comfortable as that of more responsible people, but they lived as well as people who are wholly dependent on Social Security today.

REAL REFORM OF SOCIAL SECURITY

So long as Social Security remains in the politicians' hands, it will be unsafe. We can't leave our retirement money lying on the table, for them to grab and spend.

The only way to make Social Security safe is by getting the government out of it.

And the only way to get government out of it is to do so now — completely and forever.

Millions of Americans have paid into Social Security. But since the politicians have already spent that money, they now tax *you* to make good on what they promised to others.

That seems to leave only two alternatives: either (1) you continue paying the tax collector for the retirement of senior citizens or (2) elderly people will lose their pensions.

Political methods always involve using force to take from one and give to another. So political methods can't free you and other Americans from servitude to Social Security without impoverishing those who are already dependent upon it.

But we don't have to solve this problem with political methods.

Real Security for Seniors

If you're retired now or about to be, the present system makes you dependent on the politicians' ability to take more and more money away from your children and grandchildren. No wonder you worry about your future.

In place of Social Security, I want you to have your own individual account with a private company that can guarantee to deliver a lifetime income to you without fail — an income equal to what Social Security has promised.

The politicians will never be able to touch that account or reduce it or borrow from it for their pet programs. It will belong to you and you alone, just like your car or your clothes.

Financing the Transition

It isn't necessary to tax younger people to provide private accounts for each person on Social Security now.

The federal government owns trillions of dollars worth of

assets it doesn't need and shouldn't have. These include power companies, pipelines, idle military bases, business enterprises, over 400,000 buildings, oil and mineral rights, commodity reserves, and much more — including 29% of all the land in the United States.[5]

When the federal government is reduced to just its Constitutional functions, there will be no reason for it to continue hoarding those assets. They can be sold to the public, putting them in the hands of people who will use them more responsibly and more productively. And the sales will generate the money to clean up the financial mess the politicians have made.

So that the market for these assets won't be depressed, I believe the sales should take place over a six-year period. I'd prefer that it be six days, but that would reduce the proceeds.

It is impossible to know in advance how much money the assets will bring because nothing like this has ever been done before. Estimates of the assets' market value have ranged from $5 trillion to $50 trillion. But if selling the assets brings even $12 trillion, it would solve two thorny problems.

First, the initial proceeds should be used to buy private retirement accounts for everyone now on Social Security — lifetime annuities from stable insurance companies that have never broken their promises.

The government will have no further Social Security liability to anyone. No retiree will be left in the lurch or dependent on the solvency of Social Security. And neither you nor your children will ever again have to pay the 15% Social Security tax.

Anyone between age 50 and retirement can receive an annuity that will begin paying out at age 65.

Anyone under 50 will save more from the elimination of the Social Security tax than he gives up in future Social Security benefits.

Second, the remaining proceeds from the asset sales will pay off the entire accumulated federal debt. You, your children, and your grandchildren will be free of the enormous burden of debt the politicians have piled on you. The government's yearly interest costs will be reduced to zero.[6]

---

[5]Starting on page 155, we will see how the government has misused much of that land, causing severe environmental damage.

[6] The table on page 231 shows the estimated year-by-year sale proceeds and the cost of the private retirement accounts.

This is *real* reform.

It's the only plan that takes Social Security completely away from the politicians and gives you control over your own money.

It's the only way your retirement, that of your parents and grand-parents, and that of your children and grandchildren, will finally be secure.

It's the only solution worthy of a free country.

CHAPTER 10

FREE FROM THE NIGHTMARE OF PROHIBITION

Until the early 1900s, the federal government did little to regulate or control the sale or use of alcohol or drugs — except for taxing alcohol.

It may be hard to believe today, but early in the 20th century a 10-year-old girl could walk into a drug store and buy a bottle of whiskey or a packet of heroin. She didn't need a doctor's prescription or a even note from her parents. Any druggist would sell to her without batting an eye; he would assume she was on an errand for her parents.

While that may seem amazing now, it wasn't to anyone then. Heroin was sold in packages as a pain reliever or sedative — just as aspirin or other analgesics are sold today. The measured dose didn't make anyone high, and rarely did anyone become addicted — certainly no more often than with sleeping pills today.

Given such easy access to liquor and drugs, we might assume that America's adults and children were all high on booze and drugs. But that wasn't the case.

There were alcoholics and drug addicts then, just as there are today. But there were far fewer of them — because there were no criminal dealers trying to hook people on drugs or turn them into alcoholics.

There always will be people who are susceptible to addiction, and who take a big risk by consuming any alcohol, drugs, or tobacco. But when there's no money to be made pushing those items on school grounds and street corners, fewer of the susceptible get hooked.

America wasn't a Utopia. But it was quite different from today. For one thing, the violent crime rate was only 15% of what it is today. Gangs didn't rule the cities or neighborhoods, because there was no black market in drugs or alcohol to make gangs profitable. After all, anyone could buy what he wanted cheaply at the corner drug store. And because of the low prices, drug addicts and alcoholics didn't have to steal the money to buy what they craved.

Just as today, alcohol and drugs were food for tragedy — bringing hardship and ruin to those addicted, and often to their families as well. But before government regulation, the circle of tragedy reached no further than the addict and his immediate family.

Enter Prohibition

Then, as now, some people believed that the only way to save addicts was to prohibit *everyone* from using liquor or recreational drugs.

This is a familiar approach. Because some people can't save for their old age, everyone must be forced into a shaky Social Security system. Because some people might take up smoking if Michael Jordan were to show up in a TV ad with a cigarette in his hand, no one can be allowed to see a tobacco ad on television. Because some people might react sinfully to the sight of a naked woman, no one should be allowed to look at such pictures.

This approach is alien to a nation of free, responsible citizens. But it is the normal recourse of the reformer and the politician.

The reformers' crusade to save America from drugs and alcohol succeeded only slightly with drugs. The Harrison Act, passed in 1914, was meant to take drugs off the free market, but it was enforced only loosely. In fact, drug prohibition was barely enforced at all by the federal government until the 1960s.

Alcohol Prohibition

But alcohol was a different story. In 1919 the 18th Amendment to the Constitution was ratified, prohibiting:

> . . . the manufacture, sale, or transportation of intoxicating liquors within, the importation thereof into, or the exportation thereof from the United States and all territory subject to the jurisdiction thereof for beverage purposes.

The advocates of alcohol prohibition thought they were making America a better place — an alcohol-free zone, a land without alcoholics or drunken brawlers, a land with stronger families, a more stable society.

But they were wrong. The "Noble Experiment," as it came to be called, began in 1920 — and by the time it had ended, only the bootleggers were better off.

The Nightmare of Prohibition

Prohibition did little to reduce the demand for alcohol. It simply replaced law-abiding brewers, distillers, vintners, and liquor stores with moonshiners, smugglers, and bootleggers who were willing to flout the law and risk prison. The alcohol industry became the province of gangsters operating a black market.

Prohibition spawned many evils:

- People bought from bootleggers, with no knowledge of where the products came from, and no company staking its reputation on the quality and safety of the products. As a result, many people died from drinking bad liquor.
- Having committed themselves to a life of crime, bootleggers were prepared to break more laws to control liquor territories. Gang warfare, drive-by shootings, and the killing of innocent bystanders became commonplace.
- People still wanted to patronize bars and restaurants that served alcohol, and such places continued to operate. But they could do so only by paying off the police.
- Corruption of law enforcement went far beyond the payoffs from speakeasies. Selling black-market liquor through monopolies enforced by Tommy guns was much more lucrative than the legal, competitive sale of liquor had been. And a good deal of the money passing through the hands of gangsters was used to buy "protection" from prosecutors and judges.
- Because the demand for alcohol couldn't be stopped, the uncorrupted police who tried to enforce Prohibition turned to law-breaking themselves. They resorted to ever-more-draconian attacks on the individual liberties the Constitution was supposed to protect.
- Because alcohol Prohibition eventually was seen as a farce, respect for the law in general went downhill. Prohibition encouraged the idea that all laws could be ignored.

Peace at Last

Prohibition finally ended in 1933. The Noble Experiment had lasted 13 years. Many people died, and a few became very wealthy. But Prohibition hadn't made America an alcohol-free zone. It hadn't even come close to doing so.

The return of legal liquor didn't turn America into a nation of alcoholics. Alcohol consumption increased as liquor became more easily accessible, but the dire forecasts of social instability from Prohibition die-hards proved incorrect.

Even though Prohibition ended in the middle of the Great Depression of the 1930s, the crime rate began falling immediately. And it continued downward for 30 years.

Almost no one wants to go back to alcohol Prohibition — with the black markets in liquor run by criminal gangs, drive-by shootings that killed innocent children, innocent people dying from drinking contaminated liquor, over-worked law enforcement agencies, and widespread corruption.

But a new Prohibition came in through the back door thirty years later.

Rebellion

In the 1960s, marijuana became a token of rebellion for many young people who, in a less tumultuous generation, might have been content swallowing goldfish.[1]

Although there has never been a reported death from marijuana, the idea of youngsters smoking an illegal substance alarmed many people. Pressure grew for the drug laws to be enforced. And most politicians will happily give in to any pressure to make the government larger and more powerful.

And so the War on Drugs was born.

In the more than 30 years since then, tens of billions of dollars have been spent fighting drugs. And the campaign has been no more successful than alcohol Prohibition was.

TWO TYPES OF CRIMES

It's not difficult for a free society to keep violent crime to a minimum — with little intrusion on individual liberty and at relatively low cost.

But governments also prosecute "victimless" crimes. These are acts that (1) are illegal, (2) involve no intrusion on anyone's

---

[1] All but one of the 1960s marijuana smokers inhaled.

person or property, and (3) about which no injured party files a complaint with the police.

These acts include such things as prostitution, gambling, and drug use. They are activities in which all parties participate voluntarily. No violence or threat of violence is used. No one has been robbed, or been attacked, or lost a loved one to violence.[2]

Still, victimless crimes can hurt people other than the participants. But that injury doesn't come from force or the threat of it. It may be difficult for a spouse to leave an alcoholic or a gambler, but it is the spouse's own free will that determines whether to stay or go. All parties are there voluntarily, however dismal the situation.

If you accept that the unhappiness suffered by non-participants is a reason to make alcohol, gambling, or drugs illegal, you remove all limits on what can be labeled a crime. Should it be a crime to make your parents unhappy by marrying the wrong person? Or to make bad investments and lose the family savings? Or should it be a crime against your family to run up debts, move to the wrong neighborhood, invite your relatives to dinner too often?

Where does crime stop and simple bad behavior begin? Perhaps you have a clear idea in your mind, but the politicians won't consult you when they decide that prohibiting something is in their interest. The only dividing line that can't be fudged by politicians is the line that separates voluntary relationships from violence.

Either individuals are responsible for their own acts — including their choices of relationships — or the government is responsible for everything you do. There is no middle ground. Giving government the power to outlaw consensual activity allows the politicians to impose any laws they want on you. And they will use that power.

OUTLAWING PRIVATE BEHAVIOR

While it has been relatively easy for a free society to keep violent, intrusive crime to a minimum, it has been virtually impossible to control victimless crime. Prostitution is found in most societies, there has always been gambling, and government has never been able to stamp out alcohol, drugs, or nicotine.

Individuals simply will not allow the state to choose their tastes and values. For centuries governments have tried to con-

---

[2]If someone using or selling drugs commits violence against someone else, that isn't a victimless crime; it's a crime of violence.

trol private behavior, but with little success.

Government fails to alter conduct because there is so little public cooperation in prosecuting most victimless crimes. No one registers an accusation, identifies the culprit, or testifies in court that he's been injured. And while a woman might call the police to report being assaulted by her spouse, she isn't likely to report her spouse's drug use.

People outside the family are no more likely to help out by informing. You might tell the police that someone is breaking into your neighbor's house, but you aren't likely to report your neighbor's drug use.

The difficulty of enforcing victimless-crime laws leads to three bad consequences.

The Rise in Violent Crime

The first consequence is the diversion of more and more law-enforcement resources into the fight against victimless crimes.

As the vice squad grows, fewer police resources are available to deal with violent crime. And so it becomes easier to steal, mug, murder, assault, rape, or burgle and get away with it. More people find a way to make crime pay.

Prosecutors swamped with drug cases have to process violent crimes more quickly. Plea bargains abound for thieves and attackers. Instead of facing a trial for murder, with a life sentence at stake, a violent criminal pleads guilty to manslaughter and serves only a five-year sentence.

And the prisons fill up with "criminals" who threaten no one — such as pot smokers taking up cells for 25 years or more. Meanwhile, a violent criminal who may have terrorized many people — and perhaps even killed someone — gets out in seven years or so, because of a shortage of cells.

In 1978 Lawrence Singleton kidnapped a 15-year-old California girl, raped her, chopped off both her hands with an axe, and left her to die. But she happened to survive to testify against him. He was sentenced to 14 years, and then released after only eight years. Eleven years later, he killed a woman in Florida. Meanwhile, some casual drug users are serving life sentences.

Rodney Kelley robbed and killed two people in New Orleans in 1991. He was allowed to plead guilty to manslaughter and receive an 8-year sentence — making him eligible for parole in only four years.

Should we be surprised at the terrible rate of violent crime, when so much of the criminal justice system has been diverted to the prosecution of victimless crimes — most notably the War on Drugs?

Black Markets

The second consequence of outlawing private behavior is that the prohibited activity spawns a black market run by criminals. Drugs are sold only by people willing to risk being caught and sent to prison. The business becomes the province of gangsters.

Instead of competing with their rivals by offering superior products, better service, or lower prices, drug dealers compete by gang warfare. And the more the government cracks down on drug operations, the more drug activity is dominated by the most brutal elements of society.

Consequently, violent crime rises as the government steps up its insane War on Drugs.

Didn't America learn this lesson from alcohol Prohibition?

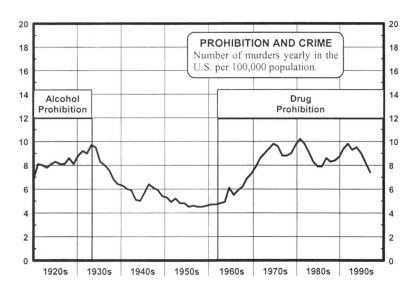

PROHIBITION AND CRIME
Number of murders yearly in the U.S. per 100,000 population.

Police State Tactics

The first two consequences of outlawing bad behavior are bad enough, but the third is worse yet. It is the destruction of our Constitutional liberty. The politicians justify this as the price of winning the War on Drugs.

Because there are no victims to help the prosecution, the Drug Warriors resort to police-state tactics:

- The police and prosecutors rely on informers — who almost always turn out to be criminals bargaining for a lower sentence.
- Sting operations become commonplace. Policemen actually buy and sell drugs and then arrest those they deal with. The government trains the police to be effective liars.
- The government can no longer tolerate your privacy. Government agents routinely rummage through your bank records, without your knowledge, looking for suspicious transactions. Politicians continually lower the standards for warrants to search your mail or tap your phone, and judges rubber-stamp the warrants. Judges allow SWAT teams to invade your home to search for drugs — based only on an anonymous tip, perhaps a tip from someone who just happens to dislike you. Your home is no longer your castle.
- Policemen can stop your car because of a bad tail light, and then search for drugs because they find your statements to be "suspicious."

These intrusions don't happen only to junkies and drug dealers. They happen to people just like you and me. For every successful drug search, many innocent people must be inconvenienced, embarrassed, or injured.

The drug-enforcement tactics erode your liberty. But the Drug Warriors — inside and outside of government — believe your Constitutional rights are a small price to pay for the victory they promise is coming.

However, they don't usually tell you what the price is. They bury provisions to violate your Constitutional rights deep inside anti-crime bills while focusing public attention on their high-minded objectives.

And with each new addition to the drug-enforcement laws you become less and less a free citizen whose life is your own:

- You can be convicted of drug dealing without any physical evidence such as drugs or money in your possession. All that's necessary is the testimony of an accused drug dealer who will get a reduced sentence for fingering you. So you'd better hope that no one you know ever gets entrapped by drug agents and decides to buy his freedom by giving away yours.

- The police easily can obtain a warrant to enter your home, search it for drugs or suspicious amounts of cash, and turn it upside down. All they need is an anonymous tip — for example, from a neighbor who's upset about your barking dog.

- The police can seize your property on the claim that it *might* have been used in a crime — even if you haven't been convicted of a crime, even if you haven't been indicted for a crime, and even if you haven't been accused of a crime. To get your property back, you must sue the government — at your own expense. Law enforcement agencies use the proceeds from the sale of your property to supplement their budgets.

- If a drug agent at an airport happens to believe you're too well dressed (or too poorly dressed or too middling-dressed) he can take you into custody, order you to take off all your clothes, and force you to have a bowel movement in front of drug-enforcement agents — just in case you've hidden a package of drugs in your stomach.

HOW THE INNOCENT ARE HURT

You may think it's unfortunate that such things happen to other people, but that your lifestyle and law-abiding history protect you from such trouble. Understand, however, that these things happen to people just like you — people who have never taken drugs, never dealt drugs, and never been in trouble with the law.

Lonnie Lundy

One such person was Lonnie Lundy, a businessman. At 32, he had never smoked, drunk alcohol, or used drugs. In 1993 an employee of his was prosecuted for drug-dealing, and the employee succeeded in getting his sentence reduced by naming Lonnie as his drug source.

No drugs, no money, no physical evidence of any kind were produced. His accuser later recanted his testimony, saying, "My life may be a mess but I'm not going to live the rest of my life with this on my conscience." And yet Lonnie Lundy languishes in prison, *sentenced to life imprisonment with no chance of parole.*

His only hope for freedom is a Libertarian President who will pardon all non-violent drug offenders in federal prisons.

Compare Lonnie Lundy's sentence with that of Jose Tapia, who in 1996 intentionally burned down a house in Rhode Island, killing two adults and four children. Tapia will be eligible for parole in 21 years. But Lonnie Lundy who wasn't even accused of using violence will never be free again unless he receives a presidential pardon.

Mario Paz

In the middle of the night on August 9, 1999, 20 police officers wearing masks surrounded the home of Mario Paz in Compton, California, fired grenades through the windows, shot the locks off the front and back doors, charged into his bedroom, and shot him to death. The victim had never used or dealt drugs, never been accused of a crime, and never been in any trouble with the law.

The police raided the home as part of a drug investigation of a former next-door neighbor who had used Mr. Paz' address to receive mail.

Even after the mistake became apparent, the police confiscated all the cash they found in the house, and took seven members of the family to jail in handcuffs. The police didn't read them their rights because they weren't accused of any crime.

Unfortunately, even a Libertarian President can't raise Mr. Paz from the dead.

Debbie Vineyard

In 1994 Debbie Vineyard was accused of dealing drugs, even though no drugs or money were ever produced as evidence. She was convicted solely on the say-so of an admitted drug dealer — a man who was given a reduced sentence in exchange for naming other people.

The drug agents pressured her to name other conspirators in exchange for leniency. But, of course, she couldn't name anyone because she wasn't involved in any criminal activity.

She was told (as many people in her situation are) that if she pleaded innocent and asked for a jury trial, she would get 30 years to life if she lost — as a penalty for tying up the judicial system. Afraid of being separated from her family for so long, she gave in and pleaded guilty. Even though she was a first-time "offender," she was sentenced to ten years in prison.

Debbie was sent to a prison in Alabama — separated by 2,000 miles from her husband, son, and disabled father in California.

There were no drugs, no money, no evidence of any kind — just the misfortune of being acquainted slightly with someone who was secretly dealing drugs.

She describes the experience:

> I was never given the opportunity for a bond, and I was held for eight months before pleading guilty. Before this happened to me, my family and I would never have believed something like this could actually happen. There was absolutely no evidence against me, and a crime had not even been committed.
>
> Even though I was pregnant, I was handcuffed, shackled, and flown via airlift with the Federal Marshals. I was housed in four different county jails before finally reaching my destination, an Alabama jail. In court, I was provided a court-appointed attorney (I was his first client). Due to my pregnancy, my court date was postponed and the Marshals drove me, handcuffed, belly-belted, and shackled, for ten hours to a Kentucky Prison to give birth to my child.

Suzan Penkwitz

In 1997 Suzan Penkwitz helped her friend Jenny retrieve Jenny's car from Tijuana, Mexico. They were stopped at the border, and drug agents found 43 pounds of heroin hidden in a secret compartment welded inside the gas tank.

Jenny immediately confessed to being a drug smuggler, and told the authorities that Suzan knew nothing about the drugs. But after several hours of intimidation, Jenny changed her story and implicated Suzan — in order to obtain leniency for herself.

For her cooperation, Jenny — the actual drug smuggler — got off with a 6-month sentence at a minimum security prison. Suzan — who was completely innocent — was sentenced to 6½ years in federal prison. Suzan couldn't cooperate, because she had nothing to admit to — and no one to finger.

Suzan had no criminal record of any kind. And both the judge and the prosecuting attorney acknowledged that Suzan didn't know there was heroin in the car. But still she was convicted and sentenced as a conspirator — receiving a sentence ten times as long as that for the real drug smuggler.

Richard Allen Davis

Richard Allen Davis is a different sort of prisoner. He is a violent man who has been in and out of prison all his life. Davis has raped women, terrorized families, and robbed banks.

He has spent nearly half his life in prison — but, no matter how badly he hurts people, he has never served a complete sentence. He has always managed to get parole or early release because the prisons are so crowded. On the other hand, Lonnie Lundy (described on page 97) has never been accused of hurting anyone, but he now serves a life sentence with *no* chance of parole.

The life of Richard Allen Davis has been one continuous horror story. On June 27, 1993, he was paroled from prison after serving only eight years of a 16-year sentence for assault with a deadly weapon. His frightening life reached its climax just three months after his release from prison, when he kidnapped 12-year-old Polly Klaas from her bedroom and murdered her.

But don't worry: law enforcement agencies are aggressively locking up pot smokers, minor drug dealers, and innocent people fingered by drug smugglers — and throwing away the key.

Some Are More Equal Than Others

In 1995 Republican Congressmen nearly broke their arms patting themselves on the back for passing a rule that all laws and regulations applying to ordinary American citizens apply as well to members of Congress. At last we're all equal under the law.

Except that some of us are more equal than others.

Lonnie Lundy (described on page 97) was given a life sentence for supposedly dealing drugs, even though no money or drugs were ever produced as evidence. He was convicted solely on the say-so of an admitted drug dealer, who later recanted his testimony. Lonnie's father wrote to Senator Richard Shelby (R-Alabama) to ask his help in getting Lonnie's sentence reduced.

On February 25, 1998, Senator Shelby replied:

Drug abuse and drug-related crimes are among the greatest ills that plague our nation. We must take a strong stand against drugs, and I support strict punishment for individuals involved in the possession or distribution of illegal drugs. While I understand your concerns about mandatory penalties for nonviolent offenders, I believe that our nation's drug problem is serious enough to warrant harsh sentences.

Five months later Senator Shelby's 32-year-old son was arrested at the Atlanta airport with 13.8 grams of hashish in his possession. He pleaded guilty to a misdemeanor possession charge, paid two fines totaling $860, performed 40 hours of community service, and was on probation for one year. He didn't spend a single hour in jail or prison.

Representative Randy Cunningham (R-California) has been an avid Drug Warrior. He wants mandatory prison terms, tougher judges, and the death penalty for big-time drug dealers. He has repeatedly criticized the Clinton administration for being soft on drug dealers and users.

In January 1997 his son was caught with 400 pounds of marijuana. In November 1998 the Drug Warrior father pleaded with a judge to show leniency — saying his son is basically a good person who made a bad decision. "He has a good heart. He works hard," said the father (as though that couldn't be said as well about thousands of young people serving sentences of 5, 10, 20 or more years for smaller drug offenses).

The son received a sentence of only 2 years — half the mandatory sentence. He also was given the opportunity to reduce the sentence to 18 months by completing a drug rehabilitation program while in prison. (Prosecutors originally had agreed to a sentence of only 14 to 18 months in a half-way house. But while out on bail before the trial, the Congressman's son tested positive for cocaine three times.)

Another aggressive Drug Warrior is Senator Rod Grams (R-Minnesota). While he has been calling for harsh sentences for drug offenders, his son Morgan has been involved with drugs for years — a problem the senator has acknowledged publicly. The senator claims that harsh sentences for drug dealers would save people like his son from drug abuse.

In July 1999, Senator Grams asked the local sheriff to look for the senator's son, who was on probation for drunk driving and had disappeared while driving an overdue rental car. Sheriff's deputies found him driving the rental car with two companions but no driver's license. They also found ten bags of marijuana in the car. A deputy drove the son home. Despite the son's probation for drunk driving and the marijuana in the car, no charges were ever filed, and the son has spent no time in custody.

The Honorable Hypocrites

As though the hypocrisy involved in family drug dealing wasn't sufficient, Congressmen themselves have been caught with drugs and managed to slither out of the justice system. According to *Capitol Hill Blue* (a Washington publication), 14 members of the current Congress have been arrested on drug-related charges. Would you like to guess how many of them have gone to prison?

And, of course, it seems as though virtually every contender in the 2000 presidential primaries acknowledged that he had used drugs in his younger days.

But not one of them claimed that he should have been sent to prison for his "youthful indiscretions."

Politicians "experimented" with marijuana when they were younger. But today's youths aren't allowed to experiment; they're charged with felonies and sent to prison for smoking marijuana with their friends.

The Innocent & the Guilty

The Drug Warriors will tell you that sentences like those imposed on Lonnie Lundy, Debbie Vineyard, and Suzan Penkwitz strike fear in the hearts of America's drug kingpins.

In fact, however, cases in which a big-time drug dealer receives a long prison sentence are very rare. But one-time offenders and innocent bystanders get sentences ranging from a few years to life without chance of parole.

This is not just a technical problem that needs to be corrected. These injustices are inevitable in any plan to prosecute victimless crimes. Without victims to testify, the state must offer bribes to truly guilty people to provide testimony against truly innocent people — padding the arrest and conviction records of drug agents and prosecutors.

The drug kingpins have plenty of names to give the prosecutors, and so they obtain reduced sentences by fingering others. But the low-level drug runner has only one or two contacts to offer, and the innocent bystander knows no one he can turn in — so these people wind up with the worst sentences.

The drug warriors may want you to believe that only drug kingpins go to prison. But in 1998 alone, according to the Justice Department, 682,885 Americans were arrested on marijuana charges — 88% of whom merely for possessing marijuana. A

recent study by the Center on Juvenile and Criminal Justice estimated that the total prison population of the U.S. reached 2 million sometime around February 15, 2000. More than half of those
are non-violent offenders according to the report.

The stories recounted in this chapter aren't rare exceptions.
Such tragedies occur frequently to people just like you and me.
Some may have been involved in a single drug incident, and
some are completely innocent.

If your child should make one silly mistake and be caught, or
just happen to be acquainted with the wrong person, it could
mean a prison term of 5, 10, 25 years — or even a life sentence.
Would your child deserve that?

Police-State Tactics

We aren't making America safer by violating the Bill of
Rights.

Such violations are far more likely to hurt you than to hurt
drug dealers. Serious criminals know every aspect of the law that
might affect them, and they do whatever is necessary to avoid
problems. They wouldn't think of leaving money in a bank
account where it could be seized by a federal agent or police officer.

But because you're ignorant of these and millions of other
laws, you're a sitting duck for any law-enforcement officer or
prosecutor hoping to pad his arrest, seizure, or conviction statistics. So one day you find that your property has been taken from
you — or, worse yet, that you're accused of a crime by someone
who is desperate, or who just doesn't happen to like you.

It is the innocent — not the guilty — who are hurt most
when the Bill of Rights is ignored.

THE FUTILITY

And what's the point of all this? No matter how aggressively
and oppressively the Drug Warriors fight their war, the drug
trade continues unabated.

Despite the invasions of your civil liberties; despite over $25
billion a year spent to chase drug smugglers, dealers, and users;
despite cruel and unusual punishment for small offenses; despite
all the "just say no" propaganda, despite all the news stories pro-
claiming drug seizures and other supposed victories, the Drug
War continues to be a massive failure.

It was supposed to keep drugs away from your children, but the results have been quite different:

- In 1972 only 14% of teenagers had ever tried marijuana. By 1997 the number was up to 50%. The number regularly smoking marijuana more than tripled, from 7% to 24%.
- In 1972 only 2% of teenagers had ever tried cocaine. By 1997 the number was up to 9%. Regular users increased from 1% to 6%.
- In 1972 only 1% of teenagers had ever tried heroin. By 1997 the number was up to 2%.
- The percentage of teenagers who had tried hallucinogens, stimulants, or inhalants all more than doubled between 1972 and 1997.

But this doesn't deter the politicians. They don't reevaluate their misguided, destructive Drug War. They don't repeal a single law that failed to achieve its purpose. They don't cancel the oppressive sentences that have achieved nothing but prison overcrowding. They don't give back the civil liberties they took from you.

No, they press ever onward with ever more intrusions on your Constitutional rights.

They push for even longer drug sentences. Some even want to publicly hang drug dealers — by whom they mean anyone caught with more than a week's supply of marijuana.

Would that be any more effective than the stringent sentences drug dealers are already willing to risk? And if it *did* work, think of the terrible precedent it would set. Politicians would cite the success of hanging drug dealers as the model for dealing with any public problem.

TIME TO END PROHIBITION II

America woke up in 1933 and ended the "Noble Experiment" — the nightmare of alcohol Prohibition — that had triggered the worst crime wave in the nation's history.

It is long past time to end the even larger crime wave sponsored by drug Prohibition. It is time to end the insane War on Drugs. It is time to return peace to American cities.

Libertarians understand that ending the Drug War would eliminate the criminal black market — ending the incentives to hook adults and children.

Ending the Drug War will end most of the violence, the gang warfare, and the drive-by shootings.

It will make it possible to restore your civil liberties.

Ending the Drug War will end the deaths of addicts taking contaminated drugs or overdosing on drugs of unknown strength.

Legal competition will quickly reduce prices to a fraction of today's prices — ending the muggings and burglaries by addicts, who will no longer need to steal to support their habits.

Ending the Drug War will allow law-enforcement resources to be redirected toward protecting you from violence against your person or property — the reason you tolerate government in the first place.

It will end the overcrowding of courts and prisons — freeing the criminal justice system to deal with the people who are hurting and terrorizing others.

Ending the Drug War will end most police corruption by taking the big profits out of the drug business.

It probably will end the epidemic of crack babies. Crack (highly concentrated cocaine) became a profitable commodity for drug dealers only when the government succeeded temporarily in reducing the supply of simple cocaine, which is somewhat less dangerous. In fact, cocaine itself became a profitable commodity only when the government succeeded temporarily in reducing the supply of marijuana, which is much less likely to harm anyone.

Ending the Drug War will make our schools safer. Brewers and distillers don't recruit children to sell beer or hook other kids on liquor. Nor do they give them guns to take to school. Nor would legal drug companies. When I grew up in Los Angeles in the 1940s, the worst schools were safer than L.A.'s best schools are today.

Ending the Drug War will make marijuana readily available to people afflicted with cancer, glaucoma, AIDS, and other diseases — to help them digest their medicines, relieve their pain, and restore their appetites.

It will allow addicts to seek help from doctors — who today must report addicts to the police or risk going to jail themselves.

It finally will be legally possible to do truly scientific studies to better measure the effects and biological mechanisms of drug use — without making scientists conform to political correctness.

And it will be possible for children to get more realistic information about drugs — for example, that marijuana is far less harmful than harder drugs. Today the obvious exaggerations about marijuana lead teenagers to discount the official warnings about more dangerous hard drugs.

After Prohibition

Don't misunderstand me. We shouldn't expect a sweet world of low drug use to return immediately upon the end of the War on Drugs. The Drug War has gone on for over 30 years, and the bad habits it taught won't be unlearned overnight.

But just as America didn't become a nation of alcoholics in 1933, it won't become a nation of junkies in the coming years. Within a year we should see drug use drop significantly, because there no longer would be drug dealers on the streets and in the schools. And the crime rate should drop just as dramatically.

Will some people ruin their lives with drugs? Of course — just as some people ruin their lives now with drugs, alcohol, tobacco, or pizza — or by making bad investments, running up debts, or marrying the wrong person. But when the government tries to stop someone from ruining his own life with drugs or anything else, it expands a personal tragedy into a national disaster.

No, we won't have a crime-free, drug-free America. But we don't have that now and we never will. What we *will* have when the insane War on Drugs is ended is less drug use, a more peaceful America, and a less oppressive government.

Should We Be Afraid?

Understandably, many Americans fear that ending the Drug War would result in tens of thousands of addicts, crack babies, and children trying drugs. *But that's what we have now.*

Are we afraid there will be ads for heroin on television? We shouldn't be. Why would any pharmaceutical company tarnish its reputation by running such ads, and why would any broadcast network offend its audience by accepting them?

Are we afraid our children would have easier access to drugs? How could they have more access than they do now? Drugs are being sold in our schools. And most street dealers are themselves teenagers. But the money to finance the corruption of the young would disappear if we ended the Drug War.

What about people who use drugs and commit crimes or cause accidents? They should be held responsible for what they do, just as people who don't take drugs should be responsible for what *they* do. It isn't the drug that's the problem, it's the person who injures others — with or without drugs. Everyone should be held responsible for what he does to others, but what he does to himself is not the government's business.

Legal Status of Drugs

The most important step we must take is to end the federal government's involvement with drugs.

The Constitution recognizes only three federal crimes — treason, piracy, and counterfeiting. The federal government has no Constitutional authority to deal with any other crimes. Every crime occurs in the jurisdiction of a police or sheriff's department somewhere, and that's where it should be legislated, investigated, and prosecuted.

Once the federal government is out of the picture, each state will choose its own approach to the question of drugs. Most likely, every state will have far more liberal drug laws than exist today, since the trend is already in that direction.

Some states may legalize all drugs, while others continue partial Prohibition, and some may legalize only medical marijuana.

What I Want

My own hope is for complete legalization everywhere.

Whatever part of the market remains illegal will be a breeding ground for black markets, gangs, and violence. Criminals, unable to compete with legal companies selling safer drugs at much lower prices, will focus their attention on any area that remains illegal.

We can say anything we want about the "message" legalization sends to children, or that government should protect them from some drugs, or that some other high-minded objective should be pursued. But the fact remains that government doesn't deliver what we want, and Prohibition breeds crime and higher drug use.

I want an end to just-pretend wars against sin.

I want a return to the safe, peaceful society in which violent crime is much rarer, but prosecuted vigorously, while innocent people are free to live their lives in peace.

I want to empty the prisoners of the nearly one million inmates whose only crimes were to buy or sell drugs.

I want people with drug problems to be able to seek help without fear of being arrested.

I want your children to be able to play in safe streets and attend safe schools.

I want to end the insane War on Drugs.

CHAPTER 11

FREEDOM FROM WAR

In 1914 Austria was Europe's "superpower." The Austrian Empire included the territories of present-day Hungary, the Czech Republic, Slovakia, Slovenia, Croatia, and Bosnia, as well as parts of Italy and Romania.

Serbia, an independent country, wasn't part of the Empire. Many Serbs (both in Serbia and Bosnia) wanted Serbia to annex Bosnia, but the Austrian Emperor refused to let Bosnia go.

When the Emperor's heir apparent, Archduke Ferdinand, visited Bosnia, he was shot and killed by a Bosnian Serb.

The assassination was a crime, of course, but it was committed by just a handful of men. Since Bosnia was part of Austria, it would have been a simple matter for Austria to prosecute the assassin and his collaborators. But instead the Austrian Emperor accused Serbia's government of arranging the murder, and Austria mobilized for war against Serbia.

At the time, governments inside and outside of Europe were joined together in a web of mutual defense treaties, and so a local quarrel became a world war. Britain, France, Belgium, Romania, Greece, Portugal, Montenegro, Russia, and even Japan supported Serbia. On the other side, Germany, Italy, Bulgaria, and Turkey supported Austria. The awful war quickly consumed most of Europe.

Eventually, 15 million soldiers and civilians would be killed and at least 20 million wounded — all because one person had been assassinated. What a testament to the irrationality of war.

Stalemate

After three years of fighting, the two sides were bogged down in a bloody stalemate — with neither able to gain a decisive advantage.

The armies on both sides were exhausted, and Europeans were ready for an armistice that would stop the terrible bloodshed. Germany put out feelers to end the conflict.

If that armistice had materialized in 1917, the history of the past 80 years would have been quite different and much happier. There might still be monarchs in Germany, Austria, Belgium, and even Russia. That may be distasteful to some, but it might have saved the lives of tens of millions of people.

With Russia and Germany again at peace, the Germans would have had no reason to help Lenin take over Russia, and the Soviet Union never would have been born. And with the German Emperor still on the throne, Adolf Hitler would never have had the opportunity to seize power.

Although no one can say for sure, it seems very unlikely that there would have been a second World War. And without that war and without a Soviet Union, there would have been no Cold War, no Korean War, no Vietnam War. The 20th century wouldn't have been an era of perfect peace, but it would have avoided being history's bloodiest 100 years.

American Intervention Changes History

But such was not to be.

Instead, in 1917, after winning reelection for keeping America out of the war, Woodrow Wilson pulled America into it — and that intervention changed history irrevocably for the worse.

Millions of fresh American soldiers streamed into Europe — tipping the balance of power and overwhelming an enemy exhausted from three years of war. Germany and Austria surrendered, the German emperor fled to the Netherlands, and the Allies imposed devastating conditions upon a defeated Germany.

So, instead of a functioning Germany with Kaiser Wilhelm on the throne, America produced a prostrate Germany eager for revenge.

The humanitarian spirit that propelled America into a war to "end all wars" laid the groundwork for two of history's worst murderers — Josef Stalin and Adolf Hitler.

Could Woodrow Wilson — or anyone else — have foreseen all this in advance?

No, and that's the point. Once you embark on the use of force — for any purpose — you have no idea what will fly up out of Pandora's box.

Lessons to Be Learned

At least, one could learn a lesson from the deaths of 15 million people. In fact, World War I offered two unmistakable lessons:

- George Washington and Thomas Jefferson were right to say America would achieve nothing but ruin by meddling in the ancient quarrels of Europe.
- When mutual defense treaties fail to deter wars, as they usually do, they enlarge war and make it bloodier. A mutual defense treaty easily becomes a mutual suicide pact.

Unfortunately, memories are short, and history seems to be such a dull subject.

So when the politicians tell us we have a chance to bring about world peace if we just send more of our children to die, or just bomb more innocent civilians overseas, or just bully a few more smaller countries, many people don't realize they are listening to a story that has been told many times before — and seldom produced a happy ending.

THE PERMANENT WAR FOOTING

America returned to peace and independent policies after World War I. But after World War II our government enmeshed itself in mutual defense treaties all over the world, put us on a permanent war footing, undertook numerous military adventures, and took sides in almost everyone's conflicts — much of which activity had little to do with the Soviet threat.

Here are a few examples:

- In the 1980s our government sent military equipment to Iraq's Saddam Hussein to help him fight the Ayatollah in Iran. Much of the American equipment was used in 1990 to help Iraq invade Kuwait. So our children were sent to Iraq to depose our one-time ally Saddam Hussein — now described by our politicians as a modern Hitler.

However, even after the U.S. killed thousands of civilians and soldiers, Hussein remained in power.

- Our government enlisted Panamanian dictator Manuel Noriega in the fight against communism. But in 1989 the U.S. military invaded Panama, killed a number of people, kidnapped Noriega, took him to Florida, and imprisoned him — supposedly to stop the use of Panama as a relay station for the drug trade. Noriega still sits in a U.S. prison, but there's no indication that the drug flow through Panama has abated. In fact, the drug cartels of South America move freely into Panama because America destroyed Panama's army in 1989.

- American politicians went to the Philippines to monitor elections, pressure the Philippine people to get rid of Ferdinand Marcos, and end corruption. Marcos lost the election, but corruption is as rampant in the Philippines today as it was then — and the subject no longer seems to interest American politicians.

- Our government bombed Libya in 1986, killing a number of civilians, to force Muammar Khadaffi to end his support for terrorists. But two years after our government supposedly taught Khadaffi a lesson, a bomb destroyed a Pan American Airlines flight over Scotland, killing 259 people — and our government says Khadaffi was responsible.

- During the 1980s our government helped the "freedom fighters" take power in Afghanistan. In 1998 our government bombed those same Afghans, claiming they were now harboring terrorists.

- In Rwanda, Somalia, Bosnia — wherever our government has meddled — the only consistent outcomes have been American deaths, American tax dollars wasted, the sacrifice of thousands of innocent foreigners, and no lasting solution.

In country after country, American intervention either failed to achieve its objective or succeeded in making matters worse.

A DANGEROUS WORLD

Because America has taken sides in so many conflicts, because America has armed so many countries' enemies, because America has imposed so many "solutions" on so many people, because American troops occupy so many countries, the world has become dangerous for America.

Foreigners generally love McDonald's but hate our government. Foreign politicians exploit that hatred. And now and then foreign terrorists try — or pretend to try — to change our government's polices by bombing American targets here or abroad.

But our policies don't change, because politicians never respond to problems by letting go of their power. So, instead of doing something to eliminate the motive for actual or threatened terrorism, our politicians "fight" it with even more foreign adventures.

And they issue a steady stream of alarms about frightening problems around the world — all of which supposedly require our immediate attention and intervention.

But why should we have anything to fear? Our country is bounded by two friendly nations and two oceans that protect us from invasion. We are open only to the sky. Our first military concern should be to defend ourselves against missiles launched from overseas.

Weak Defense

And therein lies the rub.

Today we have a very strong national offense, but a very weak national defense.

American taxpayers have coughed up trillions of dollars for the military since World War II — giving the politicians the power to destroy any country in the world. But we are still almost completely helpless before any dictator who decides to lob a low-budget missile at your city.[1]

The basic technology to defend against incoming missiles has been available for close to 30 years, and perfecting and implementing it becomes easier every year. But by leaving us vulnerable, the politicians can justify more power for themselves.

They tell us we must arm ourselves to the teeth with weapons that can threaten any would-be attacker with annihilation. We must station American troops in nearly a hundred countries around the world, as though your children were a Roman army of occupation. We must intervene in every foreign dispute

---

[1] A Brookings Institute study concluded that since 1940 the U.S. government has spent on nuclear weapons and the bombers, missiles, and submarines made to deliver them $5.8 trillion dollars (in 1999 dollars), roughly $58,000 per American household.

to prevent it from escalating into a wider war. We must react with fright when India or Pakistan tests a nuclear weapon. We must intimidate other countries and impose our "solutions" upon them. And although the Cold War is over, we must continue to support a huge, bureaucratic Defense Department and military.

In reality, we need only two things to make you, me, and every American safe from the world's turmoil: (1) a missile defense that will repel a nuclear attack, and (2) a border patrol that will protect us from those rampaging Canadians when they charge across the border from Ontario.[2]

With a proper defense against incoming missiles, we'd have no need to intimidate the world with offensive missiles — threatening to kill millions of civilians in an aggressor country. We'd have no reason to bomb Serbia, Iraq, Afghanistan, the Sudan, or any other country — and then give it billions of dollars to repair the damage. Instead, we could let others nurse their age-old grievances they seem to love so much — knowing that their problems can't hurt us.

Mutual Suicide

And even without a missile defense, we have no need to participate in NATO, the United Nations, or any other foreign agency that wants to bind you and me to its decisions. And there is no reason to risk disaster with mutual defense treaties. (Or do you really believe Turkey and Italy will rush to help us if we're attacked?)

Our federal government was formed to protect Americans, not foreigners.

If we're responsible for the defense of Europe, what are the Europeans responsible for — the defense of Asia?

POLITICIANS & DEATH

War is justified by blurring the distinction between foreign rulers and their subjects. Our politicians cite the sins of foreign rulers, and then ask us to join in killing their downtrodden subjects.

The politicians want us to forget that wars and "police actions" kill innocent people. They talk about teaching a foreign dictator a lesson, but the dictator never gets hurt. Instead,

---

[2] Only kidding about the second.

American bombs kill thousands of innocent civilians who may hate the dictator even more than our politicians claim to.

For example, since the Gulf War in 1991, our government has brow-beaten other governments to ban trade with Iraq — in order to force Saddam Hussein from power. In the eight years of trade sanctions through 1999, it is estimated that at least 1,700,000 Iraqi civilians have died for lack of imported foreign food and medicine.

And, although it doesn't seem to make the newspapers very often, from time to time American planes continue to drop bombs on innocent Iraqi civilians.

Politicians call the deaths of the innocent "collateral damage." And President Clinton and the Republican Congress have steadfastly supported the policy of starving and bombing, even though it has achieved nothing but death and disease.[3]

And after ten years of delivering death by air freight, the U.S. has left Saddam Hussein still firmly entrenched in power. But American politicians never admit the failure or cruelty of their policies — or even discuss the matter.

The war against Serbia in 1999 was little different. When it ended, the hated Slobodan Milosevic was still ruling the country. And it became apparent that American bombing had done little to cripple Serbia's military. But hundreds, and maybe thousands, of civilians died — including many of the Albanian civilians who supposedly were the objects of our government's "humanitarian" mission.

Isn't there a better way?

SOLUTIONS

Yes, there is.

Like the Founding Fathers, Libertarians know that war is the first resort of political scoundrels, but the last resort of a free people. Libertarians know that government's role isn't to police the world — or even to win wars. Government's role is to *keep us out of wars* — and to protect us from foreign enemies, *not create* them.

How would a Libertarian government assure our safety?

---

[3] The traditional method of explaining away collateral damage is to say "You have to break a few eggs to make an omelet." But it's always someone else's eggs that get broken, and somehow the omelet never materializes.

Our foreign policy would be simple:

> *We are always ready to defend ourselves, but we threaten no one.*

America's foreign policy should rest on four principles.

1. Non-Interference

Our government should express good will and a desire for peace toward all — threatening no foreign country, interfering in no other countries' disputes, arming or aiding no foreign governments, and giving terrorists no motivation to influence our government.

Any American who wants to volunteer to a foreign government to fight in its war, to negotiate its peace, or to send money to help defend it should be free to do so with no interference from the U.S. government.

But no American should be forced to participate in or pay for such activities. And our politicians should quit committing Americans to these futile attempts to settle other people's problems.

When the politicians drag us off to someone else's war, they always offer plenty of reasons — too many, in fact, to be taken seriously. The typical menu of justifications for a single intervention might be: We must interfere to keep the conflict from spreading, to head off the emergence of a new Hitler, to protect our allies, to do the moral thing, and to end violations of human rights.

But how can our politicians protect human rights in other countries? They don't even respect *our* rights. They try to disarm you, they allow the police to invade your life and property, they use the insane War on Drugs to impose police-state surveillance on all of us, and they try to censor the Internet. So how can they claim to care about human rights in other nations?

2. No Foreign Aid or Military Assistance

The Constitution grants our government no authority to take your money to support foreign governments.

Not only is it unconstitutional, it is unfair by almost any standard. As Fred L. Smith pointed out, foreign aid taxes poor people in rich countries for the benefit of rich people in poor countries.

Little of the money reaches the average citizen in the target country. Most of it enriches the rulers — and it helps them stay in power and continue the policies that keep their countries poor.

Foreign aid originally was justified as a way of arming countries against Communist encroachment. But Cuba, China, and Vietnam all fell to the Communists *after* receiving massive amounts of American money and weapons. In fact, much of the military equipment given to fight the Communists eventually fell into their hands.

So the politicians no longer bother trying to justify giving your money to foreign governments. They just do it. And, not surprisingly, most of the money has strings attached — requiring that it be spent with politically connected industries in the U.S.

Much foreign aid is spent to fix problems that might not exist but for our government. For example, many Americans understandably worry about Israel's security, fearing that without American aid Israel will be overrun by its neighbors. But the most effective thing our government could do to help Israel would be to *stop arming Israel's enemies.*

Our government's eagerness to take sides in Middle East disputes has put billions of dollars of weapons in the hands of Saudi Arabia, Syria, Iraq, and Iran. Small wonder that it seems necessary to rush to Israel's defense when hostile governments can use American weapons to intimidate Israel.

Every American should be free to send money or weapons to Israel or any other government in the world. But our government has no business taxing you for the benefit of any foreign government.

3. Security against Attack

Are there bad people in the world who would conquer America if they could?

Most likely, there are. But how would they do it?

They would have to pulverize American cities to the point that we submit to an invasion and occupation. Or they would have to threaten to pulverize us and be believed.

In other words, all we have to fear are incoming missiles.

In 1983 Ronald Reagan made the most sensible military suggestion of the past 50 years — that America should have protection against missile attacks. Unfortunately, he assigned the job to the Department of Defense, and now — 17 years later — we are no closer to being protected than we were then.

The Constitution asks the federal government to defend the nation. But we should rely as little as possible on the political and bureaucratic worlds if we want to achieve anything useful. Instead, we should look to those who know how to solve problems and can be motivated to do so by the lure of big profits.

The government should simply post a reward — say, $25 billion — to be given to the first private company that can produce a working, functioning, fool-proof missile defense. Not a prototype, not a plan, not a cost-plus contract — but a demonstration of the actual system successfully bringing down missiles. If such an offer were made, we probably would have a missile defense within five years.

Remember all the reasons given in 1997 that the Y2K computer problem couldn't possibly be solved by 2000? Even many computer experts said there wasn't enough time, there weren't enough programmers, and there were too many lines of computer code to be examined, altered, and tested. But somehow, people in search of profits found ways to overcome all the barriers and reduce the problem to a minor inconvenience.

In the same way, private firms competing to win a huge reward will achieve missile-defense goals that bureaucrats (and even scientists) working for the government might consider impossible.

Even the companies that don't win the race can profit if they find the answers eventually — by selling them to other governments that want protection from terrorist missiles.

What if the missile-defense technology fell into the hands of a savage dictator? That would pose no threat to us. We shouldn't be afraid of any country's ability to defend itself — only afraid of our inability to defend America.

When India and Pakistan tested nuclear weapons, there was nothing the U.S. could realistically do about it, short of bombing or invading them. None of our government's admonitions could change anything, so our politicians should have kept their mouths shut.

If we had a missile defense, such nuclear tests wouldn't frighten us. We can't prevent other nations from fighting each other or developing weapons of mass destruction, but we can make sure their disputes and their deadly arms don't reach us.

Will a missile defense make us perfectly secure? Of course not. But neither will any other policy.

What a missile defense *will* do is make us far safer than we are today, eliminate the excuses for meddling in other countries' affairs, and remove one big reason for taxing us so heavily.

4. Target the Aggressors, Not the Innocent

Suppose that, even with a missile defense, America truly were threatened by a foreign ruler.

A Libertarian President would target the ruler himself. He wouldn't order bombers to kill the ruler's innocent subjects.

A Libertarian President would warn the ruler that any actual attack would be met by the offer of a mega-reward to anyone who could kill the ruler. Everyone would be eligible to collect the reward, including the ruler's guards and wives. And the reward would be very big — perhaps $100 million or more.

Would this prompt the foreign ruler to respond by putting a price on the head of the Libertarian President? Possibly.

But *anything* the U.S. President does to interfere with the ruler's plans could provoke an assassination attempt. Posting a reward for the dictator's death wouldn't add to the risk.

In addition to sparing innocent people in foreign countries, the assassination response would spare innocent Americans. Only those who want to try for the reward would be at risk. Americans wouldn't be drafted to fight and die invading a foreign country. And Americans wouldn't be taxed to pay for volunteers.

Please understand the limits of this proposal. It isn't a way to force dictators to change their spots or accommodate the U.S. It is only a means to prevent a direct attack on America. If the dictator withdraws his threat, the U.S. would withdraw the reward.

If our government followed a libertarian foreign policy, it's unlikely that any foreign ruler would want to threaten us. So it's unlikely that any such reward would ever be posted. But if a foreign ruler *were* tempted to threaten us, the fear of assassination would be more likely to deter him than the fear of losing some of his civilian subjects to U.S. bombs.

If you don't believe that's true, if you think assassination isn't nice, what is the alternative? Is it to kill thousands of innocent foreigners and to assure the deaths of innocent Americans?

That to me is the cruelest, most reckless approach.

DO WE TRUST GOVERNMENT TO MAKE US SAFE?

Those who tell us America can bring peace and democracy to the world don't seem to recognize that they're talking about the same American government that can't keep the streets safe in Washington, D.C. It's the same government that bleeds us with taxes, pits group against group in battles over quotas and privileges, and has devastated our cities with a futile War on Drugs.

If it fails to achieve any of its domestic goals, if it imposes alien values on its own people, why should you expect it to attain lofty goals overseas?

Politics Is Usual

And don't forget: we're talking about the government, after all.

Military decisions are made politically — just as new pork-barrel projects are chosen politically. The government's foreign policy is determined with reference to polls, voting blocs, rewards, and punishment. For example, Bill Clinton sent troops to Haiti in 1994, killing people along the way, just to gain the support of the Congressional Black Caucus for his domestic political agenda.

It's easy to imagine how our government could intervene to bring peace to some foreign region or to support "American interests" overseas. But the actual policy will never be the one you imagine, implemented in the way you envision. Instead, the politicians will define those interests by relying for "counsel" on those who have the most political influence.

To expect foreign policy decisions somehow to be separated from politics is as unrealistic as to expect politicians to refrain from buying votes with your tax money.

In short, foreign policy is as much a political boondoggle as any other government project. So be careful what you urge the politicians to do.

PEACE FOR ALL TIME

When America can defend itself against missile attack, the politicians will lose their best excuse for butting into the affairs of other countries and making demands upon you. That's probably why so little has been done to construct such a defense.

But it should be the first priority of anyone who pledges to support and defend the Constitution and the American people.

And when our government no longer interferes in other countries with military adventures and foreign aid, foreign terrorists will have little reason to threaten your city.

If in spite of these policies, some foreign leader still tries to make trouble for America, we should target the foreign leader for assassination, not target innocent civilians for bombing. But I doubt that an American government that minds its own business and provides a secure defense will ever have to resort to assassination.

These policies don't appeal to Democratic and Republican politicians, who see foreign crises as opportunities for greater power and more government spending, who demonstrate their courage by sacrificing the lives of others, and who see clearly what we too easily forget — that "war" is just another word for "big government," a way to make politicians more important.

The policies I've outlined should make it possible to defend this country successfully for no more than $50 billion a year — contrasted with our current vulnerability, which costs nearly $300 billion a year. In 1952, at the height of the Cold War and the Korean War, the federal government spent less than $50 billion a year on the military.

But, more important than the savings in taxes, you will know that your children will never fight and die in a foreign war — and terrorists will never target your city.

Finally, we will have a strong national defense, instead of a strong national offense.

And then we must find a way to keep politicians away from loaded weapons forever. That's the one kind of gun control that really will save lives.

CHAPTER 12

FREEDOM TO MAKE
YOUR OWN CHOICES

You wouldn't want to take a medicine that makes you sick, or fly in an airplane with a drunken pilot, or buy an investment from a crook. Preventing such things from happening is what we think of as regulation.

Your first defense against accepting something dangerous or fraudulent is the *personal regulation* that you enforce through your own buying decisions — especially your decisions to *avoid* various items and situations.

When you pass up a product or service, in effect you tell the seller that you've tried it once and you were disappointed, or that you heard something bad about it from a source you trust, or simply that the seller hasn't convinced you that the product or service is safe, reliable, effective, and worth the money to you.

In the same way, when you buy a product or service a second time, you're providing an informal endorsement that encourages the seller to continue offering the features that pleased you.

Your second defense against bad products and services is *consumer regulation*. This is the total effect of all the buying decisions you and millions of other consumers make. As those choices are made, manufacturers and other sellers look for clues about what you really want. If safety is a factor in a product or service, the sellers will want to know which safety features are important to you, how much safety you're willing to pay for, and how to assure you — by your standards — that what they're offering really is safe.

Consumer regulation is like a free gift from your neighbors. You might not have a clear understanding of what makes a particular type of product safe or unsafe, effective or ineffective, reliable or unreliable — but many other consumers do. And their decisions to buy or not to buy will push sellers to provide better products to everyone.

One advantage of personal and consumer regulation is that you and others don't have to agree on such questions as which products suit you best, how much safety you're willing to pay for, what risks you're willing to take and what risks you'll avoid at all costs.

The variety of suppliers available allow you to buy the product that suits you best while someone else can buy from a different supplier and get what suits *him* best. You can make your choice and everyone else is free to make his choice.

In the same way, you might rely on the advice of a particular expert you believe is the best authority on the value and safety in a particular type of product, while someone else chooses to rely on a different expert.

The expert source might be something as simple as a magazine article explaining the relevant subject or just a company's general reputation — or it could be a doctor, scientist, insurance company, consumer testing service, academic study, or consulting firm. You not only choose what you want, you choose whose opinion you value in selecting among the available alternatives.

Enter the Politicians

A third kind of regulation is *political regulation* — by which politicians impose their choices upon you and everyone else. Political regulation says, in effect, that you aren't competent to know what's best for you. Nor are you competent to choose a source that can help you make decisions.

By contrast, political regulation says that politicians not only are competent to choose what's best for *themselves*, but to choose what's best for *you*.

We've been taught since childhood that we need political regulation to force sellers to provide safe products. But the history of regulation demonstrates exactly the opposite. Here are just a few examples.

- Consumer regulation asked for safer cars, and so automakers developed radial tires, safety glass, disc brakes, cruise control, turn signals, seat belts, and dozens of other features that make your car much, much safer than cars of 50 years ago. But political regulation has produced such things as mandatory airbags — which killed dozens of little children.

- Consumer regulation asked for safer ways to smoke — prompting tobacco companies to develop filtered, low-tar, and low-nicotine cigarettes. The companies competed with each other by advertising tar and nicotine levels and other safety features. But then political regulation prohibited such advertising, reducing the incentive for tobacco companies to make their products safer.

- Consumer regulation encouraged pharmaceutical companies to develop beta blockers that reduce the chance of a heart attack by keeping blood flowing to and from the heart. But political regulation kept these products off the American market for six long years — although in other countries they were readily available with no reported problems. The delay allowed at least 60,000 people to die prematurely from heart attacks.

- Consumer regulation made banks and savings & loans safer because wealthy investors monitored the safety of these institutions. But then political regulation raised the government insurance level to $100,000 per account, removing the incentive for wealthy investors to monitor the institutions. Imprudent managers were then free to make even riskier investments, bringing on the savings & loan crisis of the early 1980s.

Which is better, more helpful, and safer for you:

- Consumer regulation — whereby competition prods companies to provide the features and benefits important to you. Or . . .

- Political regulation — whereby politicians force companies to provide the features important to those with the most political influence.

With consumer regulation, you can change brands at any time. You can accept or reject the claims companies make, according to your own standards. Or if you're not sure what's right, you can refuse to buy until some company finds a way to prove to you that its product is safe and beneficial.

With political regulation, you can't change regulators, and your choice of products is restricted to just those the regulators like. Decisions are made by politically motivated people and imposed on you by force.

If you try to buy something the political regulators don't approve of, you might face fines and imprisonment. People have gone to prison for smoking marijuana to relieve nausea or to ease glaucoma symptoms — or for bringing into America medicines recommended by reputable scientists but vetoed by political regulators.

Whom Do You Trust?

If you had a dangerous illness and needed to decide whether to take a newly developed medicine, whom would you want to help you make the decision — your doctor or Bill Clinton?

Most likely, you'd choose your doctor. But, unfortunately, Congress has already made the decision for you — and it chose Mr. Clinton.

No, Bill Clinton doesn't test medicines and render decisions. But, as President, he has the power to choose who *will* make the decisions. And politics plays an important part in every decision he makes — including his choice of who will be the Commissioner of the Food and Drug Administration (FDA).

The Bureaucrat's Choice

And when the FDA decides whether you can use that new medicine, politics plays a big part.

Picture the situation. A new medicine has been tested and seems to work as expected. It could save thousands of lives. But no amount of testing could uncover every conceivable side effect — what might happen when the medicine is taken along with combinations of other medicines a patient could be using, or when the medicine encounters other medical conditions a patient might have, or when it has been taken for a longer time than the tests considered.

So how will the FDA regulators decide whether to allow your doctor to offer you this medicine? They have two choices:

1. *They can approve the medicine.* Many lives will be saved, but the administrators won't be congratulated for saving them. After all, the administrators didn't invent the medicine; their only job is to keep bad medicines away from us. So no one will congratulate the FDA for approving the medicine.

On the other hand, if just one person suffers a serious side effect from the medicine, the mishap probably will be highly publicized; Congress will hold hearings and compel the Commissioner to justify the decision; some FDA regulators may be fired; and most likely new laws and regulations will be enacted.

2. *They can turn down the medicine or delay its approval while further tests are conducted.* Many people may die for lack of the medicine, but *that* event will receive very little public notice, if any. And the administrators will never be criticized for being "too cautious." "After all, you can't be too safe, can you?"

Consequently, the regulators have good reason — good *political* reason — to play it ultra-safe. That may sound like a prudent policy, but it isn't. It assures that many people *will* die in exchange for the lives of a few people who *might* have died from taking the medicine.

Do you think this doesn't happen?

The FDA kept Propranolol off the market from 1968 to 1976, even though the drug was already effectively treating angina and hypertension in European countries without problems. A study by Arthur D. Little, Inc. estimated that 30,000 Americans died of heart attacks waiting for the FDA to approve Propranolol.

It might take a hundred years for that many people to die from taking unregulated drugs.

As with any other function, if you turn the regulation of food, medicines, and safety features over to the government, they become political issues. It can't be otherwise.

Real Regulation

Suppose there were no FDA. What would happen? Would we be afraid to walk into a drug store?

Of course not. Imagine this conversation:

Your doctor: You have a severe medical condition that requires treatment. I'm going to recommend a relatively new medicine.

You: Is this medicine safe?

Your doctor: I don't know.

You: You don't know????

Your doctor: No, I don't know. After all, no political agency tests these things. We just have to take our chances. If you survive it, let me know how it works.

Does it seem likely that your doctor would recommend a medicine he knows nothing about? Is your health insurance company going to pay for a medicine that could kill you? And are you going to bet your life on a medicine whose safety is open to question? Hardly.

So pharmaceutical companies would be unable to induce doctors, insurance companies, or patients to accept a product without proof that the medicine is safe.

How can the companies provide that assurance? There are many possibilities. They could have a medicine tested by one or more independent agencies — the same way the Underwriters' Laboratory seal of approval guarantees that electrical appliances are safe.

Or the companies could back up their products with their own insurance policies. Anyone suffering adverse results from using a medicine would have all his rehabilitation costs paid. An insurance company would use the best scientists and researchers to test each new drug, and it would stand behind a drug only if satisfied there would be no major problems.

Most likely, a system we can't even imagine now would evolve — because there would be a market for such assurance. And a small fortune would go to the founder of the system that provides the best balance among safety, cost, convenience, and availability.

You're in Command

Most important, a system that doesn't involve government coercion would let you decide whose advice to take — your doctor's or Bill Clinton's. A handful of political appointees in Washington wouldn't have your life in their hands.

Should your health and your very life be dependent upon politics? It's one thing to let politicians take some of your money and waste it on the building of a subway system that goes nowhere. But let them mess around with your very life?

In fact, should anything you value be dependent on political whims?

You automatically regulate companies far more effectively than government does. If you don't think meat for sale is safe, you don't buy it. If you aren't confident an airplane is safe, you don't get in it.

When people worried that computer problems might make airplanes unsafe on January 1, 2000, many of them altered their travel plans to work around that date. But others who saw no Y2K problem were free to travel on New Year's Day. Each person regulated the airlines in his own way. Would it have been better if politicians had made a single choice and forced it on everyone?

Because you don't *have* to buy, the burden of proof is always on the sellers to prove that their products are safe. This is far superior to political regulation that gives people false assurances about products — even though the assurances stem from political considerations.

So, really, should *anything* you need and want for your life be regulated by political considerations?

POLITICAL REGULATION BACKFIRES

Campaigns for more political regulation rely primarily on anecdotes — simple stories that seem to offer proof of something. An accident happens, people die, Congressmen rush to the TV cameras to strut and proclaim their concern for public safety, new laws are passed, and the matter is forgotten as everyone turns his attention to the next crisis.

Or politicians cite statistics demonstrating that large numbers of people are hurt or die because of some cause. New laws are passed to use government force to reduce the cause of the problem. And the politicians move on to the next crisis — satisfied that they've won another victory for safety, benevolence, and The American Way.

Rarely is there any follow-up to see whether the new laws really achieve their purpose, whether they make no difference at all, or whether they actually make things worse.

Instead, the politicians rely on "self-evident" propositions. For example:

1. Wearing a seat belt reduces your risk of being killed in an automobile accident.
2. Government can force everyone to use a seat belt.

Therefore:

3. A law to force people to use seat belts will reduce traffic fatalities.

The logic seems so simple. How can anyone argue with it? You can't, unless you look beyond the obvious.

Before there was a mandatory seat belt law in England, the British Department of Transport studied accident patterns in eight European countries that had such laws. It found that the accident rate *increased* in every one of the eight countries *after* it enacted a seat belt law.[1]

The study was completed in 1981, but it wasn't made public until 1985. In the meantime the British Parliament enacted a mandatory seat belt law. Just as in the other countries, higher traffic fatality rates quickly followed.

How could this happen?

The most likely explanation is that many drivers *feel* so much safer wearing a seat belt that they are willing to take greater risks — and so have more accidents. If a driver has an accident, the seat belt may increase *his* chance of survival, but that doesn't help his passengers or anyone hit by his car.

After Britain passed its law, fatalities increased by 27% for back seat passengers, by 14% for pedestrians, and by 40% for the enormous population of English cyclists. So even though fatalities for drivers declined, more lives were lost than saved.

There are other bad effects of such laws. When police are diverted from fighting violent crime to ticketing people for not wearing seat belts, we shouldn't be surprised that violent crime increases — also leading to more fatalities.

None of that matters to the politicians. They just go on congratulating themselves and exploiting individual accidents to force new laws and regulations on you and me.

Politicians and reformers are fond of saying, "If this saves even one life, it will have been worth it." Change "even one life" to "the life of just one child" and you double the emotional impact. It doesn't matter to politicians and reformers that the life may be saved at the cost of *several* other lives — just so long as the life saved is on camera and the lives lost are offstage.

Political vs. Consumer Regulation

Getting government out of the business of regulating foods, medicines, and other products would undoubtedly save lives, save you money, make you healthier, and greatly expand your choices.

---

[1]Statistically, there was no more than 4/10 of 1% possibility that this resulted from chance.

We can get an idea of how much better off you'd be just by looking at what's happened in other areas after the politicians quit regulating them.

1. Before banking services were deregulated, banks were open only from 10a.m. to 3p.m., Monday through Friday. Every bank provided the same accounts and services, and they paid the same interest rates. You chose a bank only by its location, the choice of check designs, the size of the free toaster, or the length of time you had to wait to get a safe deposit box.

After banking services were deregulated, banks competed for your business with real choices. Now there are longer operating hours (including Saturday service), ATM machines, after-hours outdoor tellers, debit cards, banking with your computer, better interest rates on deposits, many more choices among checking and savings accounts, mutual funds and life insurance available at the bank, and much, much more. [2]

2. Before long-distance telephone service was deregulated, the average cost of a cross-country call ranged from 20¢ to $1 a minute. Today most calls cost 10¢ a minute or less.

3. At one time it was illegal for private companies to provide overnight nationwide courier service. The Postal Service didn't offer guaranteed delivery or any of the other features that private carriers like Federal Express and UPS provide today. The ability to deliver something across the country overnight has undoubtedly saved a few lives, as well as many jobs.

Now imagine if we could free up health-care providers, investment companies, power companies, water companies, cable companies, and other industries so we could have services equivalent to what we now get from banks, long-distance telephone companies, and courier services.

Imagine if your food and medicines were regulated by consumer agencies that reimbursed you if you suffered because of their mistakes. Imagine if the cost of that regulation were so small that the prices of products fell by 10%, 20%, or more.

And imagine that kind of progress applied to roads, airports, mail delivery, personal safety, education, health care, home-building, food production. Think how much more your paycheck could buy. And how it could elevate the poor — bringing thou-

[2]Two major regulatory impediments remain. The government's bank insurance promotes banking irresponsibility, and the government still limits the ways a bank can invest

sands of safer, more effective, less expensive, more convenient products within their reach.

WHAT DOES IT COST?

There is no way to know precisely how much political regulation costs America in lives lost, in inconvenience, or even in money. But economists have tried to estimate how much it adds to the prices of what you buy and how much it reduces your income.

A study by Thomas D. Hopkins of the Rochester Institute of Technology estimated the cost of federal regulation in 1994 to be $600 billion a year, which was then 11% of the national income. A 1992 study for the Heritage Foundation by William G. Laffer, III, and Nancy A. Bord estimated the net cost of regulation (after allowing for the benefits regulation might produce) to be somewhere between 16% and 32% of the national income.

Whatever the actual cost, regulation obviously exacts an enormous price from you — and it eats up at least 10% of the national income. Add that to the 47% that federal, state, and local governments tax away from us, and at least 57% of your earnings are diverted to satisfy government before you get to spend anything on yourself.

That means you're working Monday, Tuesday, and virtually all of Wednesday just to pay the cost of government, while what you earn on Thursday and Friday you get to keep for yourself.

Is that a bargain price for all the "good government" you're getting?

TYPICAL OF GOVERNMENT

Political regulation is handled by the same people who brought us the War on Poverty and the War on Drugs. And it demonstrates all the usual contrasts between political control and freedom.

- Because government is force, regulation prohibits you from making your own choices.
- Because government is politics, government can never be a good referee of the marketplace, since the referee will always side with the team with the most political influence.
- Because government always wants to grow, asking the government to assure the safety of food and medicines

has led to government banning pesticides that could have saved lives by making the foods you eat safer and less expensive. The government even regulates the size of your toilet.

- Because you don't control the government, the regulation you want to see will never be applied in the way you imagined.

- Because power will always be misused eventually, the regulation you hope will protect your interests will eventually be used to prevent you from pursuing your interests.

- Because regulation can't overrule the natural intention of everyone to look out for his own interests, political regulation never delivers on its promises.

- Because we won't be safe unless government is strictly limited, we must enforce the Constitution. And the Constitution authorizes the federal government to regulate trade only with foreign nations and Indian nations, and to assure that states don't erect trade barriers against each other. There is no authority for the federal government to regulate ordinary business — inside of states or across state boundaries. If we allow political regulation to remain in place, government remains unlimited.

With personal regulation and consumer regulation, you are in control.

- You don't have to know how something can be accomplished for it to be done. Companies will compete with one another to find the best ways to assure your protection, and you can choose the one you think is best.

- Competition will assure constant improvement — just as we've seen in the computer industry. No system will ever be frozen in time — the way banking regulation designed in the 1930s continued to prohibit innovation well into the 1970s.

- You will pay far less and earn far more if you and other consumers do the regulating — instead of letting politicians do whatever they find politically profitable.

- No one will force you to accept a system you aren't comfortable with. The choice will always be yours — including the choice of whose opinion to accept among competing "regulators."

As always with government, there really are only two possibilities:

- You and everyone else should have the freedom to choose whatever you want to buy and to choose whose judgment you respect, and anyone should have the freedom to try to sell to you. Or . . .
- Politicians should have the power to decide whom you may deal with, and how you may do business.

There really is no third way, no middle ground — because giving the politicians a little bit of power always leads to more.

THE GREAT LIBERTARIAN OFFER would be a giant first step toward giving back to you control over your life. It would reduce the cost of government from the three days a week you now work for the government to only about one. That means you'll be working four days for yourself instead of only two — a doubling of your standard of living.

CHAPTER 13

FREEDOM TO WORK, TO EARN, & TO BUY

Almost every politician claims to know how to run the economy.

And the differences in style from one politician to another are minor. They all believe government must stimulate the economy through spending programs, set interest rates through the Federal Reserve System, and dictate many aspects of your employment to you and your employer.

We sometimes hear a politician ask, "Are you better off now than you were four years ago?"

But, in truth, little changes from one presidential administration to the next. The economic policies are largely the same, and no President really knows how to make the economy run faster. Even those who say government should get out of the way continue the policies of government interference.

Meanwhile, the economy manages on its own because, despite all the interference and regulations, people have to produce to live and they're not going to let the politicians stop them. Despite the politicians, new jobs come into being mostly because the population grows, and because there will never be enough labor to do all the work that people want done.

Still, the politicians brag about the new jobs as though they had personally invested the money and dug the foundation for new factories, and transformed illiterate souls into productive workers.

So long as you have a decent job and your income is rising, politicians will gladly take the credit for everything you have, even though you've earned it with no help from them.

If you're better off than you were four years ago, it isn't because of some wise politician's economic policies.

135

And the comparison actually misses the point. Growth is part of the natural order of things. Barring disastrous interference from the government, you almost always will be better off than you were four years ago.

The important question isn't how you stand compared with four years ago. It is: Are you as well off as you *could* be?

And the answer unquestionably is *no* — because, while government can't make the economy run better, it can make it run worse.

Change in Economic Direction

During the 23 years from 1947 to 1970, the median income of American families increased by an average of 2.8% per year. But from 1970 to 1998, the median income grew by only 0.4% per year.

The difference is considerable. If the previous growth rate had continued, the median income in 1995 would have been 90% greater than it was.[1]

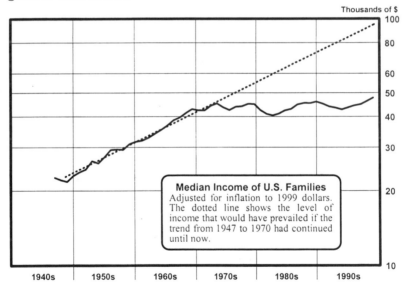

Median Income of U.S. Families
Adjusted for inflation to 1999 dollars. The dotted line shows the level of income that would have prevailed if the trend from 1947 to 1970 had continued until now.

---

[1]The median is the income of the family that ranks exactly in the middle of the U.S. population. Thus one half of American families have annual incomes larger, and one half smaller, than that of the median. The median is used rather than the average (or mean) income, because the average can be skewed by a few very large incomes at the top of the population. 1947 was the first year the median was calculated by the U.S. Census Bureau. All figures cited have been adjusted for inflation to constant dollars.

What changed in the 1970s?

That was when the government's control of the economy accelerated. The Great Society crusade of the 1960s and early 1970s (under the direction of Democrat Lyndon Johnson and Republican Richard Nixon) had brought us government programs like Medicare, Medicaid, and the War on Poverty — as well as new regulatory controls through the Civil Rights Acts, the Environmental Protection Agency (EPA), the Consumer Product Safety Commission, the Occupational Safety and Health Administration (OSHA), wage and price controls, the War on Drugs, controls on natural gas and oil, and more.

With government tinkering so furiously with the country's economic engine, it became more and more difficult for America's industries to continue growing at the previous rate. In fact, the first fruits of the government's new, much closer attention were the furious cycles of inflation and recession that beset the country during the 1970s and early 1980s.

Today some industries are booming. But compared to its performance before 1970, the economy as a whole is suffering from Chronic Fatigue Syndrome.

We shouldn't be surprised that increased government control of the economy has reduced economic growth. The effort and resources a business puts into complying with government rules and pleasing government inspectors are effort and resources that can't be used to satisfy customers.

And it should be no surprise that political management of the economy isn't a success. After all, this is the same government that has had such poor results trying to stamp out drugs and poverty.

How Much Better Could It be?

So, again: Are you as well off as you could be?

Suppose the federal government weren't taxing your income, squandering your retirement money, adding regulatory costs to everything you buy, and forcing your employer to spend money on bureaucratic mandates instead of on you. How well off would you be?

Suppose all the money you now pay in income and Social Security tax — $10,000 or more a year — were available to take care of your family? Would you work fewer hours a week? Take a longer vacation? Provide better health care for your family? Live in a better neighborhood? Spend more time helping your church or your favorite cause? Pick a better college for your children?

Are you as well off as you could be?

FREEDOM TO BUY ANYWHERE YOU WANT

The politicians not only make it harder for American companies to please you, they also tell you what you may buy from overseas.

The government prohibits some imports and taxes others. The politicians say this saves American jobs and protects American companies from "unfair" competition. But the real reason is to reward the industries with the most political influence.

The principal barriers to imports are tariffs (taxes on imported products) that make foreign goods more expensive for you to buy. The tariffs also make American products more expensive by increasing the cost of imported raw materials. And the tariffs make some foreign products so expensive they can't compete here — leaving you no alternative to more costly American versions.

In addition, when it's in the interest of companies with the right political connections, foreign products can be banned entirely from the U.S. because of questionable claims that they hurt the environment or their prices are unfairly low.

Import barriers cost Americans about $70 billion a year — roughly about $700 for every American household.

Another way of looking at it is that each American job "saved" by import restrictions costs consumers roughly $170,000 — about six times the annual wage of the average manufacturing worker. Thus the jobs and wages saved are much more than offset by the higher prices we pay for products.

Why We Need Foreign Products

Some goods are more efficiently produced outside the U.S. Anything that impedes or prohibits trade between countries lowers your standard of living. Such prohibitions preserve jobs in selected American industries, but destroy jobs in other industries. And they reduce your choices, make you poorer, and leave your life less comfortable.

Import barriers destroy American jobs because they keep dollars out of the hands of foreigners — leaving them with nothing to spend on American products. Without imports, our export industries shrivel and die.

"Fair Trade"

Because few people want to give up foreign products, no politician will admit to being against free trade — which is the freedom for you to buy any foreign product you want. Instead they mask their desire to exclude foreign products as a desire for "fair trade." That is, they want only to restrict imports from countries whose governments treat American companies unfairly. If a foreign government puts up barriers to American products, the politicians want to respond in kind.

It sounds as though we're punishing a foreign government for hurting us. But the foreign politicians don't care very much that we restrict imports from their country. In fact, they may like it. They are politicians, not producers. They don't export anything except speeches. Our import barriers just give them an excuse to subsidize their favorite exporters or otherwise increase their power.

The real victims of our government's retaliation are you and the foreign workers. The foreign workers don't get to sell to you, and you don't get to buy what you want at the lowest price.

It wouldn't make sense, for example, for you to pay $1,000 for your next VCR or an extra $5,000 for your next car just because the Japanese government makes it difficult to sell American cars in Japan. Why should our government punish you when foreign politicians act like American politicians?

Posturing on Trade

Import barriers may not make sense, but that doesn't stop politicians from playing to the crowd — posturing on behalf of their political backers who want to avoid foreign competition.

For example, Patrick Buchanan has said:

The Japanese in the last 25 years have bought 400,000 American cars and sold us 40 million. Now if that is not trade aggression, I don't know what is. You've got to wake up and start defending the national interest of the United States and of American workers, American businesses, and American auto workers.

This overlooks something. Every car sold by a Japanese company here was bought by an American. Were those Americans committing "trade aggression" against their own country?

Trade isn't aggression. Trade means that the buyer and the seller each get something he wants more than what he has to give up.

Americans sell far more airplanes to Japan than the Japanese sell to Americans — and that goes as well for aluminum, cereals, lumber, chemicals, meat, oil seeds, and tobacco products. Are Americans committing aggression against the Japanese?

Bashing the Japanese may play well to audiences that are losing customers to Japanese companies, but America does quite well in its trade with Japan. As Murray Weidenbaum has pointed out:

> It may be a surprise to most people to learn that the average Japanese spends more on U.S. products ($538 in 1996) than the average American spends on Japanese products ($432 in 1996). But we run a large trade deficit with Japan because we have far more people than Japan does.

America is a large, wealthy country. We are able to buy more goods from foreigners than they buy from us because we are better off, not because we are victims.

Competing with Low-Wage Countries

Are low wages and poor working conditions in foreign countries a reason to restrict imports? How can Americans compete with countries whose workers make only $1 a day?

In fact, American workers compete quite well with low-wage countries because Americans are far more productive.

Our two largest trade deficits are with China and Japan. Chinese wages are much lower than American wages, while Japanese wages are *higher* than American wages. So which way does it work?

Actually, it doesn't work either way. Extremely low wages reflect primitive production methods. American workers earn so much more than workers in, say, Malaysia because they are more skilled and have better machines and tools to work with. With these tools, each American worker produces far more each day than his Malaysian counterpart.

Misplaced Compassion

Those who want to exclude foreign products may try to appeal to your compassion. They call foreign factories sweat shops — where all the workers are miserable and many of them are children. They ask you to boycott the goods made in those factories.

But that kind of compassion is the cheapest product of all. It's easy to say that no child should have to work in a factory — and so we should pass up foreign products made with child labor.

Maybe no child has to toil in primitive conditions in America, but people in many other countries aren't nearly as fortunate. Children there have to work because their families can't survive, as we can, with only the parents working. The families choose the best alternative available — which may be factory work for the children. Take away their best alternative and they may starve.

Before you heed the boycotters, ask yourself what will happen to the children if those factories close down. Will they become prostitutes or thieves — or simply die? Or are the boycotters planning to adopt all the children that are thrown out of work?

We should also consider the plight of their parents. It makes no sense to boycott foreign companies whose workers toil without the comforts mandated by the U.S. Department of Labor. Refusing to buy the goods they produce may make some people here feel better, but it will make the workers there feel a lot worse.

American children stopped working in sweat shops at the beginning of the 20th century. This progress wasn't prompted by foreign boycotts of American sweat shops or intervention by our own government. The sweat shops disappeared as expanding technology made workers more productive, and as America's poorest adults accumulated better skills, became wealthier, and could afford to get by without sending their children to work.

Working conditions improved for the same reason. As basic technology advanced, as employers were able to invest in more tools and equipment, and as workers developed greater skills, labor became more productive. Using some of the increased profits to offer workers better conditions was just one more way for employers to attract and keep the best workers.

When people in poor countries can save a little from their paychecks, start accumulating capital, and take advantage of modern technology, working conditions will improve there as well.

Tariffs & Taxes

Tariffs (or "duties") are taxes on imports. A tariff isn't a "good" tax; it's just a tax. But the government can collect it without sending IRS agents to snoop through your records.

Until we find a way to finance government without taxes or a way to assure our safety without any government, some form of taxation will be necessary. And my choice is to use tariffs and excise taxes — as the Founding Fathers did.

However, tariffs today are just one more political tug-of-war. Congress imposes tariffs as high as 100% on some foreign products (doubling their retail prices) to reward their political allies. Other imports are free of all tariffs.

The use of tariffs as a political weapon must stop. I don't believe any goods should be barred from the U.S.; you should be able to buy any product or service you want from any foreign country — without exception. And all imports should be taxed at the same low rate — which needs to be no more than 2%.

By charging every import the same tax, we take a tool of favoritism out of the politicians' hands. Discriminatory tariffs are one more political game that won't be played in a Libertarian America.

PROGRESS

The politicians claim to manage the economy through government spending programs, the manipulation of interest rates, regulation, and other tools. None of this helps you or anyone else who doesn't have the right political connections. These activities are just more opportunities for the politicians to reward their friends and hurt their enemies. You pay for it in the form of higher prices. And you pay for it as well when the political tinkering leads to inflation or recessions.

The Constitution gives the federal government no authority to manage the economy, to create jobs, or to run our economic lives in any way. And politicians have exhibited no more competence in handling the economy than anywhere else.

We don't need government to tell us how to run our businesses or perform our jobs. There are much better managers — you and I and everyone who offers to buy or sell, to work or employ. Our actions and decisions make up the free market — which has produced all the good things the economy has to offer.

America progressed from an agricultural economy in the 1700s to a manufacturing economy in the 1800s, to more of a service economy in the 1900s — and now has the chance to use computer-based production to advance to even greater wealth in the century that lies ahead.

Such progress isn't miraculous. It is perfectly natural, as innovation and technology make us more productive and wealthier. Today, instead of working 14 hours a day plowing in the hot sun on a farm, or 10 hours in a factory, you probably work 7 or 8 hours in an air-conditioned office. And you make far more money than you could have made in farming or manufacturing.

The computer revolution has the potential to enhance work and living as dramatically as the industrial revolution did. But if the politicians continue to make decisions for the economy and the workplace, or if they begin to interfere with computer technology as they have with medicines and health care, we may realize that potential very slowly.

THE GREAT LIBERTARIAN OFFER will take the federal government out of every area not authorized by the Constitution — returning the savings to you by repealing the income tax. That means federal politicians will no longer be making decisions that only you and your employer are qualified to make.

I want you to enjoy the benefits that liberty can bring — a shorter work day, longer vacations, better working conditions, higher pay, a safer and more prosperous retirement, plus the ability to use your greater wealth to help others if you choose.

It is almost impossible to imagine all the exciting innovations that could be just two, three, or ten years ahead of us — provided the government gets out of the way, and provided we once again bind the politicians down from mischief with the chains of the Constitution.

CHAPTER 14

FREEDOM TO LEARN

Government schools have been deteriorating for decades. Students seem to learn less and violence has become a bigger part of the school day. Despite all the promises, education is one more political problem that never gets solved.

But help is on the way.

The President and governors from all over America have formulated a plan to fix the schools within ten years. The plan encompasses six key goals:

1. All children will start school ready to learn;
2. The high school graduation rate will increase to 90%;
3. All children will be competent in core subjects;
4. The United States will be first in the world in math and science;
5. Every adult will be literate and able to compete in the work force;
6. Every school in America will be free of drugs and violence.

Oops, sorry. These are the goals the governors set back in 1990. All were to be achieved by the year 2000.

Unfortunately, as with every other political promise for education, none of the six goals has been realized.

FIXING THE SCHOOLS

The Democrats and Republicans continually offer grand proposals to make the schools work better, but the proposals always

145

turn out to be more of the same policies that are already failing — only more expensive than before.

Democratic Plans

Here are the proposals Bill Clinton and Al Gore have made:

- Increase the amount of money that travels from your local school district to Washington and then back to your local school district.
- More federal money to hire new teachers and reduce class size.
- More federal money to modernize school facilities.
- More programs to teach students how to resolve conflicts.
- More facilities to police students more closely — to control weapons and drugs.
- More federal money to provide pre-kindergarten education.

These ideas are offered as examples of bold and innovative thinking. But every one of them has already been implemented. Between 1950 and 1995, in American elementary and secondary schools:

- Class size was cut virtually in half, with the average ratio of students to teachers falling from 27 to 14.
- The average annual expenditure per student rose 307% — *even after allowing for inflation.*[1]
- The average teacher's salary doubled, after allowing for inflation, which is roughly the same gain as for the labor force in general.
- Spending for school construction and other capital projects increased by 281%, after allowing for inflation.
- The number of non-teaching supervisors per student rose by more than half.
- The amount of education money making a round trip to Washington and back to your local school district rose, after allowing for inflation, by 1,783%.

Did these improvements make the schools a fit place for your

---

1 The annual cost per student in government schools (adjusted for inflation to 1999 dollars) was $1,814 in 1950 and $7,376 in 1995.

children to learn? Vice-President Al Gore pronounced the verdict
in October 1999:

> The teachers are overburdened. The classrooms are over-
> crowded. The buildings are falling down. The reform agenda
> is underfunded.

Now here's the part you may find difficult to understand. He
is saying that spending enormous amounts of money to reduce
class size, build more buildings, increase teachers' salaries, and
involve Washington ever-more deeply in local education has produced dismal results. So what does he propose as a remedy?
Spending enormous amounts of money to reduce class size, build
more buildings, increase teachers' salaries, and involve
Washington ever-more deeply in local education.

Republican Plans

While Democrats are focused exclusively on government
schools, the Republicans want to go further — extending the government's mechanisms of failure to *private* schools.

They don't say that, of course; they call their proposals
"school choice." But what they're proposing practically guarantees to eliminate private schools as an alternative to government
education — leaving parents with *no choice* whatsoever.

Consider, for example, the system the Republican Governor
set up in Florida in 1999. It will give some poor parents vouchers
to pay for their children's tuition at private schools. But any private school that participates in the program:

- Must file detailed reports on its own finances and the
  finances of the families of *all* its students, not just those
  using vouchers.
- Must conform to all federal anti-discrimination policies,
  which would eliminate single-sex and religion-based
  schools.
- Must accept any student who arrives at the door with a
  voucher, regardless of his academic history; so the students who were disrupting your child's class at the government school could disrupt his class at his private
  school.
- Must use roughly the same qualifications for teachers
  that are used at government schools.

- Must "accept as full tuition and fees the amount provided by the state for each student" — thereby imposing price controls on the school.
- Must abide by state regulations regarding discipline, which probably will prevent the school from expelling violent students.

It's no wonder that, in the entire state of Florida, only five private schools agreed to accept students carrying vouchers.

Vouchers = Control

Republican politicians assure us they can enact a federal voucher program that won't force private schools to change their policies. But try to think of a single government aid program that hasn't come with a thick rule book and tangled strings.

Even if the initial program were to give free rein to each school to do as it pleases, what would happen when the *next* Congress or state legislature took over?

Government programs don't stand still. They grow and change. And the politicians who guarantee that government will never cross some boundary line are eventually replaced by politicians who believe government controls are essential. The promises made at the outset of any government program are meaningless.

When federal aid to local government schools began in the 1960s, federal bureaucrats were prevented from setting any rules for local school districts. Today Washington imposes rules governing pupil-teacher ratios, teacher qualifications, "sensitivity" training, drug education, discipline policies, bilingual education, sex education, and equal funding for boys' and girls' sports.

If politicians exert this much control over government schools, why won't they do the same with private schools once they get them hooked on federal money? In fact, has government ever subsidized *anything* without controlling it?

Hooking Schools with Subsidies

Look at what has happened to colleges.

Since 1975, if a single student at a college — public or private — receives any kind of government grant (even if the money doesn't pass through the college), the school must comply with a long, long list of federal rules.

It might seem that any private elementary school could just drop out of a voucher program if the federal government began imposing oppressive controls.

In principle, it could. And so could colleges resist controls by dropping out of aid programs. But colleges don't drop out. Once it's become dependent on the manna from Washington, no college will turn it down — no matter how bad the controls become.

In recent years, the federal government has forced the Virginia Military Institute and the Citadel to overturn their most basic policies. Either could have evaded the dictation simply by rejecting all future federal aid, but neither did.

Running up Prices

Federal subsidies also run up the prices of everything they touch, and private schools would be no exception.

Again, colleges allow us to see ahead to what will happen to private schools. In the 1950s a rule of thumb was that a good college cost a student about $1,000 a year — including tuition and books. Today, the cost at a typical college is closer to $20,000 per year, with more elite schools costing as much as $50,000.[2]

This is because government "vouchers" in the form of G.I. Bill tuition, Pell Grants, student loans, and a host of other government subsidies have pushed the demand for a college education well past the supply.

As college costs rise, the politicians run to the rescue of hard-pressed families with ever-more subsidies. But each new subsidy allows colleges to raise their prices to capture most of the new money. That provokes a new round of subsidies, leading to even higher tuition costs.

In every way, federal aid has damaged American colleges. As Ronald Trowbridge has pointed out, vouchers for college education have spawned "pervasive political correctness, excessive dropouts, and exorbitant costs."

Is that what we want for private elementary schools and high schools?

There has to be a better way.

UNDERSTANDING THE EDUCATION CRISIS

And there is.

To understand the school problems, we have to realize that they have nothing to do with class size, teacher credentials, or the amount of money being spent.

---

[2]Even after allowing for inflation, the increase in college costs is more than triple.

Why does education become ever more expensive and ever more inefficient while other things get cheaper and better?

Imagine if the computer industry were like education. A typical computer wouldn't have dropped in price from over $1 million to under $1,000 — while becoming thousands of times more powerful and several times smaller. Instead, the price would now be in the *trillions* of dollars; it would do addition, subtraction, a little multiplication, but no division; and instead of sitting on your desk, it would fill up your entire neighborhood.

Why such different results between education and computers?

- Education is the province of politicians and bureaucrats who will never personally face the consequences of their own decisions, no matter how much they ruin your children's education.

- Computers are the province of profit-seeking businessmen who must continually find new ways to please you by doing more with less — or else lose their own money and go out of business.

Unlike computer companies, government schools are monopoly organizations — backed up by all the guns of government. Vouchers won't make government schools more competitive, because *government schools don't have to compete*. No matter how many students they lose to private schools or home schooling, government schools still take their money by force — and they cite their worst failures to demand even more money.

Government schools are not educational institutions. They are political agencies.

So it's no wonder that their policies are dictated by the teachers' unions, administrators' unions, and the utopian fantasies of the teachers' colleges. There are no rewards for local innovation, no opportunities to solve problems with new methods, no way to be compensated for superior performance.

Government schools wind up teaching many things that would horrify parents — if the parents were fully aware of what's being taught. Sexual techniques, drug use, death education, and sexual-abuse paranoia are just the tip of the iceberg. Students are taught to badger their parents to recycle and to practice other environmental pieties. If classic literature is ever studied, it's more likely to show how unenlightened and insensitive people once were, rather than to show students the complexity of life and the richness of the English language.

The time and resources are always available to teach children to conform to trendy thinking. But if parents complain that their children aren't learning enough math, science, history, and reading, the politicians respond that there isn't enough money — unless you vote for the next tax increase.

And why would we expect it to be otherwise? Under no competitive pressure, school administrators are free to indulge their wildest ideas for indoctrinating children to be better citizens of the New Order. In such a system, the best teachers in the world have no chance.

How to Starve to Death

If governments ran the supermarkets, we'd all have to attend food board meetings and lobby to try to make our favorite mustard the monopoly choice for everyone. And day-old bread would be on the honor roll. If government built our cars, only the super-rich could afford a Yugo — and Chevys wouldn't be available at all.

Because schooling is run by government, you're not allowed to decide what kind of education you want to pay for. The money is confiscated from you through taxes — and then you, your children, and the teachers must all beg for crumbs from government.

You don't get to decide which school your children will attend, you don't get to choose the curriculum you want. Your only role is to shut up and pay.

Why? Because you aren't a professional educator, and thus you're not competent to make such decisions. As though you haven't managed to choose an appropriate job, buy a good house, eat good food, and raise your children without being a career consultant, architect, farmer, or child psychiatrist.

SOLVING THE EDUCATION CRISIS

The obvious answer to the education problems is to get government completely out of schooling. Let people buy education for their children the way they buy the other products and services they need.

The roughly $300 billion a year spent on government schools comes from American citizens — not from Martians. Why should that money be funneled through government, subjected to waste and political maneuvering, and then doled out to schools?

Why shouldn't you keep your own money and spend it as you think best?

Schools run solely by competing private companies would have constantly rising standards, expanded choices, and falling prices. As with the computer industry, the opportunity for profit would stimulate new ways of organizing schools and teaching that we can't even imagine now. The cost of education might drop to half or less of what a private or government school costs today. And, oh yes, your children would actually learn what you want them to learn — or you'd move them to a better school.

Poor Children

Without "free" public schooling, how would the children of poor families be educated?

First, an end to the income tax and school taxes would reduce dramatically the number of poor families.

Second, poor children could acquire private schooling in the same way so many of them do now — through tuition aid provided by religious schools and private voucher programs.

Far more children attend private schools today through private voucher programs than through government voucher programs. Private agencies like the Pacific Research Institute, the Independent Institute, the Charitable Choice Trust, and the Children's Scholarship Fund administer programs to put poor children in private schools — programs paid for by such companies as Golden Rule Insurance Company, State Farm Insurance, Mobil Corp., Miller Brewing Company, and the Ford Motor Company.

And all this is achieved while government drains 47% of the national income from us in taxes. Suppose that tax load were cut in half — by repealing the federal income tax and local school taxes. Can you imagine how much money would be available to take care of any child in need of a good education?

What Can Be Done at the Federal Level?

Government schools are set up by states and communities. So changing federal polices won't get government completely out of schooling.

But there are two major reforms that can come from Washington:

    1. End all federal education programs. The Constitution doesn't authorize the federal government to be involved

in education in any way. Although government schools have never been ideal, the sharp descent in educational achievement began when the federal government moved in during the 1960s.

2. Repeal the federal income tax, so that you and other parents can afford to send your children to whatever school you want — without having to pressure the school board to respect your wishes, and without having to beg the state for a voucher to a government-controlled private school.

THE GREAT LIBERTARIAN OFFER promises the freedom to decide for yourself how to handle school and college decisions with the money you've already earned — instead of the politicians' confiscating your money and doling it back to you as though you were a child on an allowance.

True, you'll have to give up your child's student loan or Pell Grant — if you're relying on that now.

But what do you want for your child — a temporary subsidy or permanent freedom from the income tax?

Wouldn't it make more sense for your child to find a part-time job to cover part of the school costs — or to get a bank loan — or to investigate less expensive schools? And then be free to keep every dollar he earns throughout his life?

With THE GREAT LIBERTARIAN OFFER and the government out of education, you'll win three ways: (1) you and your children will be free of the income tax burden you've shouldered all your life; (2) the cost of schooling will drop considerably; and (3) schools and colleges will no longer be political institutions, but instead will provide the best education possible in order to keep you as their customer.

CHAPTER 15

SAVING THE ENVIRONMENT FROM POLITICAL DESTRUCTION

The word "environment" covers a multitude of issues — such things as pollution, conservation, recycling, global warming, the ozone layer, air and water quality, endangered species, and even population control.

Covering all these issues thoroughly — or even one of them — would take an entire book. So I will call attention only to some aspects of them that normally are ignored when the environment is discussed.

POLLUTION

When environmentalism became a popular topic in the 1970s, little attention was paid to the ownership of the properties being polluted. Important questions were never asked publicly:

- Why would the owner of a lake or river allow it to be used for dumping chemical waste — a practice that would destroy the value of the property?
- Why would the owner of a forest cut the trees for profit, and then ignore the future profits to be made by replanting?

At first glance the polluting doesn't seem to make sense. Why would anyone destroy the value of his own property? Would you intentionally pollute your front lawn, knowing this would make your home worth less than what you paid for it? It's not very likely.

And yet, many properties throughout America are losing value because the owners allow them to be polluted.

155

Who owns these properties?

In most cases, they are owned by governments —federal, state, and local.

The key to understanding and correcting pollution problems is one simple fact: most pollution occurs on government property — on government lands, and in government rivers, streams, and lakes.[1]

There are three ways pollution can occur:

1. Private companies can pollute their own property.
2. Governments can allow private companies to pollute government property.
3. Governments can pollute their own property.

Very rarely do we hear of a private company that is destroying the value of its own property. And we would be hard put to understand why a company would do such a thing.

But destroying someone else's property is a different story.

Private Polluting of Government Property

If someone dumped garbage on your property, you'd stop him the next time he showed up. And if you couldn't stop him yourself, you'd ask the police to do it. But government has rarely stopped companies from dumping toxic wastes in its lakes and streams, and clear-cutting or strip-mining its lands. In fact, it has encouraged these activities.

Why? Because no one in the government was hurt personally by the damage.

When you read that some company has polluted a river or a lake, realize that the government owns that waterway, and it has failed to keep it clean.

If an employee of a private company allowed the company's property to be polluted, he'd probably be fired. But when a government employee allows government property to be polluted or otherwise abused, he doesn't lose his job. The polluters usually have enough political influence to gain access to the government property — through leases, special arrangements, or just indifference on the part of the government managers.

---

[1] Many people don't realize that governments own most rivers and lakes in America, believing instead that these facilities are somehow owned by "all of us." But if you can't sell your share of a river — or make any of the decisions regarding its use — you obviously don't own any part of it. And if a government has the authority to stop you from fishing in its lake or sailing a boat across it, obviously that government — not you — owns the lake.

But this side of pollution is rarely noticed. Public outrage over pollution isn't directed at the government — only at the "corporate polluters." And when the outrage reaches a crescendo, governments respond by harassing private companies and property owners — those who have kept much better care of their property than the government has.

Private vs. Political Ownership

Wherever direct comparisons are possible, private ownership equals "clean" while government ownership equals "polluted."

For example, government-owned forests in the Blue Mountains of Oregon have suffered permanent damage. Nearly all the seed-bearing pines have been destroyed, and the entire forest has been devastated by insects.

But next to it is a Boise Cascade forest that has suffered practically no insect damage. And Boise uses logging practices that keep the forest replenished, protecting its investment. As a result, the Boise forest looks very much as it did a century ago.

The same comparisons exist when properties are used for mining or grazing. Private owners take special care with their own lands to preserve their value for eventual resale. But neither they nor government managers have the same incentive when companies lease government property. The government even loses money on many of the leases, which usually are granted to politically influential companies on sweetheart terms.

The most effective way to reduce pollution is to have the government sell its properties to private companies who will safeguard their future value.

Pollution by Government

The ravaging of government lands by politically connected companies has been well known for years — even if the press has ignored the government's complicity.

But now evidence is coming to light of how badly government itself is polluting its own property. Here is how David Armstrong summarized the situation in a 1999 *Boston Globe* series:

> The United States government, which acts as steward and protector of the nation's environment, is itself the worst polluter in the land.
>
> Federal agencies have contaminated more than 60,000 sites across the country and the cost of cleaning up the worst sites is officially expected to approach $300 billion, nearly five

times the price of similar destruction caused by private companies. . . .

Nearly every military base and nuclear arms facility in the country is contaminated. The pollution extends from the U.S. Mint, which released hazardous chemicals into the air when producing commemorative coins, to the national parks, where leaky oil tanks and raw sewage are polluting pristine rivers.

Even the Environmental Protection Agency [EPA], charged with enforcing the country's environmental laws, has been fined for violating toxic waste laws at its laboratories. At the EPA's lab in Lexington, for example, mercury was discovered leaching into the ground water three years ago.

From raw sewage flowing into the lakes and streams of Yellowstone National Park to U.S. Navy oil spills in Washington's Puget Sound to PCBs making fish inedible in the Shenandoah River, government managers have devastated government facilities without concern. And why should they care? Government agencies are exempt from almost all the harsh, expensive laws the politicians have imposed upon private companies.

The EPA estimates the cost of cleaning up all the sites the federal government has polluted to be at least $280 billion — five times the cost for all the privately polluted SuperFund sites.

All this devastation isn't an accident. It isn't a case of hiring the wrong people to manage government property. It is the direct result of putting property in the hands of people who have no personal interest in its future value.

The solution to America's pollution problems is to get as much property as possible out of the hands of government. Private owners will always take better care of land and other resources, because they worry about their future productivity and resale value. Government managers have no reason to care about the future value of *anything* under their care.

Love Canal

You may remember the Love Canal scandal in the late 1970s. It is a classic example of the way politicians and the press misrepresent pollution problems.

Love Canal is actually a trench, rather than a canal, near Niagara Falls, New York. It was intended to be a canal, but the project was abandoned in the early 20th century. From 1920 onward, the trench was used as a trash and chemical disposal site. In 1942 the Hooker Chemical & Plastics Company, a subsidiary of Occidental Petroleum, purchased Love Canal.

The company buried its toxic wastes in the trench, and allowed the city of Niagara Falls and the U.S. Army to dump wastes there as well. Hooker took special pains with the waste material long before toxic wastes were a public issue. The company made sure the waste was buried in a way that prevented leaks and caused no damage to the surrounding environment.[2]

In 1953 the Niagara Falls Board of Education wanted to build a school on top of the trench. Hooker refused to sell the property because of the underground wastes — afraid that any construction could allow gases to escape.

The Board of Education persisted and threatened to confiscate the property by eminent domain. And so Hooker agreed to sell to the school board for $1 — as long as the deed of sale prohibited any construction over the buried toxic wastes. The school board agreed, promising to use that area only for a playground.

But within one year the school board violated the contract and announced its intention to construct the school directly on top of the toxic wastes. Hooker protested publicly and vehemently, citing the danger involved. The school board ignored the warnings and built the school anyway. The presence of the school led to the building of new homes around it.

By the 1970s the chemical wastes were leaking, and nearby residents complained of odors and fumes. A consulting company investigated and recommended a number of measures to reseal the wastes and stop the leakage. But the city government ignored the recommendations.

Finally, in 1978 a state agency investigated and recommended closing the school, evacuating all pregnant women from the area, and banning the eating of home-grown vegetables. The state purchased and leveled 239 homes near the canal. Eventually, everyone in the Love Canal area was evacuated and relocated — paid for by the state and federal governments.

Ignoring the Real Issues

The Love Canal scandal was widely publicized. Hooker Chemical Company was condemned by politicians and journal-

---

[2]Toxic wastes are a necessary byproduct of the production of many chemical products, some of which save lives. The question isn't whether there should be toxic wastes, but how those wastes should be handled.

ists as greedy and irresponsible — as though Hooker had buried the wastes intentionally to poison little schoolchildren.

But no one bothered to ask the obvious question: why did the school board build on top of a trench that was known to contain toxic wastes — especially in the face of Hooker's public warnings? And why weren't the wastes a problem before the government disturbed them?

Hooker eventually paid out over $200 million in settlements to residents and reimbursement to government agencies — even though Hooker was the only party involved that acted responsibly.

The true story of Love Canal was always available to any "investigative" reporter who wanted to investigate. Hooker's protests against the building of the school were a matter of public record. The city archives contained the deed of sale, showing the stipulation against building on the waste site. Old newspapers carried reports of the public hearings at which Hooker warned against building on the canal.

But at the time of the scandal, the networks and wire services relied for information on the politicians' self-serving accusations against Hooker Chemical. The company's reputation never recovered.

Eventually, Eric Zuesse of *Reason* magazine dug up the truth and published it. But by then the press and politicians had moved on to new examples of "corporate greed" and no one in the national press paid attention to Zuesse' findings.

The circumstances of the Love Canal affair may seem exceptional, but only because you probably know more about it now than you do about other highly publicized environmental scandals. Reports from the press and politicians generally assume the worst about private, profit-seeking companies — while assuming that government employees have no self-interest and care only about protecting the environment.

In fact, politicians and bureaucrats have a strong interest in condemning private companies because such attacks often lead to increased government power.

Who Cares about the Long Term?

One reason government will never protect us from pollution is that government managers aren't motivated to pay attention to long-term consequences as private managers are.

For example, no government employee suffered from the Love Canal scandal. The problems didn't come to light for almost two decades after the government negligence occurred. Those who were in charge when mistakes occurred in 1954 were long gone by the mid-1970s when the scandal erupted.

By contrast, company executives must be able to show stockholders today that the company's properties won't be worth less tomorrow. Anything that will alter future dividends, no matter how far in the future, affects the company's stock price today. And a declining stock price puts a company executive's job in jeopardy.

The Solution for Pollution

The next time you hear about a corporate polluter, strip-miner, or clear-cutter, notice who owns the property that's being polluted. Chances are it's a government agency.

Realize how much cleaner that property would be if it had a private owner who cared about its value. Even if the government sold the property to the same company that had been polluting it, the property would be treated much better. At last someone would worry about its future value.

Until we get governments out of property management, we will continue to suffer the pollution problems that have become so common over the last few decades.

AIR POLLUTION

Air pollution is more complicated than land or water pollution. It isn't easy to define the ownership of air space and sort out air pollution problems in court.

But we can be sure of five points that are overlooked when people call on the federal government to clean up the air.

First, the Constitution gives the federal government no authority to regulate air quality. And to overstep the bounds of the Constitution in this area promotes the idea that the federal government should be able to overstep its boundaries for any purpose someone thinks is good.

Second, what does the federal government have to do with air quality in individual cities? Why should smog-free Seattle have to abide by costly federal air-quality mandates that were designed to reduce smog in Los Angeles? If the people in Los Angeles don't like the air quality there, don't they have enough of an incentive to solve the problem on their own — without federal dictation? And if they *don't* care, why should we? Why should people in other parts of the country, who aren't exposed to Los Angeles air, have to pay to purify the air there?

Do we really believe the Washington politicians know what's best for every part of America? Or that money sent to Washington will become more valuable than if it were left in the state from which it came?

Political Connections

Third, environmental regulations are weapons for the politically connected, just as any other government activity is.

For example, suppose the EPA forces a new factory in Tennessee to install the same new anti-pollution equipment as a plant in Los Angeles needs, even though Tennessee has no smog problem. This imposes unnecessary costs on the Tennessee company, keeping it from underselling its Los Angeles competitor.

Wasting the money in Tennessee is bad enough, but that might not be all there is to it. The EPA rule might have a "grandfather" clause — exempting existing factories from the regulation. So the regulation can force a new, non-polluting Tennessee factory to incur the cost of anti-smog devices — while an older, polluting Los Angeles factory gets off free.

Guess which of the two companies has the most political influence.

As with many laws, environmental regulations often ignore the targets that prompted the regulations, while creating enormous problems for innocent bystanders.

Free-Market Progress

Fourth, cars built in the 1960s polluted much less than the cars of the 1930s, 1940s, and 1950s. But in the 1960s there was no Environmental Protection Agency to force manufacturers to abide by federal standards. Why did the automakers build cleaner-burning cars? Because that's what people wanted — and once the technology was available, that's what they got.

Government doesn't have to force manufacturers to provide what people want. But if we let politicians decide what's good for people, we're giving the politicians the power to exploit people on behalf of those with the most political influence.

Saving Lives

And fifth, when politicians address an issue, they almost always focus only on the highly publicized areas and ignore aspects that might be more important.

For example, the EPA has forced car-makers to build smaller cars, because they burn less gasoline and because they should save lives by reducing air pollution. Both reasons ignore important considerations.

First, the desire for fuel efficiency was born in the 1970s when U.S. price controls on oil and natural gas kept oil companies from developing new petroleum sources to compete with the OPEC oil cartel. Once the government removed those controls in 1981, oil production boomed, oil prices plummeted, and there was no longer a need to conserve oil. But the EPA continues to pretend that fuel efficiency is virtuous.

And it ignores the fact that the marketplace will always provide some fuel-efficient choices for those who want them — without forcing a single choice on everyone

Second, while smaller cars may reduce air pollution slightly (by burning less gasoline), they don't save lives. Reducing their size makes cars less safe, causing more deaths than are saved by reducing air pollution. The Competitive Enterprise Institute estimated that the smaller size of cars (produced to conform to the EPA's fuel-economy standards) caused between 2,600 and 4,500 car deaths in 1998. A 1989 study produced by Harvard University and the Brookings Institute estimated that fuel-economy mandates cause a 14-27% increase in yearly traffic deaths.

Whatever may be the best remedy for air pollution, it certainly isn't to give politicians the power to force their choices on your car, your city, and your life.

RECYCLING

We are told we're running out of resources, running out of places to put trash, and in need of recycled materials to stop the pollution that comes from manufacturing.

However, government subsidies for recycling programs assure that valuable resources *will* be wasted.

There is a simple test to determine whether some resource is scarce enough to warrant recycling. If the price of a recycled item is less than the price of producing a brand new item, it's time to recycle. The higher price of a brand new item means the material needed to make it is more precious than the elements used in the recycling process. So it's profitable for recyclers to pay for your cast-offs, and you can save money by buying goods made with recycled materials. No subsidy is needed, and no one has to browbeat you to recycle; your self-interest provides all the motivation needed.

But if you don't get paid when you turn in items to be recycled, and if recycled items cost more than brand new products, it's obvious that the recycling process is using more precious resources than those that produce the item from scratch. In that case, recycling merely satisfies someone's belief that sacrificing your time and money will make you a better person. It's a religious matter, not a conservation issue.

The same principle applies to other environmental enthusiasms. If the government has to subsidize an alternative form of energy — such as solar heating or electric cars — it's obvious that the government is trying to induce us to quit using a resource in ample supply and switch to a more expensive one in shorter supply.

That's the case as well when the government imposes heavy taxes on one type of activity in order to induce people to patronize an alternative.

Landfill Shortage?

Is recycling necessary to offset a shortage of places to put trash?

No, there is no shortage of sites for landfills. Roy E. Cordato has noted:

> If all the solid waste for the next *thousand years* were put into a single space, it would take up 44 square miles of landfill, a mere .01% of the U.S. land space.

He also pointed out that the recycling process causes just as much pollution as new manufacturing does.

And recycling doesn't save trees; it eliminates them. Trees are planted in response to the demand for new paper and other timber products. Private companies plant enough trees to meet the expected demand well into the future. If people recycle paper products, fewer trees are needed and fewer are planted — just as the supply of grains, meat, minerals, or anything else is a response to the demand for these items.

So if you throw away paper products when you're finished with them, don't feel guilty. Feel proud that you're reducing pollution, saving valuable resources, and inspiring a timber company to plant more trees.

GLOBAL WARMING & OTHER ALARMS

From the cranberry cancer scare of the 1950s to the Alar-in-apples hysteria of the 1980s, from the "New Ice Age" of the 1960s to the "global warming" of the 1990s, environmental alarms almost always turn out to be false. Few non-political scientists fear ozone loss, global warming, or acid rain. These are just issues that some people hope to use to reorder the lives of the rest of us.

As William L. Anderson has pointed out:

Few among us remember the Carter Administration's *Global 2000* Report to the President, prepared by the State Department and the Council on Environmental Quality in 1980, with help from a gaggle of federal agencies like the Environmental Protection Agency and the CIA.

The report, like the discredited Club of Rome's *Limits to Growth* report of 1972 and Robert Heilbroner's 1974 *An Inquiry into the Human Prospect*, predicted mass starvation, massive amounts of pollution, and increasing hunger and poverty for all by the year 2000 unless "the nations of the world act decisively to alter current trends." "Decisive action," of course, was further government control of all resources.

Fortunately, the government didn't take greater control of our resources, and none of the scare stories proved to be even close to an accurate forecast. In fact, has *any* such scary prediction ever panned out?

Let's walk down Memory Lane and review some of them. In the 1970s, the prevailing wisdom was that gasoline prices would exceed $2 a gallon by the end of the decade, and the Arabs would soon own half the United States. In the 1980s the Arab threat miraculously disappeared (when the government removed its price controls on petroleum), and the Japanese became the new threat. They, too, were about to own most of the U.S. But then the Japanese economy suddenly went to pieces — all by itself, with no help from the U.S. government.

And there was the New Ice Age that was predicted in the 1960s. When that didn't come to pass, the alarmists decided that

Global Warming made more sense. What's next — dangerously moderate temperatures?

These scares — and many more like them — were all accompanied by urgent demands that the government take action, reduce the freedom of mankind to wantonly destroy Mother Earth, and impose oppressive controls on your life.

Fortunately, none of the proposals was enacted, and the fearful expectations evaporated on their own. So new scares were developed — complete with new demands for government action, new designs to reduce your freedom, and new proposals to keep companies from providing the products and services you need and want.

A great deal of what you hear about the future of Planet Earth isn't science, it's politics. Notice that with every alarm — about global warming, the ozone layer, air pollution, dwindling resources, endangered species, or anything else — the preferred solution is *always* the same: *more government.*

The most popular scare story today is global warming. This is the idea that human beings, by selfishly driving their cars, are releasing carbon dioxide into the atmosphere — causing the earth to heat up and leading to the melting of the polar icecaps, massive flooding, and the end of civilization as we know it.

But over 17,000 scientists — none of whom is affiliated with polluting industries — have signed a petition to the U.S. government that says in part:

> There is no convincing scientific evidence that human release of carbon dioxide, methane, or other greenhouse gasses is causing or will, in the foreseeable future, cause catastrophic heating of the Earth's atmosphere and disruption of the Earth's climate. Moreover, there is substantial scientific evidence that increases in atmospheric carbon dioxide produce many beneficial effects upon the natural plant and animal environments of the Earth.

The supposed struggle to save the planet is really a struggle for power — power over your life. So politicians and environmental extremists never wait for their claims to be proven before demanding to turn your life upside down.

They tell us we can't afford to wait for proof; we must do something *right now* — even if no one is sure what the problem is, even if no one knows whether the changes they demand really will help, and even if a solution might be discovered tomorrow that wouldn't require upsetting everyone's life.

If these weren't at bottom political issues, occasionally the reformers would suggest solutions that *don't* call for increased political power over your life.

SAVING THE ENVIRONMENT PROPERLY

The politicians and the environmental extremists make most of the noise, but there are tens of thousands of Americans who are doing things that actually make a positive impact on the environment.

While politicians keep reaching for more land to be controlled by the government mismanagers, organizations like the Nature Conservancy raise the money from voluntary donors to purchase properties and remove them from development.

People concerned about animal species becoming extinct are buying up lands where those species flourish. If they turn out to be wrong in their expectations, only they will lose; you won't be taxed to pay for someone's guess.

Companies building new plants make them more energy-efficient, simply to save on costs. No one has to browbeat them to do what's in their self-interest.[3]

Other people are working to deregulate the electric power industry, so that power companies will have an incentive to reduce energy costs. Today almost all government-regulated power companies are required to charge on a cost-plus basis — that is, electricity rates are based on how much it costs the companies to produce the power. There is no incentive for the companies to become more efficient and reduce costs, since their profit margin is guaranteed by the government.

THE GREAT LIBERTARIAN OFFER seeks to increase these private efforts by leaving more money in the hands of the people who earn it, so they can do their good deeds without being tempted to call on the government for help.

As with every good thing we enjoy today, future environmental blessings will come from people acting voluntarily in their own interests — not from politicians imposing unproven, untested designs upon you and me.

---

[3] Too often, however, environmental regulations apply to new plants but not to old ones. Thus a company defers building a new energy-efficient plant in order to avoid being subject to the regulations.

WHY THE ENVIRONMENT IS SO
IMPORTANT TO POLITICIANS

Everything you do, every move you make, each step, each breath affects the environment in some way.

That's why so many politicians and reformers are enthusiastic about "saving the environment." Virtually the entire crusade is about you.

- "Conserving resources" means taking them from you and putting them under political control.
- "Ending global warming" means forcing you to pay higher taxes for gas, oil, and electricity.
- "Recycling" means vast power for those who will decide what you must recycle and what you'll be allowed to throw away.
- "Protecting endangered species" means the power to seize your land.
- "Controlling pollution" means controlling you.

For the politicians, the environment is the perfect issue. They can use it to gain more power while appealing to your desire for health, to your appreciation for the natural beauty around you, and to your concern for your children and future generations.

But when you get past the pseudo-science and quasi-religion that accompanies their crusades, you find that the only real environmental problems come from government itself.

And if government is unable to keep its own properties clean, why should we give it control over *your* property? Shouldn't we instead reverse the process and get as much property as possible out of the hands of government?

Shouldn't we choose a system in which every property manager is personally responsible for the results? Shouldn't we discard a system in which politicians are free to give politically connected companies the license to pollute land — without either the politicians or the polluters having to pay for the damage?

The answer to environmental problems isn't to expand the reach of government, but to shrink it. No problems will be solved by the people who gave us the U.S. Postal Service and the Savings & Loan crisis.

But a great deal will be improved by getting property out of the hands of politicians, reducing the federal government to its

Constitutional limits, telling the politicians to stop playing Junior Scientist, and letting motivated individuals deal with the problems society discovers.

In other words, by accepting THE GREAT LIBERTARIAN OFFER.

CHAPTER 16

FREEDOM TO COME AND GO AS YOU PLEASE

Today's critics of immigration want to slow the influx of foreigners or stop it completely. They worry that immigrants take jobs away from Americans, go on welfare, or dilute our culture.

Some politicians demand that the borders be closed; others want them open. Some politicians say legal immigration is okay, but they want to crack down on illegal immigrants.

The arguments about immigration overlook one critical fact: no matter what the politicians say or do, the immigrants keep coming. Immigration policy hasn't changed noticeably in almost four decades. And whatever changes that *are* made don't alter the rate at which immigrants come across the borders.

We can argue about open borders vs. closed borders. But the truth is that America's borders are open and they will remain that way — no matter who's in the White House or Congress.

In Case You Hadn't Noticed, Government Doesn't Work

This is because government is no more capable of keeping immigrants out of America than it is of keeping drugs out.

No matter how much politicians posture about immigration, there's little they can do. They could triple the border guard. They could dig a mile-wide moat along the Mexican border or erect a new Berlin Wall there. They could trash what's left of your privacy by making you carry an identity card.

But they won't stop people who want to get into America. Government immigration policy works no better than its other policies.

So politicians continue to pretend they'll keep out the undesirables if you'll just give them a little more power and a few

171

more of your civil liberties. But no administration in decades has successfully stemmed the flow of immigrants — and no administration is likely to.

TWO TYPES OF IMMIGRANTS

People are drawn to America by one of two motives.

The first type of immigrant sees America as the land of opportunity where hard work is rewarded. It's a place where he can raise his family in peace, free from armed bandits, both private and governmental, and free to speak and worship as he chooses. All he wants is a chance to prove himself.

The other type sees America as the land of the big free lunch — where anyone can get free education, free health care, and free welfare. Those things may be available in his home country, but the helpings here are much larger.

The opportunity-seeker is a boon to America. In most cases, he is willing to do work that no American citizen wants to do — such as picking lettuce, cleaning hotel rooms, mowing lawns, or running a store in a rough neighborhood. In other cases, he has exceptional skills — perhaps in high-level computer engineering or other scientific work.

The welfare-seeker is a different story. He is here to get on the gravy train. And he won't be disappointed. The Welcome Wagon will be waiting for him at the border, offering a basket of goodies.

If we put the Welcome Wagon out of business by shutting down the welfare state, the welfare-seekers will stop coming, while the opportunity-seekers will continue to arrive with their energy and talent.

On the other hand, if we could even find a way to close the borders securely, we'd still have to put up with the welfare state.

So if you don't like having the doors open to free-loaders, the solution once again lies with *less* government, not more.

FEARS

Four worries drive most of the opposition to immigration.

Jobs

The first is that immigrants take jobs away from Americans.

It can happen. If an immigrant is willing to work longer hours, work for less pay, or do tasks an American shuns, he could take your job away from you. But the same competition operates even without immigrants. And a new immigrant doesn't alter the balance between supply and demand for labor.

While each working immigrant increases the supply of labor, he also increases the *demand* for labor. He brings with him a need for products and services — which his job gives him the money to buy. So the immigrant has no *net* effect on the competition for jobs or the level of wages.

Higher wages don't come from restricting the supply of labor — either through restrictive immigration, labor unions, or government regulation. Higher wages come from investment in tools and machines and training and technology that make workers more productive.

The more a worker can produce, the more revenue his employer has available. Part of the increased revenue always finds its way into the employee's paycheck because the employer doesn't want to lose well-trained workers to other employers.

Immigrants don't take jobs away from Americans. They increase the demand for labor and they help to meet that demand.

Welfare

A second worry is that taxpayers will have to provide free health care, free education, and other services to the immigrants.

Needless to say, the answer is to stop providing taxpayer-supported welfare to anyone — immigrant or citizen.

THE GREAT LIBERTARIAN OFFER will end government welfare, at least at the federal level, and add to your take-home pay the resources to support those you believe deserve your help.

Culture

A third concern is that immigration pollutes our culture and replaces America's traditional values with those of other cultures.

It is true that in some parts of the country the culture seems to be changing. Large segments of the population fail to learn English, for example. And fewer and fewer immigrants seem determined to become Americanized in the way most immigrants used to do. But both these problems stem from government.

Where immigrants neglect to learn English, it is because the local or federal government caters to the use of their native tongues. Government schools provide foreign-language teachers, and government forms and signs are printed in two or more languages.

More immigrants would want to become Americanized if America was the distinctive country it once was. But our nation has become more and more like the Old World — where everyone's life is run by a government rulebook.

The answer to the culture problem isn't to keep immigrants out, but to restore the America of free individuals, each responsible and self-governing. Immigrants will embrace our culture more quickly when government stops trying to dissolve it.

Not Enough Room

The fourth concern is that America will become overcrowded.

But the United States is still a country of wide open spaces. The western states contain hundreds of thousands of square miles of unused land — kept off the market and out of use by the federal government.

Advocates of government land ownership imply that the properties are largely beautiful forests and gorgeous canyons. But in fact most of it is flat land, kept off the market for no good reason.

America could triple its population without our existing cities growing any faster than they do now. Wonderful new cities could spring up if we just forced the federal government to give up the open land.

WHICH DO YOU WANT?

It's easy to imagine that the federal government could keep out undesirable immigrants if it just made the effort. But no government program ever works out the way you imagine it will. An attempt to close the borders would be far more complicated than you might have thought.

Tighter immigration laws would mean higher taxes for you, more corruption in law enforcement, and more attacks on your privacy. You'll be required to carry an identity card, and to submit to searches of your car and home. Increased harassment of companies will add to the costs of what you buy. And all the while, the people you thought were being kept out will keep showing up to tend your yard and wash the dishes at the local restaurants.

As with any other issue, turn this over to the politicians and they'll play politics with it. They will do the picking and choosing of who gets to come in and who is kept out. Their choices will bend, as always, to political influence — to the industries that spend the most on politicians, to the unions that can deliver votes, and to the best organized minorities.

Most likely, the people you wanted to keep out will come in, and those you'd welcome will be shut out. The one thing we know for sure is that you won't be the one who gets to make those decisions.

On the other hand, ending the pretense of closed borders and tight immigration would lower your taxes, restore some of your privacy, reduce the costs of many products and services you buy, and increase the demand for your services.

TWO CHOICES

We really have only two alternatives. Either we:

1. Spend our energy trying to dismantle the welfare state and repeal the income tax, so you no longer will be forced to buy lunch for every immigrant. Or . . .
2. Give the politicians the power to decide who gets to come and who will be shut out, and continue to pay for the welfare state.

If we try to close the borders before ending the welfare state, it's very unlikely we'll succeed in keeping many people out — and we will give government new powers to intrude into your life. Overall, the situation will be even worse than it is now.

But if first we dismantle the welfare state and allow you to live in freedom, most worries about immigration will disappear. If they don't, *then* we can examine the issue of immigration more closely.

Even if it turned out that a new wave of immigrants were hurting America, the nation wouldn't be transformed overnight. We would have time to deliberate and find a better policy.

More likely, as people experience the benefits of smaller government, they will become more skeptical of any plan to put more power and money in the hands of politicians. But they can decide that when the time comes.

In the meantime, Libertarians won't join in pretending that some political policy will keep America Simon pure. We don't pretend that the government that's failed at everything else can successfully control our borders.

WELFARE VS. FREEDOM

Trying to limit immigration is an admission that the welfare state is a failure.

It is a confession that America is no longer the most prosperous country in the world — no longer a country so big, so free, and so open-handed that it can accommodate anyone in the world who wants to come here and work to improve his life.

A free and prosperous society has no fear of anyone entering it. But a welfare state is frightened of every poor person who tries to get in and every rich person who tries to get out.

CHAPTER 17

FREEDOM
FROM CRIME

Politicians have been congratulating themselves that crime rates fell during the 1990s.

Unfortunately, that doesn't mean you can safely walk the streets late at night — as you once could in most parts of most American cities. Nor does it mean you can leave your front door unlocked — as once was the rule in America.

As we can see from the graph on page 95, the murder rate in America is still more than 50% higher than it was in the 1950s.

In 1943, there were 44 homicides in New York City. In 1995, with roughly the same population, New York City had 1,170 homicides — and this was celebrated as an improvement.

The truth is that our cities are still unsafe.

Liberal politicians say the crime problem is caused by widespread poverty. But the federal government has thrown trillions of dollars at poverty in the past 30 years while the crime rate continued to rise. By contrast, the crime rate *fell* dramatically during the poverty-stricken Great Depression of the 1930s.

Conservative politicians say the crime problem stems from lenient judges, the coddling of criminals, and a lack of prisons. But the prison population *quadrupled* between 1980 and 1997. How many people have to be locked up to make America safe?

How do we reduce crime without the same old futile proposals for more prisons, tougher laws, more federal handouts, higher taxes, more trampling on the Bill of Rights?

Why Crime-Fighting Is Ineffective

To answer that question we first have to ask: Why is crime such a problem?

Primarily because we rely so much on government for law enforcement.

Government is government. It doesn't matter whether government is performing a function you want it to perform or one you think it should avoid. Anything government does will be organized, financed, and carried out using force — not just force against criminals, but force against taxpayers and innocent bystanders. Any program based on force will be inefficient, expensive, misdirected, and intrusive of individual liberty.

It doesn't matter how conscientious the crime fighters are, government — by its nature — can't be very efficient at anything. It never has been and it never will be[1].

Even where you believe government must be utilized, you should minimize its role and maximize reliance on individual citizens acting voluntarily.

That's the key. Crime rates were much lower when we relied far less on government — and far more on individuals acting in their own self-interest.

And if we want to bring back the safety of those times, we need to make big changes in five areas. Each of them involves a reduction in government, not an increase.

1. STOP DISARMING INNOCENT CITIZENS

There was a time in America when criminals had to fear law-abiding citizens. If a criminal thought about attacking someone on the street, he had no way of knowing whether his victim was armed. If a criminal wanted to rob someone's home, he had to wonder whether the homeowner would meet him with a gun.

But the ability of innocent people to defend themselves and repel attacks has been vanishing steadily — thanks to misguided gun-control laws.

These criminal-friendly laws include federal, state, and local requirements that you wait several days before touching a gun you've purchased, age restrictions on gun purchases, prohibitions on mail-order sales, gun registration or licensing, and mandatory gun locks.

---

[1]The example of supposed government efficiency I've heard most often is the winning of World War II. However, that's a poor example because the U.S. government was fighting other governments.

As a result of these restrictions, gun ownership didn't increase during the 1960s and 1970s, and violent crime did. Consequently, innocent citizens have become more and more at a disadvantage to criminals.

Concealed-carry Laws

But the late 1980s saw a new development. In 1987 Florida passed a law that allowed anyone who met certain minimal qualifications to carry a concealed weapon. Other states followed suit — and by early 2000, 31 states had such laws.

The laws act as a deterrent to street muggers and rapists who have to wonder whether an intended victim is carrying a weapon. And they provide the means to fight back when a vengeful or deranged person opens fire on people in a public place.

In 1996 law professor John R. Lott, Jr., and economist David B. Mustard published an extensive study of these laws. Examining the period 1977 through 1992, they found that states with "concealed-carry" laws have significantly less violent crime, with no increase in accidental gun deaths.

A similar study was made by the Cato Institute, which found that the 24 states that had concealed-carry laws in 1992 had 7.7% fewer murders, 5.2% fewer rapes, 2.2% fewer robberies, and 7% fewer assaults. The report concluded that if such laws had been in effect in every state, there would have been 1,414 fewer murders, 4,177 fewer rapes, and 60,363 fewer assaults nationwide in 1992.

Understandably, some people fear that someone carrying a weapon might shoot an innocent person by accident or in anger — at a traffic accident, for example. But in the 14 years since the first concealed-carry law was passed, there is no reported incident of someone with a concealed-carry permit wrongfully killing anyone — in anger or by accident.

And there are thousands of examples in which someone carrying a gun has stopped a crime or defended himself against attack.

For example, in October 1997 a gunman went on a shooting spree at a high school in Pearl, Mississippi. He killed two students and could have shot many more. But an assistant principal ran to his car, got his gun, and kept the gunman at bay until the police arrived. How many lives do you suppose were saved?

Contrast this with the 1991 mass shooting in Luby's Cafeteria in Killeen, Texas. Suzanna Gratia Hupp was in the restaurant at the time. She had a concealed-carry permit in her home state, but she wasn't carrying her handgun because at that time it was illegal to do so in Texas. So everyone in Luby's was unarmed except for the murderer, who was free to kill eight people — including Suzanna's mother and father. Four years later, Texas passed a concealed-carry law, and there have been no mass shootings since. Had the law been effect in 1991, Suzanna Gratia Hupp could have saved her parents' lives.

The greatest benefits of concealed-carry laws are bestowed on the people who are society's most vulnerable. Women, the disabled, the elderly, and the weak have always been easy prey for muggers and other predators. But would-be attackers in states with concealed-carry laws know that any potential victim might be carrying a handgun. As Barbara Goushaw has pointed out, "Handguns are a girl's best friend."

One great advantage of a concealed-carry law is that you don't have to own a gun to benefit from the law. As long as *some* people are carrying concealed weapons, criminals have to fear that you are one of them.

Gun Control

The concealed-carry laws cut against the trend of ever-expanding gun-control laws. While concealed-carry laws empower some innocent citizens, gun-control laws disarm others — making them easy prey for criminals who carry whatever weapons they please. After all, criminals don't care about permits, gun registration, or buying through legal channels. They steal the guns they want or buy them from other criminals.[2]

Gun-control advocates believe their laws will prevent deaths. And they are fond of saying that if just one child's life is saved, it's worth all the intrusions on your liberty.

But they overlook the lives saved by citizens who brandish a gun at an attacker or intruder. A 1994 Department of Justice study estimated that guns interrupt or avert about 1.5 million crimes each year. That translates into not just one child's life, but thousands of lives that guns save each year.[3]

---

[2] A recent Justice Department survey of convicted felons showed that 93% had obtained their guns illegally.

[3] Another Department of Justice study estimated that the 10-year period ending in 1997 produced 36,395,000 violent crimes, resulting in 221,412 murders — or one murder for every 164 violent crimes. If about 1.5 million violent crimes are averted each year by the use of guns, the ratio of one murder to every 164 violent crimes suggests that 9,146 murders are averted every year through the defensive use of guns.

For example, someone telephoned Doug Stanton to tell him that a man who once had stalked Mrs. Stanton was on his way to the Stanton house. Sure enough, the stalker arrived in the driveway, holding a pistol and wearing a bullet-proof vest.

He shot at the back door, kicked it open, and sprayed bullets into the kitchen. Stanton fired two shots at the attacker with his .45 automatic. The intruder staggered, despite his bullet-proof vest, and then fled. He was captured by the police shortly afterward.

As Doug Stanton said, "Because the Stanton family had a gun, six lives were saved. Had there been restrictions on gun ownership, the Stantons would be dead. This is a fact, not a hypothetical situation."

How many children at Columbine High School would have been saved if one of the teachers had a gun close by? When a lunatic starts shooting in a restaurant, how many lives could be saved if just one customer has a concealed weapon?

How many women could have saved themselves from rape, kidnapping, or recreational torture by carrying a gun?

It's nice that gun-control advocates talk about saving the lives of children. But it's not nice when their own distaste for guns forces disarmament on the people who could save the lives of children.

Gun-control laws make the world safer for criminals, and less safe for you.

Politicians Don't Believe in Gun Control

When politicians say they favor gun control, they mean they favor it for you — not for themselves.

If you should visit the Capitol Building in Washington, notice how many guards are carrying guns. The politicians say you must be disarmed to make America safer, but they don't disarm government employees.

Members of the federal agencies that protect politicians are always well armed. But it doesn't stop there. Employees of the EPA, the U.S. Fish and Wildlife Service, the Army Corps of Engineers, and many other agencies now carry guns.

If guns cause crime, why do so many government employees have them? Maybe they have a compelling need to carry guns, but is it more compelling than your need to defend your home and family against criminals?

Who Needs What Guns?

Gun-control laws have been disarming America inch by inch. Any one step may seem reasonable (if you don't look at it too closely), but the cumulative effect has been to put innocent Americans at a dangerous disadvantage to criminals.

For example, it might seem reasonable to say that individuals should have the right to own handguns (with appropriate restrictions like gun locks, registration, and such), but who needs such things as assault weapons or mortars?

Maybe you don't. But some people do.

During most riots, the police have been outnumbered and have intentionally stayed clear of gangs that were looting and vandalizing. Suppose your life savings are invested in a store the gangs are about to loot. And suppose you have little or no insurance because your store is in a dangerous section of town. How will you defend the store against the looters? With a knife? With a handgun against a dozen attackers? Or with an assault weapon?

If you prevent innocent citizens from acquiring assault weapons, criminal gangs will still acquire them — even if they have to smuggle them into America from thousands of miles away. So why pass laws that disarm only the innocent?

You might be able to imagine the perfect law that allows just the right people to own just the right types of guns, while prohibiting other citizens from owning inappropriate firearms. But remember, you're only imagining such a law; it will never be a reality. Once the issue is turned over to the politicians, it will be decided by whoever has the most political influence — and that will never be you or me.

The only valid policy is to have no laws regulating the ownership of guns, but to hold every citizen responsible for whatever harm he initiates against others — with or without a gun.

As always, you really have only two choices. Either:

- Politicians will decide what people can own — and they will never stop their prohibitions at the point you believe best. Or . . .
- People will decide for themselves what they can own.

Any apparent middle ground between the two actually gives the politicians the power to do as they please.

And all such decisions will be made on the basis of who has

the most political influence. So attempts to limit gun ownership do more to promote the political interests of well-connected people than to reduce crime.

No More Laws

Gun owners have fought back against gun-control laws, but ineffectively.

The gun-grabbers exploit every well-publicized shooting to advocate another new gun-control law — even if unrestricted gun ownership would have prevented the shooting, and even if the shooter was breaking existing gun-control laws.

Gun-control laws don't stop criminals from acquiring guns. And it weakens the case for gun ownership if we call for existing gun laws to be better enforced before passing new laws. This implies that the existing laws have merit.

They don't. Such laws have caused people to die when a waiting period has kept someone from acquiring a gun to scare off a stalker — or a gun-lock requirement prevented someone from using a gun in time to stop an intruder or attacker.

If we want Americans to be safer, we need to take the offensive and repeal all the gun-control legislation on the books. Criminals will have no more guns than they do already, but it will allow Americans to defend themselves — and it will probably inspire a number of criminals to seek a safer line of work.

Restoring your Right to Defend Yourself

The 2nd amendment to the Constitution says:

> II. A well regulated Militia, being necessary to the security of a free State, the right of the people to keep and bear Arms, shall not be infringed.

There are arguments over whether this means only a duly authorized state militia has the right to keep and bear arms — even though when the amendment was passed, there were no restrictions on anyone's right to keep and bear arms.

But the arguments are irrelevant. The 9th amendment states clearly that the Constitution does not deprive anyone of the right to keep and bear arms:

> IX. The enumeration in the Constitution, of certain rights, shall not be construed to deny or disparage others retained by the people.

Nothing in the Constitution authorizes Congress to limit gun ownership, and so the right to defend ourselves is "retained by the people."

Unfortunately, politicians only talk about the Constitution, they don't respect it. And we aren't going to secure your right to defend yourself by pushing this issue in isolation.

We must show Americans the harm that comes to their own lives when *any* Constitutional right is violated — the right to say unpopular things, to practice unpopular religions, to defend yourself against predators, to be safe against vindictive cops and prosecutors, to keep your property safe against demagogues invoking the "public good," to have all your rights secured by strict adherence to the Constitution.

If you're a gun owner, you are always on the defensive — defending some weapon as legitimate, and then watching as your favorite politician agrees to a compromise that takes more of your freedom from you.

Your only hope is a President and Congress who believe the right to bear arms isn't a negotiable issue — that it's one of many fundamental Constitutional rights that can't be traded away.

You have to support candidates who believe in the entire Constitution, not just in the 2nd amendment. You need champions who will go on the offensive — who will say there are far too many laws in America, and that we must repeal all the useless, oppressive, dangerous, unconstitutional laws passed in the last 70 years, including those that limit the right to bear arms.

You will restore the right to keep and bear arms only when we put the gun-control advocates on the defensive.

And we will make America safer only when we end the government's ability to disarm innocent citizens.

Less government means less crime.

2. GET THE FEDERAL GOVERNMENT OUT OF LAW ENFORCEMENT

All crime is local. It occurs in the jurisdiction of a police department or sheriff's department somewhere. The Founding Fathers wisely provided no Constitutional role for the federal government regarding common crimes of any kind.

But, of course, the politicians never lose sleep over Constitutional limitations. They have passed federal laws against carjacking, vandalism, "hate crimes," kidnapping, discrimination, fraud, pornography, gun ownership, drugs, and almost anything some politician doesn't happen to like.

A federal police force provides no additional safety for you. Local-law enforcement agencies help each other capture fugitives, share fingerprints, and otherwise cooperate across state lines. They don't need federal police to help them protect you.

In fact, a federal police force makes you *less* safe. The federal government's involvement in law enforcement gives politicians another excuse to spend more of your money, it gives federal bureaucrats the power to dictate politically correct polices to your local police department, and it does more damage to your Constitutional liberties.

The Founding Fathers would be shocked to see today's federal police forces — such as the FBI, the BATF, and the DEA. They explicitly warned against giving the federal government the power to deal with common crimes. They knew that federal police forces could lead to events like the BATF-FBI massacre of the Branch Davidians at Waco, and the shooting of an innocent woman and her child at Ruby Ridge.

Loading up the Bills

Every federal law includes intrusive and expensive provisions you never hear about. Crime bills are no exception.

After the Columbine High School massacre, the House of Representatives passed the "Juvenile Crime Bill" — supposedly to reduce teenage violence.

Conservatives supported the bill because they didn't notice its gun-control provisions, and probably because they didn't want to appear insensitive in the midst of a supposed crisis.

Liberals supported the bill because they didn't notice that it gave the government more power to use warrantless wiretaps, allowed police to intercept messages going to your pager, promoted drug-testing of all school children, and gave increased immunity to police who might commit violent crimes against you.

As usual, the politicians had practically no idea what they were voting on.

Not only is federal law enforcement dangerous, it is very expensive. As with any other kind of bill, the politicians see anti-crime bills as opportunities to enact unrelated programs for their political allies.

For example, Bill Clinton made a big show of a proposal for the federal government to pay for 100,000 new local patrolmen. The final version of the law, passed in 1994, appropriated $8.8 billion for the new policemen along with a load of non-crime goodies for anyone with the political clout to get on the gravy train.

In 1999, the Inspector General's Office audited the program. It found that all the subsidies had been duly paid, but where were the cops? Only about 40,000 had been added to the nation's police forces.

The President often congratulates himself on the success of this program. He thinks so highly of it that in 1999 he asked Congress to appropriate another $6.4 billion to put an additional 50,000 cops on the streets by 2005.

Getting the federal government out of local law enforcement will mean less government, not more — and it will reduce the cost of local law enforcement, reduce your taxes, restore many of the liberties you've lost, and make your neighborhood safer.

Once again, less government means less crime.

3. REPEAL ALL ASSET FORFEITURE LAWS

Asset forfeiture laws allow government agents — federal, state, or local — to seize your property if they suspect it may have been related to a crime.

It doesn't matter that the property was only incidental to the crime. It doesn't matter that you didn't commit the crime. It doesn't matter that you didn't even know a crime was occurring — or perhaps saw the crime and risked your life trying to prevent it. It doesn't matter that no one is ever convicted of the crime — or even *charged* with the crime. It doesn't even matter that no crime actually occurred. If government agents suspect that your property might have been related, however remotely, to a crime that might have occurred, even if you had no knowledge it was occurring, the agents can seize the property.

For example, if drug warriors learn that your child's friend brought a marijuana cigarette into your home without your knowledge, your house could be seized under the asset forfeiture laws.

Roughly 80% of the people who lose property to seizures are never charged with a crime. All of them have to sue the government to get their property back.

At the federal level, asset forfeiture is used by the Drug Enforcement Agency, the IRS, the FBI, the Coast Guard, the

Postal Service, the Bureau of Land Management, the Fish and Wildlife Service, the Securities & Exchange Commission, the Department of Health & Human Services, the Food & Drug Administration, the Customs Service, the Immigration & Naturalization Service, and the Department of Housing & Urban Development. And over 3,000 state and local governments have their own forfeiture laws.

Although the laws were enacted to fight organized crime and large-scale drug operations, they have turned into a brutal fund-raising tool for law-enforcement agencies. For any department that wants to augment its appropriated budget, asset forfeiture is a gift from Heaven. And human nature dictates that many law-enforcement officials pay more attention to cases involving property that can be seized, and less to cases in which your life or property may be threatened.

Seized property usually is sold at auction, and the law-enforcement agency keeps all or most of the auction proceeds for its own use. However, sometimes the agency will keep the assets and use them — especially cars and buildings. Sometimes the seized property is stolen by government employees. Or it may simply be left forgotten and moldering in a government warehouse.

Asset forfeitures total over $2 billion a year in property — allowing many state law-enforcement agencies to be self-funding. These agencies no longer plead for money from the legislators; their seizures provide the money to buy whatever they think they need.[4]

Asset forfeiture is a mockery of the Bill of Rights. There is no presumption of innocence, no need to prove you guilty (or even charge you with a crime), no right to a jury trial, no right to confront your accuser, no right to a court-appointed attorney (even if the government has just stolen all your money), and no right to compensation for the property that's been taken. Somewhere hidden in the 4th and 5th Amendments there must be a clause saying these Amendments don't apply to asset forfeiture.

Asset forfeiture laws allow an angry neighbor or a desperate business competitor to make your life a living Hell by telling the police *anonymously* that you're storing drugs or illegal weapons in your closet. You can lose not just your closet, but your entire house or any cash kept in the house — even if the police don't find any drugs or weapons.

---

[4] The U.S. Drug Enforcement Agency alone confiscated $551 million in currency and property in 1997.

To reduce crime and protect your right to property, it's important that we repeal all federal asset forfeiture provisions. I hope this will lead to the repeal of all state and local asset forfeiture laws.

Reducing government power by getting rid of these laws will refocus police on chasing violent crime, instead of lucrative seizures — making your life safer.

Once again, less government means less crime.

4. STOP PROSECUTING VICTIMLESS CRIMES

The crime rate can be reduced dramatically by ending the War on Drugs and stopping the prosecution of other victimless crimes. This will free up resources to control true crime — the kind that hurts and terrorizes people.

Our prisons are packed with non-violent criminals — which frees violent murderers, rapists, and robbers on early release and through plea bargains. We need to send the pot smokers and other non-violent prisoners home, and make room for the thugs who terrorize innocent people.

This is covered in more detail in chapter 10, and my proposals to free non-violent prisoners are on page 237.

Mandatory Minimums

One of the cruelest consequences of the War on Drugs has been the invention of federal sentencing formulas. These are rules established by Congress that require judges to impose fixed sentences, without hope of parole, for various crimes.

Beyond a very narrow range of discretion, a judge can reduce a defendant's sentence only if the defendant provides "substantial assistance" in convicting others — and only if the prosecutor approves (a clear violation of the separation of powers between the executive and judicial branches).

In 1986 basketball star Len Bias died of a cocaine overdose. House Speaker Tip O'Neill saw this as an opportunity to show that Democrats are just as tough on drugs as Republicans. He exploited Bias' death to rush through a bill before the 1986 elections. The bill fixed the minimum sentences for a whole range of crimes, but mostly concerning drugs. Republicans eagerly embraced a bill that responded to their long-standing complaints that judges are "soft on crime" — especially drug crime.

Few Congressmen took the time to read any part of the bill.

There were no hearings, and there was virtually no discussion of the bill before it was passed. This reckless legislating has caused gross injustices in the sentences imposed on non-violent criminals and innocent bystanders, overflowed the nation's prisons, and destroyed thousands of lives.

Laws are rarely repealed — not even bad ones. Instead, a law is "fixed" by passing an additional law — which usually makes matters even worse. When it was found that the 1986 bill wasn't putting away big-time drug dealers for long sentences, Congress passed a 1998 bill that held everyone in a drug organization responsible for every crime committed by anyone in the group. That meant the errand boy who never carried anything more important than sandwiches and coffee could receive the same sentence as Mr. Big.

I know you won't be surprised to learn that this law didn't catch any big fish either. In fact, it did just the opposite. When a major drug dealer was caught, he provided "substantial assistance" by ratting on everyone underneath him — allowing him to get a light sentence. Because of the 1998 law, groups of smaller fish went to prison with long sentences that had been intended for the big barracuda.

This has caused the prison population to explode — with more and more people entering prison and staying longer. The Justice Policy Institute has estimated that the prison population of the United States reached 2 million on February 15, 2000.

But this explosion in the prison population hasn't taken violent criminals off the streets. For the most part, it has scooped up only low-level drug offenders or innocent people who were fingered by high-level dealers providing "substantial assistance."

One example was Clarence Aaron. In 1992 he was a 23-year-old college student in Mobile, Alabama. He had never been in trouble with the law when he agreed to drive some friends to a drug transaction in Baton Rouge. When caught, the friends provided "substantial assistance" by testifying against Clarence. *Although he had never dealt drugs himself or even touched any, Clarence was given three life sentences without possibility of parole.*

His only hope now is a Libertarian President who will pardon him. If I am elected President, I will provide that pardon from the inauguration platform.

The mandatory minimums are a travesty, spawned by the travesty that is the War on Drugs. They must be eliminated, and sentencing discretion must be returned to judges who can consider all the circumstances when passing sentence.

Wiping victimless crimes off the law books and ending the mandatory minimums will not only end the cruel and unusual punishment of people who are either innocent or who have committed minor offenses. It also will dramatically reduce the prison population and make room for the violent thugs you don't want to meet on a dark street.

Once again, less government means less crime.

5. RESTORE RESPECT FOR THE RULE OF LAW

Every senseless law enacted by big government erodes the public's respect for the rule of law. And there have been plenty of senseless laws.

With government invading your bank account, your bedroom, your bathroom, and your closet, many people can no longer see the difference between laws to punish violent criminals and laws to regulate your private business. With the line blurred, it's too easy for individuals without much moral training to step over it and hurt others. If it's okay to smuggle into your home a toilet larger than the federal government allows, maybe it's okay to smuggle out of the office a little of your employer's property.

Respect for the law also means insisting that police, prosecutors, and courts respect your civil liberties. Without the rights promised you in the Bill of Rights, you are living in a police state. Among those rights are:

- Your right to be secure in your person, house, papers, and effects against unreasonable search and seizure. (4th Amendment)

- Your right to be safe against double jeopardy, to remain silent if suspected of a crime, to due process of law, and to just compensation if your property is taken for public use. (5th Amendment)

- Your right to a speedy and public trial, to know of every witness against you, to cross-examine those witnesses, and to have the assistance of counsel for your defense. (6th Amendment)

- Your right to a trial by jury. (7th Amendment)

- Your right to be released on reasonable bail, and to be free of excessive fines, and cruel and unusual punishment. (8th Amendment)

- Your right to privacy or any other common right that hasn't specifically been forfeited in the Constitution. (9th Amendment)

These rights have been sliced and diced by asset forfeiture laws, by the practice of retrying in federal court individuals who have been acquitted in state court, by search and arrest warrants issued on anonymous tips, by confiscation powers given to the EPA and other federal agencies, and by mandatory minimum sentences imposing cruel punishments.

The abuses of civil liberties by the police, prosecutors, and courts have done little to keep violent criminals off the streets. But they have turned the lives of many innocent people into nightmares.

Professional criminals are versed in the laws they break; they know how to limit the risk of prosecution. The innocent know little about the 1,001 new laws passed each year — and so they're shocked and helpless when a government agent moves in on them. This is why tough new laws aimed at crime always seem to hurt the innocent more than the guilty.

The Declaration of Independence says that "Governments are instituted among Men" to "secure these rights" to "Life, Liberty, and the Pursuit of Happiness." A government that does that and no more will be immeasurably more just, more efficient, and more respected than our government is today, and you will be freer and more prosperous.

THE GREAT LIBERTARIAN OFFER will reduce the federal government to just its constitutional functions — automatically removing thousands of federal laws from the books, automatically restoring hundreds of lost rights, and automatically restoring the rule of law.

This will do far more to reduce crime than all the new prisons, new money for law-enforcement agencies, and new intrusions on your liberty.

Once again . . .

LESS GOVERNMENT MEANS LESS CRIME

Crime rates will drop to the level of a generation ago only when we reduce our dependence upon government.

- Repeal gun-control laws and criminals will start fearing innocent citizens.

- Get the federal government out of local law enforcement,

and local law enforcement will be much more effective and less expensive.

- Repeal the asset forfeiture laws, and crime-fighting agencies will refocus on the most dangerous criminals, rather than on the most valuable property.

- End the prosecution of victimless crimes — especially drug crimes — and the courts will tell the truly violent criminals to step to the head of the line.

- Reduce the enormous number of pointless and harmful laws and regulations, and citizens will respect the laws that remain.

Will these five proposals do away with crime entirely? Of course not. Even the freest and most prosperous country in the world will have people who try to get what they want by taking it from others.

But you *can* have a peaceful city and a peaceful neighborhood. And you can have it without making big government any bigger — but instead by reducing our reliance on government and relying more on citizens who have an interest in minimizing crime.

Libertarian solutions are sometimes accused of being too extreme. But what could be extreme about wanting to reduce crime, making our schools safer, and setting our citizens free?

The real extremists are those who continue to let children die in school shootings and drive-by killings rather than give up their love affair with big government.

CHAPTER 18

FREEDOM TO FOLLOW YOUR DOCTOR'S ADVICE

There was a time in America when your doctor knew you well, when a hospital stay wouldn't bankrupt you, when low-cost health insurance was available to virtually everyone — even those with pre-existing conditions. For those in need, doctors gave free or low-cost care, and there were free clinics and charity hospitals. Few people went without adequate health care.

Today we hear about such care only when politicians use their imagination to make promises. They never notice that what they promise and never deliver is precisely what Americans took for granted just a few decades ago — before politicians presumed to make things better.

No political program will ever bring the kind of care the politicians promise, because you can't organize health care by force and expect people to function as they did when they worked together voluntarily.

Today 51% of all health-care dollars in America are spent by governments — not insurance companies, employers, or individuals, but by governments. If there is a crisis in health care — and there certainly is — the government, not the free market, is responsible for it.

If we want to restore good health care, the answer is simple: get the government out of the way.

How Health Care Became So Expensive

Politicians and reformers want us to believe there are more than enough goods and services to provide a good standard of living for everyone in America, and that all we have to do is redistribute them more equally. They assume the shopkeeper in Boston, the wholesaler in Denver, the manufacturer in Cleveland will continue to get up at 5 a.m. every day and work until midnight producing those goods and services — just so the government can confiscate them and give them to someone else.

Once the government takes from those who produce and gives to those who don't, people inevitably will produce less, the supply will diminish, and the demand will become much greater. So don't be surprised when government intervention into any market causes prices to skyrocket.

Nowhere is this more evident than with health care. Medical prices have escalated because government subsidies push up the demand for medical services, while government regulations chase medical providers out of the market.

There are five principal tools the federal government has used to make it harder for you to get good medical care:

1. The federal income tax code, which has skewed the payment for health-care services.
2. Laws that forbid health insurance companies to offer low-cost policies that exclude certain medical treatments.
3. Medicare — a government health insurance program for senior citizens.
4. Medicaid — a program to provide medical services primarily for the poor.
5. Government regulations on doctors, hospitals, insurance companies, and drug companies.

We'll look at each of these tools in turn.

1. THE TAX CODE

Employer-based health-care coverage began during World War II, when wage and price controls prohibited employers from attracting better workers by offering higher wages. To circumvent the controls, employers offered new fringe benefits — in particular employer-paid health insurance.

The wage controls ended after World War II, but most employers continued their health insurance programs. The tax code allowed employers to deduct the costs of health insurance, but didn't allow individuals to deduct much of the medical expenses they paid out of their own pocket. So employer-based medical insurance continued to make sense.

Insurance is an efficient way to protect against bad luck. But it's a clumsy way to pay for routine expenses. You don't use car insurance to pay for oil changes or gasoline; you have it in case your car is stolen or badly damaged in a collision. You don't use homeowners' insurance to pay your electricity and water bills; you have it to cover a fire or other catastrophic loss.

Obviously, an insurance policy that covers every small, routine expense is going to be far more expensive than one that covers only extraordinary expenses. And the difficulty of administering a policy with frequent claims will run up the cost even more.

Tax incentives have led employers to offer broader and broader health-care coverage, and the same incentives have led employees to prefer such coverage over higher wages.

So medical coverage has become less like traditional insurance, and more like a total health-care service paying all your medical bills, big and small. To the employees, this seems like free health care, and so they use it much more than they would if they were paying for routine care out of their own pockets. This has put much greater demands on health-care providers — running up the price for everyone.

When we repeal the income tax, there no longer will be a tax incentive for employers to furnish health care, or for employees to prefer health benefits to higher wages. Incomes will go up. And you'll be able to purchase relatively inexpensive insurance to cover extraordinary expenses — such as those connected with a bad accident or a life-threatening disease. Routine doctor visits will be much less expensive because people paying for what they use will be more sparing with their money.

You will be able to handle routine costs out-of-pocket — just as you now pay for gasoline for your car or utility bills for your house. And most people will find that they are paying less than the wage increase they received in place of employer-provided medical insurance.

Until the income tax is repealed, all medical expenses should be fully deductible — whether you pay for them directly or through your employer. This will help to take the pressure off broad employer-provided coverage, and reduce the demand that is running up medical costs.

2. HEALTH INSURANCE YOU CAN'T AFFORD

Health insurance has become progressively more expensive and thus less accessible for many people.

Politicians love to posture as friends of particular groups — women, children, and people suffering from a particular disease — by insisting that health insurers must cover some medical procedure that is important to the target audience. But every time the government (state or federal) forces insurers to include another benefit in your policy, the company has to raise your premium. Not surprisingly, the cost of health insurance has risen spectacularly over the past quarter-century.

Depending on the state you live in, your insurance company may be pricing your policy to allow for mandatory psychiatric coverage, chiropractors, acupuncture, naturopathy, marriage counseling, abortions, drug abuse, alcoholism, treatments to stop smoking, cosmetic surgery, weight loss, wigs and other hairpieces, Christian Science practitioners, and dozens of other possibilities.

I have nothing against any of these treatments. But it makes no sense for the government to force you to pay for such coverage if you would prefer a cheaper policy.

For example, a Catholic nun buying health insurance may live in a state that requires every policy to cover abortions, and she must pay accordingly.

You should be able to buy a policy that requires you to pay only for what *you* need and want — not what the politicians think you need.

The alternative we have now keeps pushing up the cost of insurance. And as it becomes more expensive, every medical interest group suffers. So most of them go to Washington (or the state capitol) to lobby the politicians to provide relief by forcing insurers to include *its* favored treatment in all policies — pushing the price up further.

Expensive health insurance hurts young people in their 20s and 30s the most. Generally, they belong to no special interest group, and as insurance becomes progressively more expensive, more and more of them decide to risk going without insurance.

This graph shows that health insurance coverage grew until the 1970s, when politicians began imposing mandates on the insurers. Since then, premium costs have been spiraling upward, and more and more people buy no coverage at all.

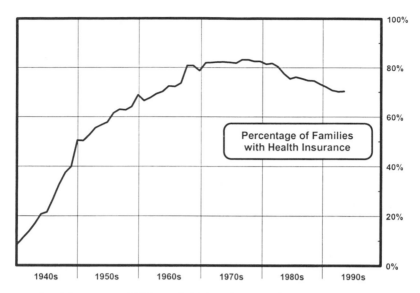

| 1940s | 1950s | 1960s | 1970s | 1980s | 1990s |

Just between 1990 and 1996, the number of insured people decreased by about one sixth. The largest block of uninsured is in the 18-35 age group.

Rising costs also have lead many employers to drop health coverage. In 1980 fully 97% of the companies with 100 or more employees provided medical coverage. By 1995, only 77% were doing so.

The growing number of uninsured people gives the politicians more ammunition for more programs to force more costs onto insurance companies — and to push the price of insurance still higher.

More people will have medical insurance, and the insurance will cost much less, when we get government out of the way.

How HMOs Became So Powerful

In 1999 politicians pushed for a "Patients' Bill of Rights," supposedly to give patients certain privileges in dealing with health maintenance organizations (HMOs).

No one was pushing for a "Bill of Rights" to protect patients against doctors — or against druggists, appliance stores, computer makers, or gardeners. So how did HMOs become so powerful and dictatorial that their customers need protection?

In 1973 Congress passed the HMO Act — which subsidized HMOs and forced any company providing employee health insurance to offer an HMO as an option. This requirement was finally repealed in 1995, but by that time the government's favored treatment had made HMOs the centerpiece of employer-sponsored health programs.

Once again, the politicians are seizing the opportunity to rescue us from their own handiwork.

3. MEDICARE

Medical costs started moving up in earnest with the advent of Medicare and Medicaid in 1965.

By offering free or nearly free medical care, these programs increased the demand for medical services. Meanwhile, the supply of medical providers declined because the new programs overloaded doctors and hospitals with forms to fill out and bureaucratic regulations to obey.

The result, not surprisingly, was dramatically higher prices for anyone who didn't qualify for free service. Since the 1960s, health care costs have been rising generally at twice the rate of inflation.

Medicare is so complicated, no one person could possibly explain the complete system to you. The rules, guidelines, and instructions cover 111,000 pages. And whenever you hear that Congress has reformed the system to make it easier to deal with, to eliminate waste and corruption, or to provide more choice, you can be sure that it has become even more complicated.

Medicare has overloaded doctors with regulations, forced them to undercharge for many services, and driven a large number of them out of the medical profession entirely.

Some doctors have remained at their posts but have resigned completely from the Medicare and Medicaid systems — refusing to perform any service that will be paid by Medicare or Medicaid. The savings to the doctors are so great that they now charge their patients only half or less of what they had to charge before.

But it isn't just doctors who have been hindered by Medicare. If you're a senior citizen locked into Medicare, you have my sympathy:

- Medicare routinely turns down roughly 20% of all the procedures physicians decide are needed. The skyrocketing costs of "free" medical care have led to rationing of various kinds. Many treatments that might relieve your discomfort or even save your life are rejected to save money.

- If Medicare refuses your request for a particular test or treatment, even one your doctor thinks is essential, you can't pay your doctor for it out of your own pocket. If the doctor were to accept your money, he would not be allowed to treat any other Medicare patients for two years thereafter. To get the treatment you need, you would have to find a doctor who refuses all Medicare and Medicaid patients — and you might have to travel several hundred miles to find him.

- If Medicare denies your hospital claim, your appeal can take as long as a year to be processed.

- Because Medicare regulations are so complicated, ignorance of the law could easily get you or your doctor in legal trouble. Penalties for mistakes include fines and imprisonment.

- You most likely pay out of your own pocket at least twice as much for health care as seniors did before Medicare began — even after allowing for Medicare's contribution and after adjusting for inflation.[1]

You will be much healthier and spend less money on health care once we replace Medicare and all other federal programs with the kind of health care that was available before the politicians decided to become doctors.

You'll be able to get private insurance that is tailored to your specific needs, without paying for government mandates. Government programs will no longer run up the price of medical care. And your doctor will be free to treat whatever ails you.

4. MEDICAID

Medicaid is a federal subsidy for state government programs that provide free health care to people below a specified income level and to nursing homes for the elderly.

Each state designs and names its own program. However, 50-75% of the money comes through the federal government, which doles it out according to formulas set by Congress.

With most of the cost paid by the federal government, the states have an incentive to spend as much on Medicaid as federal rules will allow. This generates still more upward price pressure on medical care.

---

[1] In 1961 the average elderly family spent $1,933 per year on health care (in 1999 dollars). By 1991 this had risen to $4,042 per year (also in 1999 dollars).

Like so many federal-aid programs, Medicaid is an invitation to waste and corruption. State programs are continually under fire for exceeding their budgets. In 1994, for example, Oregon instituted strict rationing of health-care services in order to bring medical costs under control. And in Tennessee in 1999, the Republican governor cited out-of-control Medicaid costs as his excuse for breaking his word and proposing the state's first income tax.

Before the government stepped in, poor people found solace with charity hospitals, free clinics, and doctors who knew and cared for their patients. One way or another, there was always medical care for those who needed it urgently. But some people didn't like that system.

So instead we now have a health-care system that even fewer people can afford.

5. GENERAL REGULATIONS

Medicare and Medicaid don't just fleece you with the taxes they extract from you.

Most doctors, clinics, and hospitals are able to bill the government for only a percentage of what they would normally charge — sometimes as little as 25% to 50% of a normal bill. In order to stay in business, they have to make up the difference by overcharging their paying customers — including you.

And that's just the beginning of your extra costs. The federal and state governments have imposed all sorts of regulations on doctors, hospitals, insurance companies, managed-care providers, and others in the health-care industry.

Hospitals are forced to admit anyone who shows up at the door, with or without the price of admission. And hospitals and doctors fill out endless forms to comply with federal regulations, to justify Medicare and Medicaid bills, and to prove that they aren't discriminating.

Who pays for all the free services and for the time involved in complying with federal regulations? You do, of course; it's in the bill you receive from your doctor, hospital, or insurance company.

The "Medicare + Choice" bill in 1997 included demands that managed-care providers add more services — for free. This pushed so many providers into a loss position that over a hundred of them chose to leave the Medicare system entirely — making over 400,000 senior citizens search for new plans. The result has been less choice for the elderly — and everyone else — not more.

The supply of doctors has been diminishing as well. Almost every health-care law passed by Congress includes provisions that make it easier to sue doctors and other health-care providers. As a result, the cost of malpractice insurance has skyrocketed. Some doctors see roughly half their income going to pay insurance premiums, necessarily adding to the cost of your bill. Even worse, this prompts more and more doctors to throw in the towel and leave the profession.

As the supply of health-care providers continues to shrink and the political demands on the providers continues to grow, health-care costs continue to escalate.

All this is so unnecessary. America had the best medical system in the world before the politicians started playing doctor.

Dr. Jane Orient of the Association of American Physicians and Surgeons has pointed out:

> When medical care was mostly paid for by patients, the hospital bill for an appendectomy was the equivalent of 10 days' wages for a common laborer ($149 in 1960). Now it's at least a couple months of take-home pay for a middle-income person (about $3,000). They still do the procedure the same way, and the patient is generally home faster.

Few doctors in America ever walked away from a patient with an urgent need — no matter how poor the patient. But good works aren't good enough for politicians. And so we have today's bureaucratic, inefficient system instead.

THE FDA

As though your health weren't jeopardized sufficiently by Congressmen putting health providers out of business and putting new demands on the health-care system, we have to contend with the FDA.

The Food and Drug Administration (FDA) has routinely kept life-saving medicines off the market for years until its administrators were positive they could never be held responsible for a single death. While waiting for the FDA to approve medicines, thousands of people have died for lack of the medicines — far more lives than the FDA could possibly claim to have saved.

People have suffered unnecessarily — or even died — with such problems as heart disease, depression, schizophrenia, kidney cancer, and epilepsy, just because the FDA dragged its feet or was unsure how well various medicines would perform.

Robert Goldberg of Brandeis University has estimated that FDA delays in approving drugs that were already used safely elsewhere in the world have cost at least 200,000 American lives over the past 30 years. These delays affected Alzheimer patients who weren't allowed to take THA, people with high blood pressure who couldn't take beta-blockers, those with kidney cancer who couldn't take Interleukin-2, and AIDS patients who died while the FDA pondered whether drugs like AZT were cost-effective. [2]

Almost any doctor in the world will tell you that taking a baby aspirin or drinking a glass of red wine every day helps reduce the threat of a heart attack. But the FDA will impose fines or imprisonment if aspirin makers or wineries try to tell you that.

In effect, the FDA is in the business of keeping life-saving medicines and information out of your hands.

The people who run the FDA are politicians, appointed by other politicians for political purposes. When they keep a life-saving medicine off the market for years (as they did with Propranolol and other life-savers), why shouldn't you be allowed to get a second opinion — from your doctor or someone else?

When it's your life that's at stake, why shouldn't you be free to make your own decisions about the risks you're willing to take?

THE TWO-PARTY DESTRUCTION

Both parties campaign on the health-care issue. Each claims to have your interests at heart, and each wants to write out a prescription for you.

The Democrats: Equal Waiting Lines for Everyone

The Democrats keep pushing for "universal health care." But such a system is an impossibility.

There aren't enough resources in the world — or in the universe — to meet every health-care wish of every citizen. Choices always have to be made, and it is far better when you make your

---

[2] See the examples on pages 125 and 127.

own choices based on cost than when politicians make choices for you on the basis of political pressure.

There's a reason so many Canadians cross the border into America to get operations or other treatment. It's because Canada has "universal health care" with "free" medical care — and "free" can mean a dangerously long wait for what you need.

When patients don't have to consider the cost of anything, they deny themselves nothing that might conceivably improve their health. So in Canada waiting lines are long — very long. And an emergency doesn't necessarily put you at the head of a line. Even people needing open-heart surgery can be left waiting as long as five years.

In Toronto, hospital emergency rooms have turned away ambulances because there wasn't enough staff or space to handle the patients. Throughout Canada, hospital hallways are crowded with patients on beds or stretchers waiting for a scarce room. A vice-president at Vancouver General Hospital estimated that 20% of heart-attack patients who should have treatment within 15 minutes now wait at least an hour.

Consequently, doctors and hospitals routinely refer patients to the U.S. for treatment.

Canadian-type systems aren't unusual. They're common-place in Europe — as are the waiting lines. But unfortunately for Europeans, there are no American facilities nearby.

The contrast between government-run and private health-care systems is stark. In Canada, for example, dentistry and vet-erinary care still are privately run. Thus you can get treatment for a cavity faster than for cancer, and your dog gets better med-ical care than you do.

This is what the Democrats hold up as the model enjoyed in more "enlightened" countries — the future they have in store for you and every American. In other words, the cure for our deteri-orating health-care system is to replace it with one that's even worse.

The Republicans: Death by Degrees

The Republicans take a different approach. They claim cred-it for having stopped Hillary Clinton's 1994 attempt to impose universal health care in one giant step, and they pose as the defenders of private health care.

But the two parties differ only in the speed at which they would take us to Hell on a hospital gurney.

Republican politicians claim our system doesn't need a massive overhaul, only a few small changes — such as making health insurance portable (so that you can take it with you to a new job), or covering people with pre-existing conditions. Of course, they are talking about remedies that wouldn't be necessary if government weren't involved so deeply in the health-care system.

In recent years these "needs" have led to the Kennedy-Kassenbaum bill, the Hatch-Kennedy bill, and the "Medicare + Choice" act. These and other bills have burrowed government more deeply into your health, your insurance, and your medical treatment. The Republicans have imposed more and more mandates on insurers — hurrying the eventual destruction of the private insurance industry.

The Republicans have helped make health care so expensive and hard to get that people are eager to try anything else — even a proven failure such as government-run universal heath care. Once again, the politicians created a problem that provided a new excuse for politicians to impose a new solution.

HEALTH CARE YOU CAN TRULY AFFORD

So what is the difference between the positions of the two parties? One party runs a little faster, but they're both headed in the same direction.

It may seem prudent to support the one that's taking us to Hell a little more slowly. But continuing to support either party assures that our health-care system will never be fixed.

America had the best medical care possible until the 1960s, when the federal government moved in. Libertarians are the only political party working to restore the system that worked — so you and your family can have low-cost health insurance, a doctor whose waiting room doesn't resemble Grand Central Station, and — whenever needed — a hospital stay that doesn't cost a year's pay.

THE GREAT LIBERTARIAN OFFER will get government completely out of health care, while freeing you from the income tax. Given the advances in computers and medical technology of the past two decades, America will have a health-care system that goes beyond even the politicians' imagination.

CHAPTER 19

GOVERNMENT'S GREATEST HITS

Have I mentioned that government doesn't work?

In books, speeches, and interviews I've pointed out that government never lives up to its promises — giving us only inefficiency, injustice, waste, and loss of liberty.

Occasionally, someone counters by pointing to a government program he thinks has achieved great good for America. Here I'll touch on three of the most popular examples I've heard — federal disaster relief, the federal highway system, and the space program.

DISASTER RELIEF

It makes little sense for the people of Missouri to pay to rebuild a town in Florida after a hurricane — and then shortly thereafter have the people of Florida pay to rebuild a flooded town in Missouri. In both cases, the money passes through Washington, D.C., where the bureaucracy takes an enormous cut and adds nothing.

But the added expense of the federal government's involvement is only part of the problem. Horning in on disaster relief gives the politicians another opportunity to distribute pork to politically influential groups.

For example, in 1997 the Red River flooded parts of North Dakota and Minnesota. No politician could be so heartless as to refuse to help.

Concerned that the Federal Emergency Management Agency (FEMA) didn't have enough money to bail out the residents, Congress passed "The Emergency Supplemental Appropriations" bill.

Here are some of the "emergency" items funded, mandated, or regulated in this bill — all prompted by the need for relief from the Red River flood:

- The "peacekeeping" effort in Bosnia.
- Loans and grants for the College Station area of Pulaski County, Arkansas.

- Collection and dissemination of statistics on cheese manufacturing in the United States.
- Countering terrorism at the 2002 Winter Olympic games.
- Handling marine mammals trapped in fishing equipment.
- Foreign aid for Ukraine.
- Repairs of concession facilities at Yosemite National Park.
- Importation of polar bear parts from Canada.
- "For payment to Marissa, Sonya, and Frank (III) Tejeda, children of Frank Tejeda, late a Representative from the State of Texas, $133,600."
- Raising the limits on highway grants by $694 million.
- Fixing an error in the Department of Transportation and Related Agencies Appropriations Act, 1997 — which mistakenly appropriated $661 million instead of $661 thousand. (Close enough for government work?)
- Reimbursing the state of Colorado and the City and County of Denver for security arrangements at the Denver Summit of Eight.
- $16 million for a counter-terrorist Automated Targeting System.
- Construction of a courthouse in Montgomery, Alabama.
- An extra $928 million for the Department of Veterans Affairs.
- $500,000 for a parking garage and $500,000 to restore the Paramount Theater — both in Ashland, Kentucky.
- A new National Commission on the Cost of Higher Education.
- Exceptions to the Truth in Lending Act and the Endangered Species Act.
- Food stamps for people otherwise made ineligible by the latest welfare reform act.
- Handling appropriations if there's another government shutdown.
- Prohibition on funding national reading and mathematics testing for school children.
- Transferring $2 million from FEMA to the National Institute on Alcohol Abuse and Alcoholism.

- $2 million for the establishment of a Law Enforcement Commission.
- Leasing a building in Lexington, Kentucky.
- Prohibition on spending funds to study the medicinal use of marijuana.

The bill covered virtually everything under the sun — *except relief for the flood victims.*[1]

Show-Offs

Symbolism is everything. The President tours a disaster area and promises quick relief. In fact, the money may never arrive. And when it does, it is seldom quick — usually arriving long after the Red Cross has packed up and headed for the next disaster.

But who's counting? It's not the money that matters, it's not even the thought that matters. It's the symbolic gesture that gets votes. And a politician can make the gesture knowing neither the press nor the opposition party will ever hold him accountable later for his empty promises.

On the other hand, anyone voting against "The Emergency Supplemental Appropriations" bill of 1997 will be made to seem heartless — even though the bill is merely a cover by which the politicians can distribute more of your money to influential companies, agencies, and individuals.

This is what happens when you allow the federal government to intrude in areas where it has no Constitutional authority.

Obviously, each state would be much better off if it were responsible only for its own problems. Since it is the Red Cross and other private agencies that provide immediate, real relief to those in need, nothing will be lost by ending the public relations posturing of federal politicians.

THE FEDERAL HIGHWAY SYSTEM

The Interstate Highway System is held up as a great achievement of the federal government. Look at those beautiful 4-lane, 6-lane, and 8-lane highways. Aren't you glad the federal government builds them?

Well, actually, the federal government *doesn't* build them. Interstate highways are built by state governments — the same

---

[1] Passing all these items as "emergency" measures was deliberate. The original budget agreement allowed additional spending only for "emergency" items.

agencies that build the state highways. The only difference is that the money for a federal highway makes a round-trip to Washington, while money for a state highway doesn't.

Of course, when the federal government pays for a highway, less money comes back from Washington than was sent there. Highway expert John Semmens has estimated that federal funding of highways has increased administrative expenses from the 7% of costs that prevailed in the 1950s (before the Interstate Highway System was begun) to about 20% today. That means we pay about 13% extra for a highway just to call it an Interstate.[2]

Private Alternatives

Many governments around the world have recognized that government roads are too expensive, and they have begun relying on private companies to build, own, and operate major toll roads. A private company acquires the rights to the necessary land (usually by securing options until all the necessary land has been tied up) and builds the road.

Highway consultant Peter Samuel has estimated that the cost of building private highways is roughly half the cost incurred by government. Some specific examples — such as comparing the private Melbourne CityLink in Australia to the similar government-built Boston Central Artery-Tunnel project — show private costs as low as one third of government costs.[3]

Private roads also are more convenient. Companies are experimenting with new ways to collect tolls without slowing traffic. For example, a customer can attach a device to his car bumper that will send a signal to a toll sensor, which registers road usage and bills the customer by mail.

In addition, lower fares for off-peak hours help to draw traffic away from peak hours. Traffic slowdowns hurt profits, so private companies have a strong incentive to eliminate them — while government road administrators use slowdowns to lobby for bigger budgets.

Diverting your Money to Other Uses

Some people feel that highway programs are a model of how government should work. The highways are financed out of gaso-

---

[2]John Semmens is the Project Manager for the Arizona Transportation Research Center in Phoenix.

[3]Peter Samuels is the editor of *Toll Roads Newsletter*.

line taxes — which are paid for only by those who benefit from highways.

But that isn't the way it works. Only about 80% of your gasoline tax money goes to build and maintain highways. The rest goes to boondoggles that reward influential politicians and well-connected businessmen.

"Your highway dollars at work" means that they have been used to pay for, among other spectacular failures, a multi-billion-dollar subway system in Los Angeles that Californians laugh at, a new multi-billion-dollar airport in Denver that no one but the mayor wanted, a $2.5 billion Miami subway system that doesn't work, and the Detroit People Mover — a trolley system that hardly anyone uses because it goes hardly anywhere.

Let the federal government start anything, and it won't stop where you think it should. It is the nature of government to follow each boondoggle with something more expensive.

Why Bring the Feds in?

Some people think the federal government has to build interstate highways in order to have roads that go from state to state, and roads that go all the way across the country. But why? Before the Interstate Highway System was built, states built highways that crossed the entire country.

Too often the federal government's "interstate" highways aren't even interstate. For example, U.S. Highway 880 travels a grand total of 36 miles near Oakland, California, and is about 150 miles from the nearest state line. There are many such interstates throughout America. Why does the federal government finance "interstate" highways that don't even cross state lines?

One More Boondoggle

When you turn something over to the government, it inevitably is reworked to suit those with the most political influence — in this case, the most powerful politicians in the House and Senate, who steer the federal highway projects to contractors and unions in their states.

The highway program also allows the federal politicians to dictate policies to state governments — such as mandatory seatbelt use, speed limits, and the legal drinking age — matters that the Constitution places off-limits for the federal government.

THE SPACE PROGRAM

Perhaps they are starry-eyed, but for some reason some people believe the space program is one of the federal government's greatest hits.

They remember the remarkable moon landing in 1969 and assume that everything NASA (the National Aeronautics and Space Agency) does must be equally impressive.

But the moon landing is yet to yield any tangible benefit to the taxpayers who paid for it. And the space program has consisted since then of an unbroken string of promises and failures.

For example, President Reagan proposed the space station in 1984. All sorts of achievements and benefits were promised for it. But as of 1999, none of the promised benefits had been delivered.

The Space Station

Item	Original Promise	Result to date
Cost:	$8 billion	$100 billion spent so far
Completion : date:	1992	Still not done; current estimate is 2005
Parts completed	40	2
Missions completed	8	1

In 1972 and again in 1982, NASA made predictions about the space shuttle. Here is how well that program has turned out:

The Space Shuttle

Item	Original Promise	Result to date
Flights per year:	51	4 in 1999
Launch service customers:	All government & private customers	Government programs only
Servicing of satellites:	Expected to be one of main purposes	Done by others because it took NASA too long to learn how
Achievements	Discover cures for diseases, find miracle alloys, & lead to new products	Nothing

The space shuttle was supposed to provide great benefits to science and the American economy. As Robert Oler, Richard Kolker, and Mark Whittington explain:

> Some NASA officials even boast that for every dollar spent, nine or ten — some have even claimed fifteen — dollars go back to the federal treasury. . . . But after almost 20 years of flying the space shuttle, not a significant scientific or medical process has been discovered or perfected in space. No significant product of any kind has been produced in space. . . . Furthermore, the servicing of satellites, once the shuttle's raison d'être, has been abandoned.

In 1999 the $200 million Mars Climate Orbiter died because of "a navigation error" — which in fact occurred because NASA calculations had confused metric measurements with standard U.S. measurements.

In January 2000, NASA reported that it had lost the $165 million Polar Lander that was supposed to explore Mars. So NASA went back to the taxpayers' trough to get new funding to look for the lost Lander.

Private Alternatives

In the 1970s several private companies wanted to build their own rocket launchers and send satellites into space. But the government wouldn't use their services. And by offering cheap, subsidized rates for launching satellites, the government effectively killed all private competition.

It took the Challenger crash to change the rules, reducing considerably the number of government launches. Now government agencies use private launch services, instead of driving them out of the market.

Most other laws that inhibited private development of space have been removed. And so markets are opening up for tourism in space, as well as private mapping of the moon and far-off planets. I have no doubt that there will be other markets that will spur private space development.

Beal Aerospace has invested $200 million in the building of a new rocket to launch satellites. This is a pittance compared to what a government launcher costs. When an enterprise seems too big for the private sector to handle, it's often because we use government costs to gauge its size.

Unburden private companies from subsidized competition and they will provide the money to do what is truly worth doing. Usually they will succeed. But if a private company fails to deliver, it won't cost the taxpayers anything.

AND THE #1 HIT IS . . .

Once when I was on a radio show, a woman called in to say:

You keep saying "government doesn't work." But there are many fine government programs that have achieved a great deal.

I asked her to give me an example of one, so we could examine it. There was dead silence on the line. Then she said, "Well, there are lots of them." I asked her again for an example. Again she said, "Well there are so many."

Finally, after several repetitions, the exasperated host broke in and insisted that she give an example of a government program that works well.

After another pause, she said, "Well, there's the National Weather Bureau."

I wonder if the weatherman on your local TV station, the constant butt of jokes for missed forecasts, would agree with her.

CHAPTER 20

FREEDOM FROM MORAL POSTURING

During the primary election season, I watched the televised debates involving the Democratic and Republican presidential candidates.

They all had plenty to say and sometimes the discussions were heated. But it was apparent that all the arguments were variations on one overriding question: *Which candidate knows best how to run your life?*

Each one thinks he knows what kind of health-care system you should encounter when you visit your doctor or go to the hospital. Each one is sure he should be the one to decide what kind of school your child will attend. Each one believes he knows better than you which good works your money should support.

Each one thinks he knows what's right for you — and for every other American as well.

Instead of allowing you to keep your own money, each candidate believes he should control what you earn — and spend it on the projects he thinks best. The only real argument is over how much to leave with you to spend on your own — little or very little.

Instead of letting you plan your own retirement in the way you think best, he believes he should determine what percentage of your earnings the government must control and what percentage you'll be allowed to work with on your own.

It didn't matter whether an issue discussed was financial, ethical, or personal. In almost every area of your life, each candidate presumed to know how your life should be ordered. And he knew that what he wanted for you should be imposed on everyone else as well. The idea that each person should work these matters out for himself never seemed to occur to any of them.

The arrogance of politicians is amazing. Each one believes himself able to make decisions about the minutest detail of your life — from how to handle every dollar you have to what you should be allowed to see at the movies or on the Internet.

Mea Culpa

I'm afraid I'm not that wise.

I don't know what's right for you. I don't know how you should raise your children or how to run your child's school or how your family should approach any of the many complicated challenges you face.

And even though I've written eight books on investing, I can't tell you how to plan your retirement. I could only make you aware of techniques and alternatives you might not have known about; the final decisions, to be right, have to come from you.

Even if I don't know you, I respect your intelligence and your ability to choose and act on your own values, to work with other families and your community to achieve the goals you set for yourselves.

I respect your ability to handle these tasks because the only alternative is to let politicians handle them for you, and they will never care as much about your future as you do yourself.

I don't want to run your life, and there's no reason to think I would be any better at it than the politicians who preen and posture with answers to every one of life's questions.

America once embodied the idea that you are a sovereign individual able to make your own decisions — such as how to spend the money you earn or how to raise your own children.

The idea that politicians should run your life, the economy, or the world is the very opposite of what made America a unique and prosperous nation.

MORAL STANDARDS

Politicians claim moral authority by implying that their decisions are dictated by moral principle — and by assuming that we can't let everyone decide for himself what is moral and what isn't. That leaves only the politicians to decide what is right and what is wrong. So they claim a license to use government to compel us to do everything that's right and to forbid us to do everything that's wrong.

But the Constitution gives the federal government no authority to tell us how to live our lives. It gives the politicians no authority to make your financial decisions or your personal decisions. That doesn't stop them, however.

Democratic and Republican politicians treat us as dysfunctional children who need the attention of a strict government to decide what we can have, see, hear, and read, and what we can say publicly. Neither of the two major parties recognizes any limits on the government's authority over your life.

Of course, all politicians like to pose as supporters of your family. But their "support" really means making your decisions for you:

- Democrats invoke the "children" on behalf of every new government boondoggle and regulation — whether to censor the Internet or put a V-chip in your television set.
- Republicans claim they will restore family values by stamping out drug use or posting the 10 Commandments in schools. Somehow they think you can't instill family values in your children unless the politicians apply force.

None of the politicians believes you're capable of deciding for yourself what's best for your family. If they really trusted you, they'd repeal the income tax — so you'd have the wherewithal to make your own family decisions, so you could afford to send your children to schools that teach what you want your child to learn, and so you could afford to have one parent at home to supervise your children according to your values.

Inspiration for What?

America's politicians lament the decline in moral standards. They tell us we must raise our sights above our own shabby little lives, and give ourselves to a greater cause. They say we must practice the politics of compassion, that we must use our resources to help others, that we must solve the problems of racism, poverty, and inequality.

The oratory soars — but goes nowhere.

The politician really means that you must give up your concern for your family and whatever else you care for — areas where you might actually make a difference — and support whatever causes he's hitched his political wagon to.

He means you must stop demonstrating your compassion in ways that make sense to you, and instead give him more money to divert to programs — government or private — that have the political pull to capture his allegiance.

He means you must fight racism, poverty, and inequality not through your own kindness and decency, but by giving him more power and money to reward the squeaky wheels — the unappeasable organizations and grievance mongers who live off the ills they bemoan.

WHOSE STANDARDS WILL PREVAIL?

When a politician promises to raise moral standards in America, it's easy to think he's referring to the moral standards in which you believe. You think you've found someone who's going to use the force of government to impose your moral values on others.

But when government acts, the values imposed won't be yours and they won't be mine. Moral values will be set by whoever has the most political power — people like Teddy Kennedy or Newt Gingrich. Is that what you want to impose on others?

And don't forget that the force of government will be used to impose those values on you as well. No one is going to exempt you from the "Make America a Moral Place Act of 2001."

Even if you have some reason to believe Congress will legislate the moral rules you like, those rules are only temporary. The next Congress will go off in its own direction.

SET THEM FREE

The entire effort to wed morality and politics is based on the assumption that there are immoral or irresponsible people who can't be bent into shape unless the government does it.

Yes, there *are* people who won't act responsibly. There are people who have no regard for the consequences of their own acts. There are people who seem to be incapable of behaving wisely or benevolently.

Politicians exploit these people to justify rigid controls on *your* life. Because some people won't plan for their old age, *you* must be forced into Social Security. Because some people will do funny things after looking at dirty pictures on the Internet, *your* access to the Internet must be restricted.

So what should we do about people who won't take responsibility for their own actions? I believe the answer is simple:

Set them free.

Give them the freedom to make their own decisions, to face the consequences of their own acts, to see for themselves what their actions do to others, and how others respond to them.

Only free people have an incentive to be virtuous. Only people who bear the consequences of their own acts will care about those consequences.

A free society rewards virtue and punishes irresponsibility. Government does just the opposite.

What do we do about people who might not plan for their own retirement?

Set them free.

Let each person know that his future depends largely on his own actions. If younger people see some older people who haven't planned ahead and have to rely on charity, the young will be more likely to provide for the future. Today when someone plans poorly, the only consequence younger people see is a call for more government.

What do we do about people who are insensitive to other people?

Set them free.

Let other people shun them or respect them for what they do. Let them feel the results of being civil or uncivil.

Freedom & Responsibility

It is often said that freedom and responsibility are two sides of the same coin — that if you want freedom, you must first accept the responsibility that goes with it.

The truth is simpler. Freedom and responsibility aren't two sides of the same thing; one isn't a precondition for the other. They *are* the same thing.

Freedom *is* responsibility. Responsibility is experiencing the consequences of your own acts — not the consequences of others' acts or making others pay for what you do.

And that's what freedom is. Without government to force others to pay for your pleasures or mistakes, and without forcing you to pay for what others do, you are a free, responsible human being.

Freedom and responsibility are inseparably linked — not because they *should* be, but because they *are*. Responsibility accompanies freedom, whether or not you want it to.

We are told America must have a moral revival before we can have greater freedom — that people must be educated to be responsible before they can be free. This puts the cart before the horse.

If we expect a government program to make people responsible, we will wait forever.

We don't need a moral revival, we don't need politicians making moral decisions for us. We need do only one thing to induce people to act more responsibly:

Set them free.

ABORTION

Abortion is the most contentious moral issue of our time. Even Libertarians disagree among themselves on this issue.

- One side believes that unborn children are entitled to the same rights as those already born.
- The other side feels a natural revulsion at government intruding further into the lives of individuals making personal decisions.

In effect, both are right — or at least have understandable positions.

And because people on both sides feel very strongly about this issue, it won't be settled by inventing more slogans or repeating the old ones.

Nor will it be settled by adopting a moralistic posture. Nothing is ever really advanced by looking down your nose at those you consider your moral inferiors. Moral arguments generally succeed only in swaying those who already accept your moral premises. If that weren't so, Jesse Jackson would have won your support a long time ago.

Particularly misleading are the labels "pro-choice" and "pro-life." Aside from Libertarians, most of the politicians who say they are pro-choice or that they believe in "a woman's right to choose" would never dream of letting a woman choose to drop out of Social Security, or to choose to smoke marijuana to alleviate the pain of glaucoma or cancer treatments. The politicians are "pro-choice" on only one issue.

And most of the politicians who say they're "pro-life" see nothing wrong with our government bombing — and taking the lives of — thousands of innocent people in Serbia, Iraq, or other countries. They are "pro-life" on only one issue.

Abortion & the Government

As for me, until science can demonstrate otherwise, I must err on the side of safety and assume that life begins at conception. Thus I believe abortion, at any stage of a pregnancy, is wrong — very wrong.

I also believe that turning to the government to settle moral arguments is wrong — very wrong. And I believe that letting the federal government intrude where it has no constitutional authority is even worse.

The Constitution grants the federal government no authority to act against common crimes — such as murder or theft. In fact, only three crimes are mentioned in the Constitution: treason, piracy, and counterfeiting. Since the federal government has no constitutional authority to deal with abortion, I must oppose any federal activity in this area.

I am certain that we abandon all hope of freedom if we abandon the Constitution's limits on the federal government. So as President I would have vetoed the "Woman's Right to Choose" bill, the partial-birth abortion bill, and any other proposal from either side of the debate.

No matter what my personal feelings about abortion, it would be my responsibility to veto such proposals because the President takes an oath to uphold and defend the Constitution. Unlike all recent occupants of the White House and the other candidates who aspire to live there, I would take that oath seriously.

Litmus Tests for Judges

Every four years a great deal of political noise is made about abortion and the appointment of Supreme Court Justices. A presidential candidate usually is asked whether he will apply a litmus test to judicial appointments.

As president, I *will* have a litmus test: Does the judicial candidate believe absolutely that the federal government has no authority beyond the specific powers enumerated in the Constitution? Judges who pass the litmus test will recognize that the federal government has no business in education, health care, law enforcement, welfare — or abortion.

The judges I appoint will respect the 9th and 10th amendments for what they are — unmistakable limits on the power of the federal government.

The judges I appoint will recognize that the Roe v. Wade decision was a judicial fraud — that five of the nine justices found it in their wishes, not in the Constitution. I expect the Supreme Court to overturn that ruling someday, so that the federal government no longer will set the rules for every state.

Instead, I expect to see what Joseph Sobran called "a checkerboard of states — competing with each other to attract the best citizens." Some states may choose to outlaw abortion, and others might have few, if any, restrictions.

Taking Effective Action

Do I believe the states should outlaw abortion?

I do not, but why should my opinion matter? I'm only running for President, not Dictator. And the President has no constitutional authority to dictate to the states on this issue.

It's true, however, that I believe every abortion takes a human life. So I hope those who share that view won't waste their time trying to get government to reduce abortions. Government never delivers what you want. It doesn't protect adults on the streets. It doesn't protect children in the schools. Why should we think it will protect the unborn?

Every day we spend begging the government to stop abortion is a day wasted — a day that could have been spent doing something truly effective, such as . . .

- Working for less restrictive adoption laws.
- Encouraging private educational efforts to show young women the alternatives to abortion.
- Repealing the income tax so parents can spend more time with their children, teaching them values that will minimize teenage pregnancies.
- Repealing any law that encourages people to ignore the consequences of their actions.

As with any other problem, only a program of education and persuasion — undertaken voluntarily by individuals, not government — can work. I admire the people who work so hard to dissuade young women from rushing into abortions, who arrange adoptions for pregnant women who aren't ready to raise a child, and who spend their own money to celebrate the lives of children who weren't aborted. These are efforts that make a true difference — unlike those of politicians who pose and preach and promise, and never deliver anything.

Government doesn't persuade; it forces. And that's why it can't bring about any lasting change you might want.

To me, abortion is a horror. But giving politicians the power to run your life, hoping they will stop abortions, isn't the way to end the horror. In fact, in one way or another, it's bound to make a bad thing worse.

BEWARE THOSE WHO WANT TO USE GOVERNMENT

Politicians who claim they will use government to stop abortions — or to serve any other moral good — are telling you they believe government force can produce good results. So don't be surprised when they see government force as the solution to other problems.

Rather than look to force, if you want to change the moral climate in America I hope you'll work to solve the principal problem that feeds it — government destruction of our families and values.

The most important step we can take to solve that problem is to dramatically reduce the burden of federal taxation — a burden that forces both parents to work and that denies parents the financial means to choose schools that teach their values.

THE GREAT LIBERTARIAN OFFER provides the first step.

Let's take that step, so that people will be more responsible.

Let's *set them free.*

CHAPTER 21

GETTING FROM HERE TO THERE

Politicians have been playing games with us for decades — promising, and even sometimes delivering, cosmetic changes in government that don't really lighten your tax load or make you freer.

Recognizing that these people don't really make your life better, why would you consider giving any support to a candidate or a party that doesn't offer what you actually want?

The usual answer to that question is that the alternatives would be even worse. But, in fact, it doesn't seem to matter which of the old parties is in power because the result is always the same:

- Government gets bigger.
- Government gets more expensive.
- Government gets more intrusive.
- Even the mild, compromising, insignificant promises are forgotten once an election is over.

The only approach that makes sense is to say straight out what we want. If we never ask for it, we have no chance to get it.

- We don't want to make the best of the current health-care situation by passing a "Patient's Bill of Rights," starting medical savings accounts, or applying other Band-Aids to a sick system. We want to get the federal government out of health care — completely and immediately — to eliminate the crowding of doctors' offices, and to reduce the cost of health insurance and hospital stays. And with less tax money being eaten up by Washington, you'll be healthier and wealthier.

- We don't want to reform the Department of Education — or give the federal government the power to hand out vouchers for schools the bureaucrats approve of. We want the federal government out of education — completely and immediately — to stop the damaging interference and subsidized waste in local schools. When Washington stops taxing you to pay for its education experiments, you'll have better schools and more money in your pocket.

- We don't want more Drug War rhetoric or more lives ruined by addiction, street battles, and imprisonment. We want an end to the insane War on Drugs — completely and immediately — to call a halt to the worst crime wave since alcohol Prohibition and the worst invasion of our civil liberties in the history of the country.

- We don't want more tinkering with Social Security tax rates and benefits, or the privilege of investing for yourself a paltry 1% or 2% of the 15% Social Security tax. We want the federal government out of retirement planning — completely and immediately. A private system will finally give senior citizens a retirement they can count on, without fear of political tinkering — and it will free you completely from the 15% tax, so you can arrange a truly secure retirement for yourself.

- We don't want to slow government's growth, or make bureaucrats more accountable, or root out "waste and corruption" in government. We want the Washington politicians to get out — completely and immediately — of all activities not authorized by the Constitution.

- We don't want more justices on the Supreme Court — Republican or Democratic — who claim to respect the Constitution's "original intent" but who give your rights away whenever the government claims to have a "compelling interest." We can trust the Supreme Court only when it acknowledges that the 10th amendment to the Constitution prohibits the federal government from engaging in any activity not enumerated in the Constitution — and that the 9th amendment protects all individual rights not handed over to the government by the Constitution

- We don't want to rearrange the current burden of big government though a flat tax, a sales tax, or a tax cut that doesn't reduce the overall cost of government. We want to reduce government dramatically — significantly and immediately — so we can eliminate the income tax entirely, and you can keep every dollar you earn — to spend it, save it, or give it away as you think best.

Extremism

Of course, some people will say these proposals are extremist.

But is it extremist to believe the government should abide by the Constitution?

Is it extremist to believe 47% is too much for the federal, state, and local governments to take from you?

Is it extremist to think you should be free to invest your retirement money as you see fit?

Is it extremist to believe that every provision of the Bill of Rights should be honored?

The true extremists are those who support a $1.8 trillion budget — those who support an insane War on Drugs that's destroying our cities and our people — who allow the federal government to continue damaging our health-care system — who keep urging the same destructive government policies that have failed so miserably.

All we're asking for is a free America, where you can live by your values and raise your children accordingly.

So why should you waste your time supporting anything less?

WITH ALL DELIBERATE SLOWNESS

Of course, we have to do more than ask for what we want. We have to describe how we intend to get to where we want to be.

Some people believe progress must come slowly, a little each year in a gradual restoration of constitutional government.

But I don't believe we can succeed by trying to phase out government programs a little at time.

There are many reasons gradualism won't work. Here are some of them:

1. There will be an interminable argument over which pro-grams will be eliminated first. No one who profits great-ly from any federal program will give it up for a promise that he'll be rewarded in the sweet bye and bye. And you and I can't afford to go to Washington to offset the pres-sure applied by those who want to keep a federal pro-gram.

2. Politicians won't stick for very long to any plan that leads to smaller government. In 1981 Congress enacted a tax cut to be phased in over three years. But the fol-lowing year they raised taxes, and then raised them again in 1983.

3. A program that is immediate and complete is the only way we can assure Americans that we aren't just look-ing for government jobs like other politicians — that we intend to minimize government and maximize liberty.

4. Only a big reward will motivate people to actively sup-port our plan. THE GREAT LIBERTARIAN OFFER, with its complete elimination of the income tax, is such a reward. But we can't repeal the income tax if we don't reduce gov-ernment accordingly — and do it immediately.

Politicians will never willingly give up what they've taken from us. We must recover it swiftly, decisively, and completely.

THE TRANSITION

How bumpy would a quick transition to much smaller feder-al government be? Would it disrupt society to reduce government dramatically and repeal the income tax?

There couldn't be more disruption than the government is causing now — with its insane War on Drugs, ruinous welfare laws, dumbed-down schools, wasteful and unhealthy health-care system, and Ponzi-like Social Security system.

And the government is running up so many liabilities that we're headed for a fiscal meltdown. If we don't act quickly, the day will arrive all too soon when you might reach for your Social Security and it won't be there, when Medicare will run out of money at the moment you might need it, when your bank will close but the deposit insurance fund will be empty. How could anything be more dangerous than what we face now?

We can head off that meltdown and end most of the disrup-tions by implementing THE GREAT LIBERTARIAN OFFER.

Retraining Program?

Still, millions of people on federal welfare or on the government payroll might have to make changes in their lives. Should we have a government program to retrain them and ease the transition?

If we do, we will never get to where we want to go. Any such program would become permanent. Despite all its promises, welfare reform never really puts people to work, and retraining programs never train people for the jobs the marketplace really needs.

Fortunately, we don't need the government to manage the transition. It will come automatically.

The day a Libertarian is elected President, the transition will begin — even before THE GREAT LIBERTARIAN OFFER is accepted by Congress.

Everyone will know that passage of our program will be just a matter of time. They will know that soon the economy will be richer every year by well over a trillion dollars.

Businessmen will see growing markets coming for new products and services. Companies will want to gear up immediately to get the jump on their competitors. They'll need new employees, but there won't be enough unemployed people to fill all the new jobs. Where will they find the new employees they need?

Employers will have to try to recruit people from the ranks of government workers and the welfare rolls. They will train people to fill real jobs producing real products that real people want to pay real money for.

By the time our program is passed, the transition may already be complete. The transition will be difficult only if we let the government manage it, or if we try to stretch it out over a long period of time.

THE FEDERAL BUDGET

A government that isn't trying to dominate the world, one that focuses on national defense rather than offense, should be able to fulfill its constitutional duties to defend the country and provide a federal judiciary for around $100 billion a year.

While that may seem small next to today's $1.8 trillion budget, it's actually no less than what our government thrived on for most of America's history.

The biggest obstacle to such a budget comes from the promises the politicians have made. They have run up outright debts of

$5.6 trillion, which costs over $200 billion a year in interest expense. In addition, the government has made promises to veterans and government employees. And the federal government has underwritten insurance against low farm outputs, natural disasters, bank failures, and much else.

What do we do about all this?

First, stop the politicians from making any more promises.

Second, end all government insurance programs. To whatever extent they need it, individuals and companies can replace that insurance in the private market, paying realistic prices and making realistic business and financial decisions.

Third, sell off all government assets that don't serve constitutional purposes, and use the proceeds to liquidate the promises the politicians have made.

The first proceeds should purchase a private retirement account for everyone dependent on Social Security today, and for anyone over 50 who will be dependent on Social Security.

Without access to detailed Social Security data, it's not possible to make a precise estimate of the cost of the private accounts. But I believe the cost should be roughly $5 trillion.

Next comes the national debt — which was $5.6 trillion at the end of 1999.

(President Clinton and the Republican Congress claim to have balanced the budget. But they have done it using bookkeeping tricks that would send the officers of a corporation to jail. Each year they take about $200 billion from the Social Security "trust fund" to pay for existing pork-barrel programs, and then claim to use the same money to pay down the debt. Actually, the federal debt has continued to climb, month by month, increasing by $128 billion from the end of fiscal 1998 to the end of fiscal 1999.)[1]

To pay off the federal debt and finance the transition of Social Security to private accounts will require $10.6 trillion.

Then there are other government liabilities — such as pensions promised to veterans and government employees. Replacing these open-ended obligations with private annuities will probably require at least another $1 trillion.

Avoiding Open-Ended Liabilities

These figures are hardly precise — which demonstrates why government should never undertake an open-ended obligation.

---

[1] The debt increases from year to year because the federal government must issue new bonds to replace the money taken from the Social Security reserves.

If, for example, the American people feel they owe something to soldiers who have fought a war for them, the debt should be paid immediately. The government could either:

- Make a single lump-sum payment to each veteran; or
- Purchase annuities from private companies, so that each veteran receives payments over a number of years.

Whatever method is used, the government should face up to the cost and pay it in full immediately, so that the obligation doesn't linger and become open-ended. The exact cost of the benefit being provided should be known and paid. What we've had instead are politicians making lavish promises, and then leaving it to future generations to make good on the promises.

Asset Sales

Covering miscellaneous liabilities, financing the Social Security transition, and paying off the nominal debt will require about $12 trillion.

This sounds like a tremendous sum. And it is. But the politicians have incurred it on your behalf. And it won't go away by our ignoring it.

We can't know in advance whether the government's unneeded assets will bring $12 trillion in a series of orderly sales. Published estimates of the value of government assets have ranged from $5 trillion to $50 trillion. The only way we'll find out what people actually will pay for the land, buildings, pipelines, power companies, unused military bases, and the rest of the huge catalog of government assets is to sell them. But we can be certain that it will be the most lucrative garage sale in history.

The auctions should be spread over six years, so they don't depress prices. (I would prefer to get it done in six days, but that would be a mistake.)

If the sales do bring at least $12 trillion, the U.S. government will be debt-free, with no future liabilities, there will be no interest expense in the federal budget, and Social Security will be completely privatized.

What if the sales don't bring $12 trillion?

Then we will know that the government is insolvent — that its liabilities exceed its assets. If that's true, shouldn't we know it now — rather than let the politicians continue running up liabilities?

The Budget

The table on page 231 shows a projected federal budget through 2008. The budgets for the first two years (fiscal years 1999 and 2000) have already been passed, and the 2001 budget will be passed by Congress during 2000. The 2002 budget will be the first that the next President and Congress deal with.[2]

The table makes several assumptions:

- Social Security payments taper off during 2002 and 2003, as Social Security accounts are replaced with private retirement accounts.
- All private retirement accounts are purchased by 2004.
- In 2002 federal spending, other than for Social Security and interest on the debt, is cut in half — from $1,207 billion to $600 billion. It continues downward each year, and levels off at $100 billion in 2005. The target might be reached sooner, but there are bound to be problems liquidating some unconstitutional federal agencies.
- The income and Social Security taxes are repealed immediately and provide no revenue from 2002 onward. We can't count on a political promise to repeal those taxes at some later date.
- The asset sales begin in 2002 and continue for six years.
- During 2002 through 2005, part of the proceeds of the asset sales are used to cover current expenses — as current revenues are reduced faster than current expenses.
- The federal debt is completely gone by 2007.

Is this possible?

Yes.

Is there another way to achieve the goal of much smaller government?

I don't know of any. Do you?

---

[2]The government's 2002 fiscal year runs from October 1, 2001, through September 30, 2002.

Getting Rid of the Income Tax & the Federal Debt
The Federal Budget, 1999 – 2008 (billions of dollars)

Fiscal year:	1999	*2000	*2001	2002	2003	2004	2005	2006	2007	2008
Revenue without Social Security										
Personal income, estate, & gift taxes............	880	921	963	0	0	0	0	0	0	0
Corporate income tax...................................	185	188	190	0	0	0	0	0	0	0
Tariffs and excise taxes...............................	89	95	101	108	115	123	131	140	154	100
Other taxes & user fees................................	63	70	77	60	50	40	30	20	10	0
Sales of government assets...........................			0	3,000	2,500	2,500	2,000	1,000	1,000	0
Total Revenue without Social Security	**1,216**	**1,273**	**1,331**	**3,168**	**2,665**	**2,663**	**2,161**	**1,160**	**1,164**	**100**
Spending without Social Security										
Interest..	230	219	207	222	197	177	150	77	39	0
Other spending...	1,084	1,147	1,209	605	250	100	100	100	100	100
Purchase Social Security annuities..............				1,693	1,693	1,693	0	0	0	0
Total spending without Social Security	**1,315**	**1,365**	**1,416**	**2,520**	**2,140**	**1,970**	**250**	**177**	**139**	**100**
Surplus/(Deficit) without Social Security	**(99)**	**(92)**	**(85)**	**648**	**525**	**693**	**1,911**	**983**	**1,025**	**(0)**
Social Security tax.......................................	612	641	670	0	0	0	0	0	0	0
Social Security payments..............................	390	406	423	293	146	0	0	0	0	0
Surplus/(Deficit) with Social Security	**123**	**143**	**162**	**355**	**378**	**693**	**1,911**	**983**	**1,025**	**(0)**
Total (debt) at end of fiscal year..................	(5,607)	(5,698)	(5,784)	(5,136)	(4,611)	(3,918)	(2,008)	(1,025)	(0)	(0)
Total revenue without asset sales................	1,827	1,914	2,001	168	165	163	161	160	164	100
Total spending without annuity purchases.....	1,705	1,772	1,839	1,119	593	277	250	177	139	100
Surplus/(Deficit) without sales & annuities......	123	143	162	(951)	(428)	(114)	(89)	(17)	25	(0)
Cumulative asset sales.................................				3,000	5,500	8,000	10,000	11,000	12,000	12,000

2002 is the first fiscal year of the next administration.

* = 2000 & 2001 figures are estimates.

CHAPTER 22
THE
LIBERTARIAN PATH

Libertarians believe in individual liberty, personal responsibility, and freedom from government — on all issues and at all times.

We don't complain that government is too big in one area, but then call for more government in another area. For us, individual liberty, personal responsibility, and freedom from government aren't a "sometimes" thing — virtuous in some matters but to be disregarded in others. It's our standard for *all* issues at *all* times.

Libertarians believe it's wrong for someone to confiscate your money and give it to someone else. It doesn't matter whether the act of confiscation is called "compassionate liberalism" or "compassionate conservatism," it isn't compassionate for politicians to help someone with money confiscated from you and other taxpayers through threats of fines and imprisonment.

Libertarians believe that no government project is important enough to justify violating the Bill of Rights. They believe it's wrong for the government to paw through your bank records. They believe it's wrong for the government to impose regulations that drive up the prices of the things you buy and reduce the wages you earn. They believe it's wrong for the politicians to control important decisions in your life.

Libertarians know that using the force of government never delivers what's promised. So if someone says there's a health-care crisis, for example, Libertarians don't ask government to force employers to change their benefit plans; they don't demand that insurance companies alter their policies; they don't propose new subsidies, new commissions, or new price controls. Rather, they look for ways to solve the problem by getting government out of it.

Disagreements with Libertarians

You may not agree with the libertarian position on everything. That's understandable.

But if you disagree with Libertarians on a particular issue, it's probably because Libertarians are uncompromising in applying the principles in which you believe — individual liberty, personal responsibility, and freedom from government. And if you think about the issue some more, you may see why giving power to politicians isn't the best answer here, any more than elsewhere.

Libertarians don't want society to be governed by force in the hands of whoever has the most political power. They want a society in which people can associate with one another voluntarily to achieve what they want. In such a society, problems can be tackled by many groups — each trying different solutions, with no one forced to participate in any solution he doesn't approve of.

THE LIBERTARIAN PARTY

The Libertarian Party was founded in 1971 by former Democrats and Republicans who were fed up with the relentless growth of government. The party's growth was necessarily slow during its first 20 years. But now the party is expanding rapidly in size and influence.

In many ways, it is the dominant third party in America — and is close to becoming a major party:

- Membership in the party is now about 2½ times what it was four years ago. And while voter registrations for the Republican and Democratic Parties have been falling in many states, Libertarian registrations have been growing at a good clip.
- The Republicans and Democrats have placed tall hurdles in the path of third parties — with restrictive ballot access laws and campaign finance rules that favor incumbents. But the Libertarian Party has overcome these hurdles. As in 1996, I will be on the ballot in all 50 states in 2000.
- This year somewhere around 2,000 Libertarian candidates will be running for Congressional, state, and local seats — probably more than the total of all other third parties combined. Already over 300 Libertarians hold public office in America.

- In 2000, the Libertarian presidential campaign will be far more visible than it was in 1996. The party is now much better financed. However, the money isn't coming from taxpayers, billionaire candidates, or special interests; it comes entirely from the voluntary contributions of people like you — enthusiastic supporters who will magnify the impact of the party's advertising by their own efforts to publicize the campaign.

- My presidential campaign has produced a 30-minute TV show that will air on national networks and local stations during the 2000 campaign. We also will have 30-second and 60-second spots, as well as extensive advertising and publicity on the Internet. Because we are offering to improve people's lives dramatically, we can make an impact with a much smaller budget than that of the candidates who have more money than ideas.

The Libertarian Party now is large enough to buy national visibility. Our clear-cut proposals to reduce government in 2000 can change the terms of debate — away from government "solutions" and toward proposals to actually reduce government.

Libertarian Principles

Whereas the "ideals" of the other parties shift with the polls, the Libertarian Party's positions are permanently fixed on the principles of individual liberty and the reduction of government to the absolute minimum.

The party's platform is constant, not created anew every four years. The only changes made to the platform concern its presentation, not the party's position on basic issues concerning your freedom. The party's objective is summed up nicely in the platform's Preamble:

As Libertarians, we seek a world of liberty; a world in which all individuals are sovereign over their own lives, and no one is forced to sacrifice his or her values for the benefit of others.

We believe that respect for individual rights is the essential precondition for a free and prosperous world, that force and fraud must be banished from human relationships, and that only through freedom can peace and prosperity be realized.

Consequently, we defend each person's right to engage in any activity that is peaceful and honest, and we welcome the diversity that freedom brings. The world we seek to build is one where individuals are free to follow their own dreams in their own ways, without interference from government or any authoritarian power.

The Public Wants a 3rd Party

The press tells us that the public wants a third party to provide a "centrist" candidate — someone who avoids the "extremes" of the Republicans and Democrats. But the space between the two parties is so small that anyone trying to squeeze between them could get crushed to death.

The only good reason for a third party is to provide a choice that's completely different from the Democrats and Republicans. The other third parties don't do that. Like Republicans and Democrats, they claim they can make government work better.

Libertarians don't want to make government more effective. It's already too effective at the only thing it does well — applying force.

We want to reduce government dramatically and give control of your life back to you.[1]

THE CANDIDATE

I announced my presidential candidacy in February 2000. We have already raised more money, established a far bigger volunteer organization, and made greater inroads into the public consciousness than any previous Libertarian presidential campaign.

Can I win?

The question is irrelevant because until we do have a Libertarian President, we will never be free of big government. And so we have to start now to do what is necessary to elect a Libertarian President — whether that victory will be in 2000, 2004, or 2008. The longer we wait to begin, the longer we wait to be free of big government.

And the question "Can I win?" is meaningless until you ask yourself a more relevant question: Do you want me to win?

What a President Can Do

The President of the U.S. is the most powerful person in the world. He can personally make your life miserable, or make it much freer. And when he can't do something personally, he can lead.

[1]You can obtain information about the Libertarian Party by calling 1-800-ELECT-US or by going to its website at www.lp.org.

If I win the Presidency in 2000, there is much I will do immediately to make this a freer, safer, more prosperous country — even if there are very few Libertarians in Congress.

The First Day in Office

On my first day in office, by Executive Order I will:

- Pardon everyone who has been convicted on a federal, non-violent drug charge, order the immediate release of those in prison, reunite them with their families, and restore all their civil rights.[2]
- Pardon everyone who has been convicted on any federal gun-control charge, order the immediate release of those in prison, and restore all their civil rights.
- Pardon everyone who has been convicted of a federal tax-evasion charge, order the immediate release of those in prison, and restore all their civil rights.
- Pardon everyone else who has been convicted of a victimless federal crime, order the immediate release of those in prison, and restore all their civil rights.

I will make it clear to federal law enforcement agents and prosecutors that we want the violent criminals off the streets. No U.S. Attorney should waste his time or the taxpayers' money prosecuting people who haven't intruded on anyone's person or property. Every member of the federal criminal justice system should understand that prison space is only for criminals who have hurt someone.

Since the Constitution lists no violent crimes (except for piracy), there will be a great deal of empty prison space after the pardons. So we can speed up the elimination of the federal debt by selling federal prisons to state governments that may need the facilities.

There are other steps I can take on the first day in office:

- I will announce a policy to penalize, dismiss, or even prosecute any federal employee who violates the Bill of Rights by treating you as guilty until proven innocent, by searching or seizing your property without due process of law, by treating you as a servant, or in any other way violating your rights as a sovereign American citizen.

---

[2]Obviously, anyone who has been convicted of using violence against someone else in a drug case would not qualify as "non-violent."

- I will immediately order that no federal asset forfeiture can occur if the property's owner hasn't been convicted by full due process — and I will initiate steps to make restitution to anyone whose property has been impounded, frozen, or seized by the federal government without being convicted by due process. Over 80% of such seizures occur when no one has even been charged with a crime.

- As Commander in Chief of the Armed Forces, I will immediately remove all American troops from foreign soil. Europe and Asia can pay for their own defense, and they can risk their own lives in their eternal squabbles. This will save billions of dollars a year in taxes, but — more important — it will make sure your sons and daughters will never fight in someone else's war.

- As Commander in Chief I will remove all American troops from under the command of the United Nations or any other foreign organization.

- As President I will make sure the executive branch stops harassing smokers, tobacco companies, successful computer companies, gun owners, gun manufacturers, alternative medicine suppliers, religious groups (whether respected or labeled as "cults"), investment companies, health-care providers, businessmen, and anyone else who is conducting his affairs peaceably.

- I will end federal affirmative action, federal quotas, set-asides, preferential treatments, and other discriminatory practices of the federal government. Any previous President could have done this with a stroke of the pen. Do you wonder why none of them did?

And then I will break for lunch.

There's More . . .

After lunch, I will begin the process of removing from the Federal Register the thousands and thousands of regulations and executive orders inserted there by previous Presidents. In most cases these regulations give federal employees powers for which there is no constitutional authority.

I will call Office Depot and order a carload of pens — to use in vetoing Congressional bills that violate the Constitution or that spend more money than necessary for the constitutional functions of government.

I will submit a budget for the fiscal year 2002 (the first budget of the next presidential term), as shown in the table on page 231. I will veto any appropriations that exceed the limits shown in that table.

Dealing with Congress

Congress will undoubtedly pass a larger budget and expect me to sign it. I won't.

Will Congress override my veto?

I don't know. But we shouldn't assume that it will. If I were elected on my platform to cut government dramatically, and with my intentions spelled out in this book and in public appearances, no one could misinterpret what my election meant. No one would believe the voters chose me to make the trains run on time or to "look under the hood and tinker with the engine." It would be obvious that the people were demanding much smaller government.

That wouldn't stop the politicians from pretending to reduce government while keeping a death-grip on their favorite programs. But it would certainly give me the upper hand.

If it turned out that Congress couldn't override my veto but wouldn't agree to my budget, we would reach an impasse. Perhaps the Congressional leaders would threaten to shut down the government if I didn't give in. To which I suppose I'd reply, "Oh no, don't throw me in the briar patch!"

Even if Congress defied the electorate and passed bills over my veto, *the battle finally would be joined*. We finally would be free of what we've grown so accustomed to — a President who passively allows Congress to expand government.

At long last, there would be two sides arguing in Washington — one to increase government and one to cut it sharply — instead of the current trivial debate over whether government should grow 5% a year or "only" 3%.

Just Say No

No President in the past several decades has had the will, the determination, the courage to "just say no" to Congress.

No President in the past several decades has even had the desire to reduce the size of government. Any President who wanted to do so could have managed it — even in the face of a hostile Congress.

No President since the 1950s has proposed a single budget that would reduce the size of the federal government. And when Congress has come back with even larger budgets, no President has vetoed them.

As President, I will — for the first time — use that office on *your* behalf. I will say no to Congress. Whatever new program it wants to spend money on, I will veto. Whatever new tax it wants to impose, I will veto. Whatever new intrusion it wants to make in your life, I will veto.

Every President who has claimed to be opposed to big government has had that veto at his disposal, but none of them thought enough of your freedom to use it.

But I will do more than just defend what freedom you have now. I will go on the offensive. I will not rest until the income tax is repealed and you have control over your own money, your own freedom, your own life.

And when that's achieved, we will have a celebration. Do you remember the German youths who tore down the Berlin Wall and sold pieces of it to us?

Well, *we* can tear down the IRS building and sell the pieces — and use the proceeds to help IRS agents find honest work.

Winning

Again I ask you: do you want me to win? Are the actions I've outlined what you want your President to do?

The odds against my winning are extremely long. But just imagine how it would change politics in America if I received even 3%, 5%, 7%, or 10% of the vote. We probably would have the margin of difference between the two major parties — and they would have to pay attention to us.

That would reform those parties far more quickly than any effort to improve them from within. But even then, I believe they've become too seduced by power to be trusted.

So whether or not we win this year, we must do whatever necessary to have a Libertarian President as soon as possible. Whatever happens this year, I want my candidacy to pave the way for the first Libertarian President — whether elected in 2000, 2004, or 2008.

Every vote I get, every dollar I receive with which to buy advertising, every hour donated by a volunteer will help make that happen sooner.

And the more visible I become to American voters this year, the more we can change the terms of debate immediately. Imagine making the Republican and Democratic candidates have to defend taxing your income, defend locking you into Social Security, defend the brutality of the insane War on Drugs, defend bombing innocent people in foreign countries.

Once these issues become part of the national debate it could awaken a sleeping giant — the legion of tens of millions of non-voters who had given up on politics, having seen no hope that government would ever get out of their lives.

Matching Funds

Can you trust me to follow through on what I say?

I think you can tell from this book that my beliefs run deeper than those of a candidate who thinks he's found a few hot issues.

But perhaps there's a better way to demonstrate that I am committed forever to your freedom and mine.

I qualified for federal matching campaign funds in 1996, and I've qualified again in 2000. I didn't take the money in 1996, and I won't take it now. I don't believe in government welfare for individuals or for corporations, and I certainly don't believe in it for politicians.

Since I won't take the thirty pieces of silver to help me get elected, you can be sure I won't sell out once I'm in office.[3]

How could you trust a politician who condemns government intervention in any area but then spends campaign money that's been forcibly extracted from the taxpayers? Every contribution I receive is voluntary — from people who are looking for freedom from government, not government favors.[4]

---

[3]Your tax return asks whether you want $3 of your income tax to be used to help finance presidential campaigns. If you say "yes," this isn't a voluntary contribution, since saying "no" doesn't allow you to keep the $3.

[4]My biographical information is given on page 277.

Your Help

I hope you'll want to be part of this campaign. I hope you'll support it with your time and your money.

You can get more information by contacting:

Browne for President
P.O. Box 2347
Arlington, Virginia 22202
(888) 857-4500
www.HarryBrowne.org
email: info@HarryBrowne.org

FINALLY A CHOICE

In presidential elections you're asked to choose between candidates on the basis of minor differences over how much money the government should let you keep, how to keep Social Security afloat (so that the politicians can continue to tax you), how many intrusions in your life are justified by new federal programs.

You've known intuitively that, no matter which candidate won, government would get bigger and your liberty would shrink. I wouldn't be surprised if, down deep inside, you've felt the situation is hopeless.

You also knew that, no matter how you voted, your vote wouldn't tell the world you wanted smaller government, freedom from the Social Security tax, an end to the insane War on Drugs, or the repeal of the income tax — since neither candidate cared about any of those things. So your vote has always been treated as an endorsement of the *status quo*.

This year is different.

This year your vote can tell everyone exactly what you want.

This year, whatever the outcome of the election, we can make it unmistakable that there's a large contingent of voters whom the two old parties can no longer take for granted.

This year you have a choice.

EPILOGUE

CHAPTER 23

LIBERTY IN YOUR LIFETIME

The Republicans and Democrats have a sweet deal going.

They pay homage to the Constitution, but they violate it daily by enacting federal programs and intrusions that are authorized nowhere in the Constitution.

At election time they sympathize about the terrible tax load you bear. They criticize failed government programs and the oppressive intrusions on your liberty — and they vow to do everything possible to make things better for you. But when the election is over and your vote is no longer needed, they return to business as usual — and government continues to grow.

They see to it that alternative voices — voices calling for dramatic reductions in government and taxes — are never taken seriously, or even heard. They rig the state election laws to try to keep fringe parties off the ballot ("fringe" meaning any party other than the Democrats and Republicans). They enact campaign finance reforms that always make it easier for incumbents to be reelected.

They make symbolic gestures designed to reassure you. But they never even come close to helping you be free to run your own life in peace without interference from intrusive laws and heavy taxes.

More and more people recognize that none of today's politicians will help them in any meaningful way, and so they quit voting altogether. Fewer than half the eligible voters now participate in presidential elections — with even fewer in Congressional elections. Bill Clinton "won" the 1996 election with the support of only one quarter of the eligible voters:

245

1996 Votes as % of Eligible Voters	
Bill Clinton	24.2%
Robert Dole	19.9%
Third parties	4.9%
Non-voters	51.0%
Total	**100.0%**

The politicians claim to be alarmed by low voter turnouts. But in truth they like the trend, because the fewer people that vote, the easier it is for them to gather a "majority" for their schemes and remain secure in their power and privileges

There's no doubt the game is rigged in favor of the politicians who, whatever they may say, cherish the system just the way it is.

That makes it easy to feel that it isn't worth your trouble to fight this system — that there's no way we can turn America around.

Why We Can Win

But I'm not prepared to give up and say we've lost — that the politicians have won, that there's nothing we can do to make America the free country it is meant to be.

We *can* do something about it. We *can* have the America you want. Just look at the situation:

- Most Americans recognize that government is way too big.
- Most Americans want to be able to control their own lives.
- Most Americans would prefer to pay much less in taxes.
- We are offering to set people free to live their lives as they see fit, to keep the money they earn, to raise their children without dictation by arrogant politicians.
- THE GREAT LIBERTARIAN OFFER sets people free without requiring an initial, uncertain period of sacrifice.

So why aren't we winning?

Because up to now the American people haven't been aware of a candidate, a party, or a program that is devoted to delivering the goals they truly want — much smaller government and the freedom to pursue their own dreams. If we want them to help us, we must make them aware of my candidacy, the Libertarian Party, and THE GREAT LIBERTARIAN OFFER .

TEAMING UP TO REDUCE GOVERNMENT

As you contemplate helping to bring about liberty in your lifetime, you may be concerned that you don't agree with every stand I've taken in this book. But it would be unusual indeed for any two people to agree on everything.

Our differences undoubtedly are small potatoes compared to your differences with Republicans and Democrats — who argue between themselves only over how rapidly government should grow and over how much of your remaining liberty to take from you this year.

The critical question isn't whether we agree on everything, but whether we agree on the essentials: *Do you want much smaller government?*

Do you want to be free of the income tax? Do you want to be free of the Social Security tax? Do you want your neighborhood to be free of criminal drug dealers?

If you do, THE GREAT LIBERTARIAN OFFER provides the only chance we have to succeed. So I ask you once more:

Would you give up your favorite federal programs if it meant you'd never have to pay income tax again?

It may seem that you have many choices — perhaps eliminate a particularly obnoxious federal program while keeping one you believe does some good. But in the real world *you* aren't the one who will decide which are the good programs and which are the bad. If you let the government violate its Constitutional limits in any way, other people will pile on more violations — and you'll be stuck with the big government you have today.

And by now it should be clear that you can't cut government one program at a time. That's never happened and it never will. The pressure for government to grow is too great.

So we really have only two choices:

- We stop the federal government from doing *anything* not authorized in the Constitution, or
- You resign yourself to a government that will continue to grow ever larger, taking more and more of your income, invading more and more of your life.

Which will it be?

Will you give up your favorite federal programs if it means you'll never have to pay income tax again?

What I Want

I want you to say "yes" because I want you to be free to keep every dollar you earn — to spend it, save it, give it away as you think best, not as the politicians decide.

I want you to be able to plan a truly secure retirement as you think best, not as the politicians decide.

I want you to be able to live in a safe city and a safe neighborhood — without black markets, drug dealers, and gang warfare.

I want you to be able to live your life as *you* think best, not limited to what the politicians will allow you do.

Your Life

There is no way to put a price on your liberty — the liberty you've lost to politicians who want to run your life. But here's one way to look at it: If yours is a typical middle-class family, when we repeal the income tax your take-home pay will increase by at least $10,000 a year.

Think of the additional liberty this will provide — the liberty to spend more time with your children, more time to assure that they understand the values you cherish, the liberty to accumulate the capital to pursue your dreams without losing it to the politicians who spend it for the greater good (of politicians), the liberty to be more generous with the money you've earned.

That is why I want you to accept THE GREAT LIBERTARIAN OFFER.

WHY I AM RUNNING

And it is why I am running for President.

I am running because it's obvious that no Democrat or Republican will stop the relentless growth of the federal government. No one but a Libertarian will reduce your taxes dramatically, allow you to live your life as a free American, and make the federal government live within the Constitution.

I am running for President because the Republican and Democratic candidates argue only about which of them can best run your life. I believe *you* know best how to run your life.

As we've seen, federal, state, and local taxes today take 47% of the national income. In effect, the Republican and Democratic candidates are arguing over whether that figure should be 46%, 47%, or 48%. I want to cut it in half as the first important step — doing the same to your tax burden.

I am running for President because the federal government has its nose in virtually every area of your life. Its intrusions have made a mess of health care, of education, of welfare, and of law enforcement. If we get the federal government out of these areas, they will begin functioning efficiently and humanely again — and you'll be free of the federal income tax. You win two ways.

I am running for President to unlock the door and let you out of the failing Social Security system. I believe you can plan your future far better than any politician — and you certainly care more about it. I want to sell off unneeded federal assets to finance secure, fully paid-up, private retirement accounts for today's Social Security recipients — and free you immediately from the oppressive 15% Social Security tax.

I am running for President because the insane War on Drugs has generated the worst crime wave since alcohol Prohibition of the 1920s. It has caused our prisons to overflow with non-violent people who are no threat to anyone — so that murderers, rapists, and thugs get out on early release to terrorize our communities. I want to restore peace to your city by ending the nightmare of drug Prohibition.

I am running for President because no Republican or Democratic politician will end the dangerous foreign policy that makes America the world's policeman, the arbiter of everyone's dispute, the bully inciting terrorism, and the enemy of half the world. I want you to be able to sleep securely — knowing your children will never fight and die in a foreign war and terrorists will never attack your city.

WHAT TO DO

If you want smaller government, the first thing you must do is to say so — and stop rewarding politicians who talk a good game but always go along with bigger and bigger government. Tell them their behavior is unacceptable. Tell them you will no longer vote for any politician who isn't introducing bill after bill to make government dramatically smaller.

Second, make your beliefs public. Write letters to newspapers, call into talk shows, and let others know how you feel. Make it clear that you, like most Americans, want much smaller government and much lower taxes, and that — cold turkey — you have broken your addiction to politicians who aren't actually doing something to make government smaller.

Third, support those who *are* working to make government much smaller. How do you know who they are? If they talk only in general terms about big government, they probably aren't going to help.

But if they make specific proposals to end your forced participation in Social Security, to end the War on Drugs, to make huge reductions in government (not just "cuts" that turn out to be cuts in the rate of growth), to get rid of the income tax (not just to change it or replace it), they're the ones fighting for you.

Support these people by naming them when talking with friends or when you write letters to the editor or call talk shows — and by helping their campaigns or organizations with your time and your money.

In almost all cases, those who qualify will be Libertarians.

CAN IT BE DONE?

Are the American people ready for the dramatic changes I've advanced in this book? I believe so.

Over the past five years I've traveled throughout America — asking Americans what they want. Like you, an overwhelming majority of those I've encountered want the freedom to run their own lives, to control their own earnings, to raise their children by their own values.

An overwhelming majority of them have answered "Yes" to THE GREAT LIBERTARIAN OFFER.

Can I Win?

Does this mean I can be elected President in 2000?

Perhaps not. We may still have a way to go before we have a party big enough, strong enough, and well-enough financed to bring THE GREAT LIBERTARIAN OFFER repeatedly to the attention of every potential voter.

But asking whether I can win in 2000 begs the issue. The fact is that we will never reduce government to its constitutional limits until we *do* have a Libertarian President. And the sooner we start working to make that happen, the sooner we'll succeed.

The first big step is to win enough votes in 2000 to make the press and the nation sit up and take notice — to win enough votes to provide hope and inspiration to all those who might have given up.

And we can't take this first big step unless those who want it vote Libertarian.

If you vote for the Republican presidential candidate because you're afraid of what the Democratic candidate will do — or vice versa — you are throwing your vote away.

If you vote for either of them, it doesn't matter what your reason is. Your vote tells the party you vote for, loudly and clearly, that it doesn't need to change, that you endorse what it is doing, that its election-time promises are all you want, that no positive follow-through is required.

The politicians will treat your vote as though you've said "Well done" — that, whatever they do, they have you in their pocket — that they don't need to improve — that you endorse everything they've done to make government bigger and reduce your liberty.

Is that what you want them to believe?

But if you vote Libertarian, you're saying the Republicans and Democrats have lost you and they have to change if they want to win you back. You're telling them they can no longer play games with you.

No one will mistake a Libertarian vote as a plea to make the IRS more friendly or to just slow the growth in government or to fine-tune our foreign policy. It will be an unmistakable vote for much smaller government and much greater freedom.

Isn't that what you want to tell them?

Who Wins?

You might be tempted to say you won't vote Libertarian because Libertarians can't win this year. But you can't win either.

It doesn't matter whom you support, Republican or Democrat, you aren't going to get what you want. By now you must have figured out that — no matter what they promise you — they never deliver smaller government.

You elect Republicans to promote economic freedom — and they raise the minimum wage, make the tax code more complicated, gorge on billions of dollars in pork, and bestow corporate welfare on those with the most political influence.

You elect Democrats to promote civil liberties and peace — and they try to censor the Internet, force you to put a V-Chip in your TV set, expand wire-tapping, send your children to die in foreign wars, and regulate the most intimate details of your life.

So even if you vote for a winner, *you* still lose. And if you continue voting that way, you'll *never* get what you want. When you help the Republicans or Democrats, you throw away your vote, you reward them for ignoring you, and you guarantee that you'll never get what you want.

Voting Libertarian may not enable you to win today, but it at least will move you *closer* to the day of victory.

The Libertarian Party is building an organization big enough, strong enough, and so well-financed that soon we will be a threat at the ballot box. *Then* the changes will begin.

We want to win back our personal and economic freedom in the first decade of this new century. But to do this, we must begin *now* — not two years or four years from now. We must start by sending an unmistakable message to the politicians, to the press, and other Americans — a message that you want smaller government. And you can send that message only by voting Libertarian for every office you can.

How Well Will We Do?

Can I promise you a huge advance in 2000? Of course not. I don't make promises I'm not sure I can keep.

But if we wait to take the first step until we're certain of the timetable, we will never change things for the better.

The longer we delay taking the first step, the longer it will be until full freedom is restored in America. And the longer we delay, the more entrenched the welfare state will be — and the harder it will be to dislodge it.

Right now, most Americans are looking for something better than the politics they see on TV. They want something better than the political debates over how to run your life, something better than the parties who talk about reducing government and expanding your freedom only at election time.

If we pass up this opportunity when people are so receptive, who knows when we'll get another chance?

A FREE SOCIETY

If you need any motivation to seize that opportunity, just remind yourself what we're working toward.

A free, libertarian society means a place where you can raise your children by your values, and spend the time with them to teach them those values.

A free, libertarian society means an extra $1 trillion in the hands of the people who earned it, providing much better opportunities for those less fortunate than you — to get jobs, build careers, pull their families out of poverty.

A free, libertarian society means greater harmony and tolerance among people because no group will be able to force its values on others. Races, ethnic groups, and economic classes will have much less reason to be afraid of each other.

A free, libertarian society means a society in which people take responsibility for their lives, can be proud of themselves, and have strong motivations to reach higher.

A libertarian society is one in which everyone is free to follow his dreams, and everyone has a fair chance to succeed as government no longer aids those with the most political influence.

That is the America I want. And that is why I am running for President.

THE STATUE OF LIBERTY

The Libertarian Party chose the Statue of Liberty as its symbol because it reminds us of what America is supposed to be — the beacon of liberty, lighting up the whole world.

That America said to people everywhere:

It doesn't matter who you are, or where you are, or even what you are. You could be the King in your country or the lowest member of society.

But once in America, you'll be a free, responsible, self-governing individual. No one will ask for your papers, no one will attach a number to you, no one will extort a share of your income. You'll be free to pursue the life you've dreamed of.

I believe that's what Emma Lazarus meant when she wrote those wonderful words that are inscribed on the base of the Statue of Liberty:

Give me your tired, your poor,
Your huddled masses yearning to breathe free,
The wretched refuse of your teeming shore.
Send these, the homeless, tempest-tossed, to me.
I lift my lamp beside the Golden Door.

That is the America we once had.

That is the America we *should* have — the beacon of liberty, providing light and hope and inspiration for the entire world.

And I am determined that this is the America we will have again.

I am determined that we shall have liberty in your lifetime.

I am determined that we shall re-light the lamp beside the Golden Door.

Nashville, Tennessee, April 18, 2000

APPENDICES

A MESSAGE FROM PAMELA BROWNE

Dear Reader:

A little over five years ago my husband, Harry, announced that he was running for the 1996 Libertarian Party nomination for President of the United States.

A year later his campaign book, *Why Government Doesn't Work*, was published. The book included biographical notes and statistics about Harry, but it failed to convey much about the man — his character, personality, and mindset. Since I'd known Harry for over 25 years at that time, I felt it crucial to relay my thoughts about him. So I wrote a message to the reader in the back of his book, in which I attempted to paint an accurate portrait of Harry.

I want to assure those who read my letter four years ago that I stand by every word of my message. Harry still has a penchant for truth and plain speaking. He is as even-tempered, patient, understanding, kind, gentle, and benevolent as ever. And his natural diplomacy, passion, and enthusiasm for the task at hand is as strong, if not stronger, than it was in 1996. His love and respect for life of all forms remains unchanged. And I think he's more wise and knowledgeable than he was in 1996.

I still believe one of his greatest gifts, besides the fact that he's an original thinker, is his ability to comprehend very complex issues and explain them in terms that anyone (even a child) can understand. And that one of his greatest attributes is his quick wit — his ability to not only make people laugh, but to laugh at himself.

If you read my message in 1996 you may remember that I

spoke not only of Harry's strengths, but of his weaknesses. I mentioned that, for two reasons, he has trouble meeting deadlines. First, he procrastinates — more often than not because he refuses to act until his mind has fully assimilated all the facts and figures he's accumulated. And, second, because he's a perfectionist.

What I failed to mention is that in my estimation these traits stem from the fact that Harry is above all else not only an original thinker, but a great writer. And like a prima ballerina who appears to dance effortlessly (but only after years of dedicated practice and polishing of her technique), it is only after Harry has painstakingly processed his original thoughts and searched diligently for the precise words to convey his meaning to the reader that his writing seems totally clear and understandable. And until *he* is totally satisfied that he's relayed the exact words that convey his meaning, it is impossible for him to let go of his creation. These traits are the nature of the beast. And these "imperfections" are still intact!

When I wrote my message in 1996 I felt that I had conveyed the essence of Harry's character. However, throughout 1995 and 1996 as I campaigned across our nation with Harry and listened as he gave interviews to hundreds of journalists and spoke to thousands of citizens — some of whom personally expressed their concerns to him — I became aware of several issues that arose repeatedly that I'd neglected to address in my previous message. And since folks seemed to think these issues were important in the last election cycle, I asked Harry if I might address them now.

COMPASSION

Some folks unfamiliar with Libertarian principles hinted that Harry lacked compassion because he wanted to end government welfare, Social Security, and other federal programs not specified in the U.S. Constitution. They implied that he cared little about unmarried, unemployed mothers, the elderly, the handicapped, the poor, etc. This characterization was painful to me because I knew it to be untrue.

So this past year when Harry wrote an article entitled, "Compassion Of The Heart vs. Compassion Of The Mind" — explaining his views regarding true compassion — I urged him to include it in his new campaign book so folks would know that he and most other Libertarians care deeply for their fellow man.

But, for various reasons, at the last moment it was omitted. Because I think it's crucial for folks to understand the dynamics of compassion from Harry's viewpoint, I'd like to convey my impression of Harry's thinking regarding this subject.

Most times when politicians give gifts ("Compassion of the Heart") they promise things that make them, and the general public, feel good about what they're doing. But they ignore the bad consequences of their acts — such as giving a gift that comes at the expense of unwilling citizens. They spend money they didn't have to work to earn, they decide what's good for other people, and then they force that decision on everyone.

But when individual citizens give gifts ("Compassion of the Mind") they generally assure that their gift will make the recipient feel better, and that the recipient's life will improve at no one else's expense. Individuals who voluntarily use their own money to give gifts are truly compassionate because they achieve far more good for others.

That's one reason Harry believes that THE GREAT LIBERTARIAN OFFER is so important. It will not only restore the right of each individual to keep what he earns, but it will allow each wage-earner and taxpayer to live a better life and assure that the good he wants to do for others will be more effective and successful.

TRUST & DETERMINATION

Harry appeared on hundreds of call-in radio and television shows during the 1996 campaign. And, inevitably, near the end of each show someone would call in and say something like, "I like everything you've said, and I believe in everything you stand for. But how do I know that if I vote for you — and you become President — that I can trust you to do what you say, and that you won't give in or become corrupt like the other politicians?"

Sometimes he'd explain that he didn't really want to *be* president, but that he didn't know anyone else who possessed the will and determination to go to Washington and reduce the size of the Federal government, eliminate the federal income tax, privatize Social Security, and end the War on Drugs. And that when he accomplished those things all he wanted to do was return home and live out the rest of his life in peace and freedom.

I wish I believed there was someone in this country other than Harry who was trustworthy and capable of carrying out

Harry's Libertarian plan. I'd support him in a heartbeat, for I have no desire whatsoever to see my husband and our family involved in politics. But I truly believe that Harry is the only person I can trust to carry out all the proposals in this book. And he's the only person I know who has the unflappable determination to cut the size of our government, strictly enforce the U.S. Constitution, prosecute those who violate the Constitution, bring all our troops home from overseas, privatize Social Security, reduce the budget, end the War on Drugs, restore our freedoms, and protect our privacy.

FAITH IN PEOPLE

During the 1996 campaign people sometimes asked Harry if he believed the American people were really capable of making their own decisions and running their own lives. We heard remarks such as, "I know I'm responsible enough to make good decisions, but you should meet my neighbor down the street" or "People are just plain stupid; and most of them don't even vote, so why do you believe people are capable of running their own lives?"

In December of 1999, in an article he wrote for *WorldNetDaily* entitled, "I Believe in You", Harry expressed his faith in the citizens of our nation and their ability to make responsible decisions. He stated that he believes the American people — not the politicians running the government — are capable of deciding how to raise their children, how to spend the money they earn, how to provide for their own retirement, and how to run their own lives.

I believe that a good steward of this nation is one who helps restore our individual freedoms, prohibits the government from invading our privacy, refuses to enforce any law that violates the Constitution, enables us to keep all the money we earn by shrinking the growth of our government to its constitutional size, refuses to engage our country in a war, and holds citizens accountable for their actions. In other words, a good steward of our nation would strictly interpret and uphold our U.S. Constitution. This would provide us, as citizens and a nation, with an opportunity that no other president in our lifetime has offered — the chance to grow and blossom by means of freedom matched with personal responsibility.

I think many Americans recognize that the values and morals upon which our country was founded have greatly eroded. And that we have reached a point in our nation's history when those things we hold most dear — including freedom, personal responsibility, our family, work, the justice system, and worship — are in grave danger of slipping away.

So perhaps an important question to ask Presidential candidates is, "Do you have the wisdom, ability, experience, compassion of mind, and determination to strictly enforce the U.S. Constitution, *and* faith that the American people will act responsibly once their freedoms have been restored?"

ETERNAL OPTIMISM

Harry is by nature an eternal optimist, and I know of nothing or no one who can dissuade him from looking at individuals, situations, our nation, the world, or life in this manner. And in general his optimistic views have served him very well. So I was not surprised when during the 1996 campaign he frequently referred in his speeches and interviews to the hopes he had for his campaign — including how much money he hoped to raise, what percentage of the vote he hoped to garner, and how many new members he hoped would join the Libertarian Party before the end of the campaign.

Harry's optimistic hopes were always tempered with realism. And, in fact, he told people repeatedly that he could not predict, promise, or guarantee anything — but he could see in his mind how his campaign and the Libertarian Party could achieve great things if everyone worked diligently — and everything fell into place.

Harry has, once again, set some very optimistic hopes for his 2000 Presidential campaign. And I, for one, am glad. For as R.F. Horton said, "Success lies, not in achieving what you aim at, but in aiming at what you ought to achieve, and pressing forward, sure of achievement here, or if not here, hereafter." I personally believe that all things are possible, and that Harry and the Libertarian Party may actually exceed their hopes. And I'm the pessimist in the family!

IN CONCLUSION

Our Founding Fathers bequeathed to America a precious gift — the United States Constitution — which bestowed upon our country a way of life that no other nation in the world had been privileged to experience up to that point. We inherited a grand treasure. But over the last two hundred years (more particularly the last 40-60 years) our citizens have watched politicians devalue, degrade, and diminish our legacy.

I hope and pray that by election day the vast majority of Americans will have heard THE GREAT LIBERTARIAN OFFER. If they do, they will be given a rare and historic opportunity.

Finally they will be given a clear-cut choice: Do you want to reelect Republican and Democratic politicians who will continue to allow the Federal government to grow to such enormity that you no longer have any individual freedoms, personal privacy, or personal responsibility? Or do you want to elect Libertarians who are dedicated to dramatically reducing the size and scope of government to that specified in the U.S. Constitution, so your individual freedoms, personal privacy, and personal responsibility are restored?

Harry, his campaign staff, the Libertarian Party, and all the dedicated Libertarians who have worked so diligently the past several decades will need a great deal of help to reach the majority of American people with the Libertarian message. If you're so inclined, I hope you'll consider contributing money or volunteering your time to his campaign or to the Libertarian Party. If you're unable to contribute money or time, I hope you'll at least vote Libertarian in 2000 and take your like-minded friends and relatives to the polls on election day.

The 2000 Libertarian presidential campaign will undoubtedly be exciting. But, more important, will the vast majority of Americans hear THE GREAT LIBERTARIAN OFFER? I sincerely hope you'll help in whatever way you are able to educate Americans about this historic choice. By doing so, you will be taking a step toward reinstating America as the beacon of liberty, freedom, and personal responsibility throughout the world.

I appreciate your taking the time to read this message. And as I wrote in 1996, I consider it an honor to stand beside Harry at all times — especially now while he seeks the Presidency of the United States of America.

Best Wishes,
Pamela Wolfe Browne

APPENDIX B
ACKNOWLEDGMENTS

Since 1974, Terry Coxon has edited every book I've written. His help has been especially valuable with this book — not only in making my writing easier to understand, but also for his perceptive insights into the nature and operations of government.

I'm very grateful as well to Art Matsko of LiamWorks for publishing this book. Given my difficulty in preparing a presidential campaign while trying to write this book, the book might never have been published without his patience and his ability to be flexible with the production schedule.

I also would like to thank Perry Willis, Michael Cloud, and Jim Babka for valuable suggestions made.

I appreciate the research work done by Brian Doherty and Don Gallick. Robert Poole, John Semmens, and Peter Samuel provided important information regarding the federal highways. Stephen Moore of the Cato Institute made available valuable budget information. Arthur Bourque first called my attention to the *Boston Globe* series on the federal government's polluting, mentioned in the chapter on the environment.

Last but certainly not least, I am so grateful to my beloved wife Pamela, who has supported me through every endeavor.

APPENDIX C
NOTES & SOURCES

1. THE GREAT LIBERTARIAN OFFER

The estimate that 47% of the national income is consumed by taxes was made by the U.S. Census Bureau. It used to publish this information in an annual report, *Government Finances*, in conjunction with the U.S. Department of Commerce. But the final report in the series was published in 1996. The information on total taxation still appears in each year's *Statistical Abstract of the United States* in the table "All Governments — Detailed Finances," along with national income figures.

The graph for the percentage of national income paid in taxes was produced from the data described in the preceding paragraph. Federal government spending figures came from *Historical Statistics of the United States, Colonial Times to 1970*, tables Y336 and Y340, pages 1104-1105; annual *Statistical Abstracts of the United States*; and *Economic Indicators*, published by the Joint Economic Committee of Congress.

The five polls cited were conducted by:

1. Luntz Research Companies, November 9, 1994.
2. The Roper Center for *Reader's Digest* in 1994.
3. The Times Mirror Center for the People & the Press, July 12-27, 1994.
4. CBS News and *The New York Times*, October 29 - November 1, 1994.
5. The Times Mirror Center for the People & the Press, June 12-24, 1993.

3. HOW GOVERNMENT OPERATES

Mark Skousen's quotation concerning persuasion and force is from the pamphlet "Persuasion vs. Force," published by Phillips Publishing, Potomac, Maryland, 1992; page 2.

Michael Cloud's observation on the abuse of power was given in several speeches at which I was present.

The P.J. O'Rourke quotation is from *The Parliament of Whores*.

The 1999 bill to finance the war against Serbia was reported in *National Review*, June 14, 1999, page 4.

The Republican tax-cut plan was described in *Investors Business Daily*, August 6, 1999.

The *Capitol Hill Blue* article on Congressmen's offenses was published August 16, 1999. The report is available online (http://www.capitolhillblue.com/Aug1999/081699/criminalclass1-081699.htm).

4. GOVERNMENT DOESN'T WORK

The estimate of the number of people murdered by their own government is from "War Isn't This Century's Biggest Killer" by R. J. Rummel, *The Wall Street Journal*, July 7, 1986, editorial page.

5. THE CHAINS OF THE CONSTITUTION

The first Thomas Jefferson quote is:

It would be a dangerous delusion were a confidence in the men of our choice to silence our fears for the safety of our rights. . . . Confidence is everywhere the parent of despotism. Free government is founded in jealousy, and not in confidence. It is jealousy and not confidence which prescribes limited constitutions, to bind down those whom we are obliged to trust with power . . . Our Constitution has accordingly fixed the limits to which, and no further, our confidence may go. . . . In questions of power, then, let no more be heard of confidence in man, but bind him down from mischief by the chains of the Constitution.

It is from his draft of the *Kentucky Resolutions*, 1798.

Michael Cloud's observation that either the government is in chains or the people are in chains was given in several speeches at which I was present.

The second Jefferson quote is from *The Report to the President* (George Washington), February 15, 1791.

8. FREE FROM THE INCOME TAX

Describing the Steve Forbes flat-tax proposal, the 2000 Forbes for President website says, "A family of four earning $36,000 will pay no federal income tax under the Steve Forbes Flat Tax" (http://www.forbes2000.com/cgi-bin/fy2k_prod/fy2k/scripts/homepages/editorialContentDetail.js p?BV_SessionID=14185549.944866575&BV_EngineID=cagfghgl jlbfdlcgifcgifdik.0&name=Tax+-+How+You+Win).

George W. Bush's website says, "Under Governor Bush's plan, a family of four making $35,000 a year will receive a 100% income tax cut; a family of four making $50,000 a year will receive a 50% tax cut and a family of four making $75,000 a year will receive a 25% income tax cut" (http://www.georgew bush.com/news/1999/december/pr120199_nn.asp).

So whose taxes will go up to offset these losses in revenue?

That most of the income tax is paid by people in the $19,000 to $100,000 income range is shown in *The Statistical Abstract of the United States*, 1997, table 530, page 344.

The Statistical Abstract of the United States, 1997, table 498, is the source for state lottery payoffs.

9. FREE TO PLAN A SECURE RETIREMENT

The estimate that future generations will have to pay 70% of their lifetime income in taxes is in "Generational Accounting: A Meaningful Way to Evaluate Fiscal Policy" by Joel Kotlikoff of Boston University, Alan Auerbach of the University of California, and Jagadeesh Gokhale of the Cleveland Federal Reserve Bank, *Journal of Economic Perspectives*, Volume 8, Number 1, Winter 1994, pages 73-94.

The poll results on Social Security expectations are from *The Wirthlin Report*, January 1995, Research Supplement, page 4.

This table shows how well you can retire at age 65, based on when you start saving and how much of your income you set aside for investing.

Yearly Retirement Income
As a Percentage of Your Final Year's Working Income

	Share of your working income you invest each year					
Starting age	5%	8%	10%	15%	20%	25%
20	25%	41%	51%	76%	102%	127%
25	21%	34%	43%	64%	86%	107%
30	18%	29%	36%	54%	71%	89%
35	15%	23%	29%	44%	58%	73%
40	12%	19%	23%	35%	47%	58%
45	9%	14%	18%	27%	36%	45%
50	6%	10%	13%	19%	26%	32%
55	4%	7%	8%	13%	17%	21%
60	2%	4%	4%	7%	9%	11%

Each row is the age at which you start saving, and each column is the percentage of your income you put aside each year. The intersection of the row and column is your retirement income as a percentage of your income in your final working year. For example, if you begin investing at age 20 and set aside 10% of your annual income, your retirement income will be 51% of your final working year's income. If you earn $100,000 in your last working year, you'll have an annual retirement income of $51,000 (vs. about $17,000 from Social Security).

The table assumes you earn only a 7% return on your savings (which is less than the 10% historical return on stocks or the 8% return on bank CDs). The table assumes that — once retired — you'll live entirely off the income from your savings, without touching the capital, so that all the capital you've accumulated can be passed on to your heirs.

The Republican proposal to phase out Social Security over 60 years was put forward by Sen. Phil Gramm.

10. FREEDOM FROM THE
NIGHTMARE OF PROHIBITION

The Lawrence Singleton, Rodney Kelley, and Jose Tapia cases are described in "Why Talking about Drugs Is Worse than Murder" by James Bovard, *Playboy*, December 1997.

The Mario Paz killing was described in "Bereft Family Disputes Police Shooting Report" and "No Drug Link to Family in

Fatal Raid, Police Say," both by Anne-Marie O'Connor, *The Los Angeles Times*, August 26, 1999, page A-1, and August 28, 1999, page A-1.

The stories of Lonnie Lundy and Sen. Shelby's son were taken from "Drug Charge," *USA Today*, July 29, 1998, page 6A; "Alabama Senator's Son in Drug Arrest" by Bill Montgomery, *Atlanta Journal and Constitution*, July 29, 1998, page 6B; and from correspondence produced by Lonnie Lundy's father.

The case of Rep. Randy Cunningham's son was reported in "Son of Lawmaker Sentenced to Prison" by Bill Murphy, *The San Diego Union-Tribune*, November 18, 1998, page B-1; and "When a Father and Politician Become One" by Peter Rowe, November 24, 1998, page E-1.

The case of Sen. Grams' son was reported in "Drugs, a Senator's Son And a Hint of Favoritism," *The New York Times*, December 3, 1999, Late Edition, section A, Page 22.

The source for the 19 Congressmen arrested on drug-related charges is *Capitol Hill Blue*, August 16, 1999. The report is available online http://www.capitolhillblue.com/Aug1999/081699/criminalclass1-081699.htm).

The number of people arrested on marijuana charges was reported by Adam J. Smith in "New Bio Alleges Gore Used Marijuana for Years," *The World Online*, January 20, 2000. The study estimating 2 million prisoners by February 2000 is available online (http://www.cjcj.org/punishingdecade/punishingpr.html).

The statistics on teenage drug use are from the annual survey by The Institute for Social Research at the University of Michigan, on behalf of the federal National Institute for Drug Abuse. It is available online at http://www.nida.nih.gov/Infofax/HSYouthtrends.html.

11. FREEDOM FROM WAR

The World War I casualty figures are taken from *The First World War* by John Keegan (Knopf, 1999), and were quoted in a review by David Frum in *The Weekly Standard*, June 21, 1999, page 32.

The Brookings Institute study on the cost of nuclear weapons was reported in *National Review*, August 3, 1998, page 10.

The estimate of the deaths from sanctions against Iraq was made by UNICEF, the United Nations agency that evaluates children's health, in a report issued August 12, 1999. It was quoted in

"The War on Iraq: An Unnatural Disaster" by Llewellyn H. Rockwell, Jr., available online at http://www.antiwar.com/orig/rock well2.html.

Fred L. Smith's statement about foreign aid was quoted by Stephen Moore in *Human Events*, May 19, 1995, page 8.

12. FREEDOM TO MAKE YOUR OWN CHOICES

The tobacco companies' attempts to market safer cigarettes is discussed in the book *Fear of Persuasion* by John Chalfee. Sheldon Richman quoted examples in his article "Bad Verdicts," *FFF E-Mail Update*, August, 1999 (http://www.fff.org/editorial/ed0899f.htm).

The British Department of Transport study was reported in "Report Questions Whether Seat Belts Save Lives" by Mick Hamer, *New Scientist*, February 7, 1985, page 7, and was cited in "Auto Safety Regulations: Hazardous to Your Health" by John Semmens and Dianne Kresich, a Heartland Institute Policy Study, January 28, 1998.

The comparison of long-distance telephone rates is from *Statistics of Communications Common Carriers*, Federal Communications Commission, 1997.

13. FREEDOM TO WORK & TO EARN

The estimates of the costs of import barriers are from a 1994 study, *Measuring the Cost of Protection in the U.S.*, by the Institute for International Economics.

The assertion that Japanese car sales in America constitute "trade aggression" was made by Patrick J. Buchanan on the *One on One* television show, May 12, 1995.

Murray Weidenbaum's statement about the trade deficit with Japan was made in "The Great Confusion: A Conservative's Response to Pat Buchanan's *The Great Betrayal*," *St. Croix Review*, April, 1999, page 45.

The trade deficits with China and Japan for 1997 were taken from the Department of Commerce *Survey of Current Business*, July 1998, reprinted in the *1999 New York Times Almanac*, page 498.

The 2% across-the-board tariff rate was calculated as follows: In 1997 tariffs totaled $17.927 billion (source: Financial Management Service, Department of the Treasury), while the total value of imports was estimated to be $870.670 billion (source: Office of Trade and Economic Analysis, Department of Commerce). From *The World Almanac and Book of Facts, 1999*, pages 108 and 702.

14. FREEDOM TO LEARN

The governors' education goals were reported in "Clinton and Congress Heap More Federal Mandates on Local Schools" by Howard L. Hurwitz, *Human Events*, April 1, 1994, page 20.

Al Gore's education proposals were reported in *The Nashville Tennessean*, March 20, 1998.

The data on changes in American education since 1950 are from *The Digest of Education Statistics 1997*, Table 39: "Historical summary of public elementary and secondary school statistics: 1869-70 to 1994-95," published by the National Center for Education Statistics, an agency of the U.S. Department of Education. 1995 is the latest year for which data are available. The information is available online (http://www.nces.ed.gov/pubs/digest97/d97t039.html).

Al Gore's condemnation of America's schools was reported in "The Side Gore Must Project" by Bob Herbert, *New York Times* columnist, reprinted in *The Nashville Tennessean*, October 6, 1999, page 13A.

The Florida voucher program is described in "Voucher socialism" by Llewellyn H. Rockwell, Jr., *WorldNetDaily*, July 12, 1999, and in "Voucher Program Gets Slow Start" by Paul Wilborn, *St. Petersburg Times*, July 2, 1999.

Some of the federal controls over local education are taken from a May 1999 set of regulations issued by the Education Department, quoted by Chester Finn in "The Education Vice-President," *The Weekly Standard*, May 31, 1999; others are listed in "Devil's Deal . . ." by Ronald L. Trowbridge, *National Review*, September 15, 1997, page 58.

The information on private voucher programs comes from "Cutting out the Public-School Middlemen," *Investors Business Daily* editorial, August 28, 1997.

15. SAVING THE ENVIRONMENT FROM POLITICAL DESTRUCTION

David Armstrong's 4-part *Boston Globe* series on government pollution of its own properties was entitled "The Nation's Dirty Big Secret," and it began on November 14, 1999.

Eric Zuesse' article on Love Canal, "The Truth Seeps Out," was published in *Reason* magazine, February 1981. It is available at the *Reason* website, http://reason.com/8102/fe.ez.the.html. Further information on the Love Canal scandal is available at the Center for Health, Environment and Justice website (http://www.essential.org/cchw/lovcanal/lcsum.html).

The deaths caused by smaller cars were estimated in a report, *The Deadly Effects of Auto Fuel Economy Standards*, published by the Competitive Enterprise Institute, June 21, 1999.

Roy E. Cordato's observations on landfill space were made in "Don't Recycle: Throw It Away!," published online by the Ludwig von Mises Institute, December 1999, (http://www.mises.org/jour nals/fm/fm1295.asp#Don'tRecycle:ThrowItAway!) The italics were in the original.

William L. Anderson's statement about the dire predictions of the 1970s is in "The Other Y2K Problem," published online by the Ludwig von Mises Institute, December 16, 1999 (http://www.mises.org/fullstory.asp?control=349&FS=+The+Oth er+Y2K+Problem).

The Petition Project of 17,000 scientists rebutting the global warming scenario was organized by the Oregon Institute of Science and Medicine, and is available online (http://oism.org/ppro ject/s33p37.htm).

17. FREEDOM FROM CRIME

The Lott-Mustard study on concealed-carry laws is "Crime, Deterrence, and Right-to-Carry Concealed Handguns," published in *The Journal of Legal Studies* #26 (1997). Another study, "Multiple Victim Public Shootings, Bombings, and Right-to-Carry Concealed Handgun Laws: Contrasting Private and Public Law Enforcement" by John R. Lott, Jr. and William M. Landes was published as a John M. Olin Law & Economics Working Paper No. 73, The Law School The University of Chicago, 1999, and is available online at :
http://papers.ssrn.com/paper.taf?abstract_id=161637.

The Cato study is "Fighting Back: Crime, Self-Defense, and the Right to Carry a Handgun" by Jeffrey R. Snyder, Cato Policy Analysis No. 284, October 22, 1997.

The case of the Pearl, Mississippi, school shootings is described in "The Real Lesson Of the School Shootings" by John R. Lott, *The Wall Street Journal*, March 27, 1998.

The Luby's Cafeteria shooting is described in "The Concealed Weapons Debate," CBS Television News, July 17,1999, online (http://www.cbs.com/flat/story_167408.html?bogus=blank).

Barbara Goushaw's comment is published in "Handguns Are a Girl's Best Friend," *Liberty* magazine, January 1999, page 34.

The Clinton program for putting 100,000 new policemen on the streets is reviewed in "Hype and Glory" by Walter Shapiro,

USA Today, July 30, 1999, page 5a, and in "Clinton Goal of 100,000 Cops Far Off, Audit Finds," *The Chicago Tribune*, July 27, 1999, page 4.

The estimate that 80% of the people who have lost their property to asset seizures have not been charged with any crime was made in "Government Seizures Victimize Innocent" by Andrew Schneider and Mary Pat Flaherty, *The Pittsburgh Press*, August 16, 1991.

The list of the many federal agencies using asset forfeiture laws and the history of those laws is given in *Forfeiting Our Property Rights* by Rep. Henry Hyde, page 24.

The Clarence Aaron case was profiled on "Snitch," *Frontline*, PBS, January 12, 1999. The complete transcript of the show is online at the *Frontline* website (http://www.pbs.org/wgbh/pages/front line/shows/snitch/etc/script.html).

18. FREEDOM TO FOLLOW YOUR DOCTOR'S ADVICE

The estimate that 51% of health-care dollars are spent by governments is from *The New York Times*, June 13, 1993, Business section, page 4. A graph in *The Wall Street Journal*, July 21, 1994, page A14, indicated a similar percentage of government spending; the source was *Source Book of Health Insurance Data, 1993*.

Health insurance coverage is from *Historical Statistics of the United States, Colonial Times to 1970*, table B-408, page 82, and from *The Statistical Abstract of the United States, 1998*, table 181, page 125.

The information on declining employer coverage is from *The Statistical Abstract of the United States, 1998*, table 182, page 125.

Health-care costs rising twice as fast as the inflation rate was reported in "The Health Care Squeeze on Older Americans,"a study by the Families USA Foundation, using data from the *Consumer Expenditure Survey* of the U.S. Bureau of the Census; page 3.

The size and complexity of the Medicare program is from an article by Robert Waller and Mary Grealy of the Healthcare Leadership Council, *USA Today*, December 3, 1999, page 28A.

The report on fee-cutting by doctors who have resigned from government programs is from "Doctor: Cash only slashes prices" by Carol Carter, *The Manchester (NH) Union-Leader*, September 13, 1999.

The list of problems seniors face with Medicare (except for the final item) is from "Dangerous Remedy" by Virginia Postrel, *Reason*, October 1999, page 4. The fact that seniors now pay more out of their own pockets than before Medicare was reported in "The Health Care Squeeze on Older Americans," a study by the Families USA Foundation, using data from the Consumer Expenditure Survey of the U.S. Bureau of the Census; page 1. This also was covered in "Pay or Pay" by John Merline, *National Review*, May 29, 1995; page 45.

The Oregon health-care rationing is described in "Oregon's New Health Rationing Means More Care for Some but Less for Others" by Marilyn Chase, *The Wall Street Journal*, January 28, 1994.

Jane Orient's statement was published in a letter to *Reason* magazine, March 1997, page 10.

Robert Goldberg's statement on the number of deaths the FDA has caused appeared in *Fortune*, November 11, 1996.

All the examples for Canada are from "What Universal Health Care Brought the Canadians" by James Brooke, *The New York Times*, January 16, 2000.

19. GOVERNMENT'S GREATEST HITS

The contents of the 1997 flood-relief bill were reported in "Emergency Pork" by Leon Felkin, in his Internet publication (http://www.pissedoff.com/cgi-pissedoff/hn/get/forums/pork.html).

Peter Samuel's estimate that private roads cost half as much to build was in *Toll Roads Newsletter*, November/December 1999.

Information on the Space Station and Space Shuttle comes from "Thirty Years of Ineptitude" by Robert G. Oler, Richard Kolker, and Mark Whittington, *The Weekly Standard*, July 26, 1999, page 27.

21. GETTING FROM HERE TO THERE

The estimate of the cost to fund private retirement accounts for those now dependent on Social Security is based on two factors: (1) the current yearly outlay of the Social Security Administration, and (2) the median cost of annuities charged by private companies for men and women 65 years old. Since most Social Security recipients are over 65, the actual cost should be less, but there also may be expensive surprises once the government's books are opened.

I think also that we should encourage people who aren't dependent on Social Security to voluntarily pass up the retirement account.

The lack of a true budget surplus is demonstrated by the fact that the federal debt increased from $5.479 trillion at the end of fiscal 1998 to $5.607 trillion at the end of fiscal 1999. The source for this is *Economic Indicators*, a monthly statistical report published by the Joint Economic Committee of Congress.

22. THE LIBERTARIAN PATH

The estimate that 80% of the people who have lost their property to asset seizures have not been charged with any crime was made in "Government Seizures Victimize Innocent" by Andrew Schneider and Mary Pat Flaherty, *The Pittsburgh Press*, August 16, 1991.

23. LIBERTY IN YOUR LIFETIME

The Statue of Liberty quote is from *The New Colossus* (1886) by poet Emma Lazarus (1849-87.

WHO IS
HARRY BROWNE?

Harry Browne was born in New York City on June 17, 1933, and grew up in Los Angeles. He graduated from high school, but attended college for only two weeks. He has lived in Canada and Switzerland, and he now resides in Tennessee.

He has a grown daughter, Autumn, and in 1985 he married the former Pamela Lanier Wolfe. His main non-professional interests are classical music, opera, good food and wine, sports, television, and fiction.

He was a successful investment advisor for 30 years. He first achieved fame in the 1970s when he wrote a series of investment books that showed Americans how to protect themselves from the recessions and inflation produced by the U.S. government's monetary policy. He foresaw the dollar devaluations and the rise in precious metals prices, and he showed investors how to profit from these events. His first two investment books, *How You Can Profit from the Coming Devaluation* and *You Can Profit from a Monetary Crisis*, were *New York Times* bestsellers.

He wrote a total of eight investment books, including *Fail-Safe Investing*, his final investment book, which was published in 1999.

In 1973 he wrote *How I Found Freedom in an Unfree World*, a self-help book that shows individuals how to take responsibility for their own lives. The book remains in demand today, almost three decades later.

In all, he has written 11 books that have sold more than 2 million copies.

He has been a popular public speaker since the 1960s, and

has appeared on hundreds of national and local radio and television shows, in addition to hosting his own syndicated radio show.

In 1996 he was the Presidential candidate of the Libertarian Party. During the campaign, he traveled to 37 states and appeared on over a thousand radio and television programs. His approach to smaller government was praised in dozens of newspaper editorials and political columns. He won numerous Internet preference polls, and was endorsed for president by over a hundred radio talk show hosts, journalists, and publications.

His campaign book, *Why Government Doesn't Work*, spoke to Americans who felt frustrated by big government. It is still in print.

INDEX

279